D1597598

# GROWTH, EXPORTS, & JOBS in a CHANGING WORLD ECONOMY

# AGENDA 1988

John W. Sewell, Stuart K. Tucker,
and contributors:

Manuel Castells and Laura D'Andrea Tyson
Jonathan D. Aronson
Robert L. Paarlberg
Raymond F. Mikesell
Ray Marshall

Series editors:
Valeriana Kallab
Richard E. Feinberg

Transaction Books
New Brunswick (USA) and Oxford (UK)

ISBN: 0-88738-196-0 (cloth)
ISBN: 0-88738-718-7 (paper)
Printed in the United States of America

**Library of Congress Cataloging-in-Publication Data**

Growth, Exports, & Jobs in a Changing World Economy: Agenda 1988

(U.S.-Third World Policy Perspectives; no. 9)
1. Economic forecasting—United States. 2. United States—Economic conditions—1981. 3. Employment forecasting—United States. 4. Economic history—1971. 5. United States—Foreign economic relations—Developing countries. 6. Developing countries—Foreign economic relations—United States. 7. Technological innovations—Economic aspects—United States. 8. Microelectronics.
I. Sewell, John W. II. Tucker, Stuart K. III, Castells, Manuel. IV. Title: Growth, Exports, and Jobs in a Changing World Economy: Agenda 1988.
V. Series.
HC106.8.G75 1988
338.5′443′0973—dc19

The views expressed in this volume are those of the authors and do not necessarily represent those of the Overseas Development Council as an organization or of its individual officers or Board, Council, Program Advisory Committee, and staff members.

# Growth, Exports, and Jobs in a Changing World Economy

# Acknowledgments

*Agenda 1988 Project Directors:*
John W. Sewell
Stuart K. Tucker

*Series Editors:*
Valeriana Kallab
Richard E. Feinberg

*Associate Editor:*
Melissa Vaughn


Many individuals have contributed valuable insights and advice on the substance and presentation of this policy study, and the project directors are deeply appreciative of their willingness to devote time to this effort. Particular thanks are due to those who provided detailed reactions to ideas presented in the chapters in this volume, especially the overview essay: Harry L. Freeman, James K. Galbraith, Edward K. Hamilton, Gerald K. Helleiner, Kurt Hoffman, Daniel A. Sharp, and Robert Solomon. As always, John P. Lewis, ODC's senior advisor, provided wise insight and sage advice. None of these individuals, however, bear responsibility for the authors' conclusions.

Special thanks are also due to Gail J. McGrew, who provided valuable research assistance; to Valerie Mims for editorial and production assistance; and to Robert A. Bortner, Jeffrey L. Doidge, and Karen K. Saxon for their help in the preparation of the Statistical Annexes.

The Overseas Development Council gratefully acknowledges the support of The Ford Foundation, The Rockefeller Foundation, and The William and Flora Hewlett Foundation for the Council's overall program, and of The Pew Charitable Trusts for ODC's U.S.-Third World Policy Perspectives series, of which *Agenda 1988* is part.

# Contents

# Foreword

There is no more important task facing the next president of the United States than restoring this country's international economic strength. The twin deficits in the federal budget and the U.S. trade balance have led to an international debt burden surpassing in magnitude that of any developing country. Unless these problems are addressed and ameliorated in the near future, the ability of the next administration to promote this country's international interests will be severely circumscribed.

Fundamental changes in the world economy over the past quarter century have inextricably interwoven the future prosperity and political strength of the United States with the progress of the developing countries. If the United States is to expand exports to improve its trade balance, provide jobs for American workers, and deal with its own debt problem, decision-makers in the public and private sectors must give much higher priority to U.S. policies that support resumed growth with equity in the countries of the Third World.

These policies are the central focus of the Overseas Development Council's *Agenda 1988*—the eleventh assessment of U.S. policies toward the developing countries issued by the ODC since 1973. Because of the fundamental and unprecedented nature of the economic problems now facing the United States, the ODC Board and staff decided to make this *Agenda* about the relationship between the economic and social progress of the developing countries and the economic prospects for the United States in the decade ahead.

I want to express particular thanks to those organizations which provide support for ODC's overall program or which contribute particularly to its *U.S.-Third World Policy Perspectives* series; these include The Ford Foundation, The Rockefeller Foundation, The William and Flora Hewlett Foundation, and The Pew Charitable Trusts. The views in this publication are of course those of the individual authors, and not necessarily those of ODC's funders, or of its Board or Council. ODC's *Agenda 1988* is an independent policy study issued as a contribution to the crucial debate now under way on this country's economic and political future—and that of the developing world.

Victor H. Palmieri, *Chairman*

February 1988                                                  *Overseas Development Council*

# Agenda 1988: Overview and Summaries of Chapter Recommendations

# The Dual Challenge: Managing the Economic Crisis and Technological Change

John W. Sewell

The United States is entering a new era. The postwar period was unique in U.S. and world history. Rarely, if ever, has a country emerged from a major war as strong as the United States did in 1945, while all the other major powers, victor and vanquished alike, were left economically exhausted. U.S. economic and political preeminence was bound to diminish as the rest of the world recovered and progressed.

The United States remains a great economic power. But many Americans perceive the United States to be irreversibly losing that power, not only to Japan and Germany, but also to a number of developing countries. In politics, moreover, perceptions always matter a great deal, and in this case they have been heightened by the speed with which the current economic difficulties of the United States have arisen. As late as 1980, the current account was in surplus, the United States was a net creditor, and the federal budget deficit was manageable. By 1986, however, the current-account deficit totaled $141 billion, and it shows very little sign of diminishing in the near future. At the same time, the international debt of the United States grew to over $200 billion, making this country the world's largest debtor. These problems are compounded by the fact that policymakers thus far have been unable to come to grips with the ballooning federal budget deficit, which has been financed by foreign borrowing and high real interest rates—a policy that drove up the value of the dollar until 1985 and has worsened the trade deficit.

As a result, the United States finds itself in a position qualitatively and quantitatively without precedent in its post-World War II experience. Ironically, its situation is in some ways similar to that of many developing countries. The United States, too, needs to balance its trade accounts, to service its foreign debts, and to rebuild its industrial base; and although its position is undeniably more favorable than that of any Third World country, the United States, too, needs to develop.

The economic welfare of the United States is now inextricably linked to developments in the global economy and in the developing countries. The next administration will face a set of economically and politically difficult policy challenges as it seeks to come to grips with the economic problems of the United States. The difficulties of managing these tasks will be compounded by the fact that there no longer is a clear line between domestic and international policies, and by the reality that a growing number of developing countries will now have to be much more centrally involved in the management of international problems.

The decisions taken to improve the international economic position of the United States will have considerable implications for the developing countries. So far, however, very little analysis is available on how U.S. policy choices are likely to either damage or promote growth and equity in the developing countries. Nor is there sufficient understanding of the extent to which resumed growth in the developing countries could create important export opportunities for the United States to improve its international economic position and to deal with its own domestic problems.

The main focus of this *Agenda* is on the relationship between economic and social progress in the developing countries and the prospects of the United States for increasing exports, creating jobs, and servicing its foreign debt in the decade ahead. The first part of this overview chapter looks to the next few years. It argues that policymakers concerned with exports, jobs, and debt must take into account the constraints imposed on the United States by the economic policies of the last decade, the growing importance of the developing countries to the U.S. economy, and the need of both the United States and the developing countries to avoid a global downturn.

The urgency of dealing with these immediate macroeconomic issues should not, however, obscure the fact that both developed and developing countries are on the threshold of a series of changes in industrial technology and organization that serious observers are calling a Third Industrial Revolution. The new technologies are based on discoveries in microelectronics, bioengineering, and advanced materials that already are leading to fundamental shifts in relations between the United States and the developing countries. These technologies, with appropriate policies, could enable the United States to greatly strengthen its international economic position in relation to developing as well as developed countries. Only a few developing countries will be able to capitalize on the scientific and technological developments now in the making. At the same time, unless these new technologies are properly understood and anticipated by policymakers, they will place a considerable number of developing countries at an even greater disadavantage than today—an outcome that would not be in either the economic or the political interests of the United States. The second part of this overview analyzes how this technological revolution is likely to change U.S. relations with the developing countries in the 1990s. A final section sets out specific policy recommendations for both the near and longer terms.

# I. The Present Crisis: Can We Avoid Mutual Damage?

There is no essential disagreement that the main symptoms of this country's international economic problems are the trade deficit and a growing foreign debt. Considerable differences of opinion exist, however, about the relative weight to attach to the various causes of these problems, and even more sharply, over the types and duration of the policies needed to correct them.

## The State of the Debate

Virtually all analysts concur that the dollar was overvalued in 1980–85, but few agree as to how much farther and how rapidly it should drop in order to eliminate the U.S. current-account deficit. Similarly, while most analysts recognize that the federal budget deficit will have to be reduced, there is no consensus as to how rapidly this should occur and whether it should be achieved by raising taxes, cutting federal programs, accepting the automatic cuts mandated by current legislation—or some combination of all three. Further major disagreement arises over divergent assessments of the competitiveness of American industry.

Some analysts consider the current economic problems of the United States to be limited and amenable to short-term correction.[1] They hold that the American economy remains fundamentally competitive. They argue that current U.S. difficulties result from unwise policies in the industrial countries—most notably, from the failure to trim the U.S. federal deficit, which, together with a strongly anti-inflationary U.S. monetary policy, has led to high interest rates and an overvalued dollar. They also point out that the deterioration of the international position of the United States has happened extraordinarily rapidly, is spread across industries and overseas markets, and parallels the federal deficit problem. According to this view, these problems can be corrected by some combination of getting exchange rates "right" (thus improving prospects for U.S. exports and raising prices of U.S. imports), by encouraging public and private savings to alleviate the budget deficit and permit adequate investment in American industry, and by expansionary policies in other industrial countries. While taking these steps will not be easy, more fundamental policy changes are not needed and would be misguided.

Other analysts accept that part of our economic difficulties can be ascribed to budget deficits and the overvalued dollar but believe that American industry is losing its competitive position in a more fundamental sense and is ill-equipped to deal with changes under way in industrial technology and organization. They cite as evidence not only the growing U.S. trade deficit, but also our diminishing share of world manufactures exports, slow productivity growth, declining real wages, narrowing profit margins, and diminishing share of global high-technology industries. In addition, these critics see American managers as both wedded to traditional management philosophies that cannot match the organizational techniques now emerging in Japan and unable to translate the strong basic research capacity of the United States into marketable, quality products. Finally, they argue that the United States faces competition from governments operating not according to classical liberal economics, but rather from strong imperatives to "create" comparative advantage by protecting their own markets while investing heavily in world-class industrial production. The "playing field" of international trade, they maintain, is not level. These arguments lend intellectual credibility to those pressuring for the restriction of imports into the United States and threatening U.S. retaliation in order to open markets in other countries. From these analyses flow a variety of policy prescriptions focusing on domestic economic policy and "competitiveness promotion" as well as on the need for new rules for international trade to deal with a new world of "developmental states."[2]

Proponents of both views are correct in pointing to serious problems with the American economy. Judgments about future American competitiveness, however, depend in part on the time frame being considered. U.S. competitiveness will be considerably improved in the next few years if the value of the dollar continues to drop, if growth in the other OECD economies speeds up, and if the federal budget deficit is narrowed. But exports to developing countries will expand only if growth in major developing-country markets resumes. The longer-term competitiveness of the United States, in contrast, is a more open question. The United States has the potential to remain competitive, and the technological changes taking place and discussed in this volume can work to its advantage. As Manuel Castells and Laura Tyson

**Table 1.  U.S. Performance in High-Tech Trade**
**($ billions and percentages)**

|  | 1981 | | 1986 | | 1981-86 |
|---|---|---|---|---|---|
|  | Exports | Trade Balance | Exports | Trade Balance | Export Growth |
| Office, computation, and accounting machines | $9.8 | $6.8 | $16.1 | $2.2 | 64.3% |
| Drugs and medicines | 2.2 | 1.2 | 3.1 | 0.8 | 40.9 |
| Guided missiles and space vehicles | 0.5 | 0.6 | 0.7 | 0.5 | 40.0 |
| Communications equipment and electronic computers | 11.4 | 7.7 | 14.9 | 9.1 | 30.7 |
| Industrial inorganic chemicals | 3.1 | 0.7 | 3.5 | 0.5 | 12.9 |
| Professional and scientific instruments | 7.1 | 1.3 | 7.8 | -2.9 | 9.9 |
| Aircraft and parts | 16.9 | 1.8 | 18.4 | -15.1 | 8.9 |
| Ordnance | 0.7 | 0.5 | 0.7 | 0.4 | 0.0 |
| Plastics and synthetic resins | 4.8 | 4.2 | 4.5 | 2.8 | -6.2 |
| Engines, turbines, and parts | 3.8 | 1.9 | 2.8 | -0.8 | -26.3 |
| **Total High-Tech Trade** | **60.3** | **26.6** | **72.5** | **-2.6** | **20.2** |
| Total U.S. Trade | 233.7 | -39.6 | 217.3 | -170 | -7.0 |

Source: U.S. Department of Commerce, unpublished data.

# Figure 1. U.S. Trade Balances, by Sector

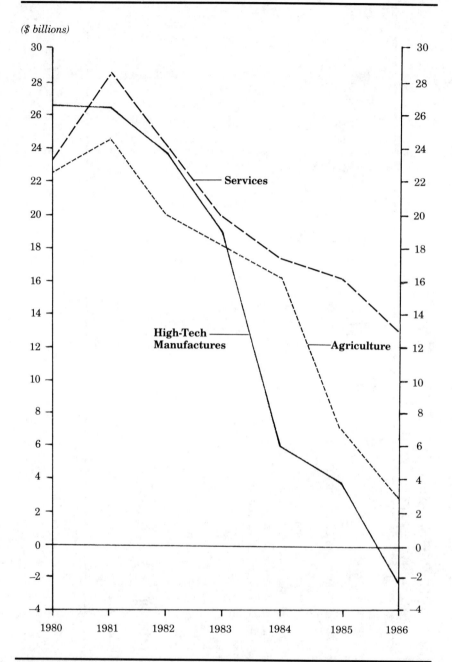

*($ billions)*

Source: U.S. Department of Commerce, *Highlights of U.S. Export and Import Trade,* various December issues.

point out in Chapter 1, the current macroeconomic difficulties of the United States are superimposed on longer-term trends of relatively low productivity growth, the attenuation of the U.S. technological lead in some industries, and intensified competition from both industrial and developing countries. Yet success is not guaranteed; it will require a conscious national effort to maintain this country's economic position. In looking at that task in either time frame, however, most analysts have virtually ignored the fact that a growing number of developing countries have now become major U.S. export markets as well as important U.S. competitors. Therefore policies designed to recapture competitiveness, increase U.S. exports, jobs, and economic growth are going to have to take account of growth—or the lack of it—not only in other industrial countries but also in a number of developing countries.

## Three Decades of Growth in the Developing World

From 1950 to 1980, the developing countries compiled a spectacular record of economic growth. As a result, their share in real gross world product grew from just over 15 per cent in 1960 to over 21 per cent in 1982. In the same period, many of these countries became important participants in the expanding global trading system. World trade increased roughly 11 per cent a year in the 1960s and 20 per cent a year in the 1970s; and the developing countries participated in that growth. In 1965, they accounted for only 7 per cent of exports of manufactures; by 1985, their share of global manufactured exports had risen over 16 per cent. (See also Table A-14, Statistical Annexes, p. 222.) The composition of Third World industrial exports also changed, with traditional labor-intensive products such as shoes and textiles diminishing in importance compared to exports of electric machinery, chemicals, and transport equipment. At the same time, the developing countries emerged as rapidly growing export markets for the industrial countries.

This progress, however, was unevenly shared among developing countries. Some countries, most notably the "newly industrializing countries" of East Asia and Latin America, were remarkably successful. A growing number of middle-income developing countries succeeded in expanding the share of manufacturing in their own economies and in enhancing their roles in the international economy. In contrast, the low-income countries—concentrated in Sub-Saharan Africa and South Asia—remain mainly producers of primary commodities and are heavily dependent on flows of concessional resources.

The emergence of the developing countries as important participants in the international economy occurred in the 1970s, as economic linkages between *all* countries were rapidly growing stronger. For the United States, this increasing interdependence with other countries was a new development. U.S. trade in goods and services as a percentage of GNP expanded from 6.4 per cent in 1970 to over 12 per cent in 1980. Both U.S. imports from and exports to developing countries grew at 6 per cent a year—far more rapidly than exports to traditional U.S. trading partners in the industrial world. By 1981, the developing countries were purchasing 41 per cent of American exports—a greater share than Japan and Western Europe combined. (See also Table A-9, Statistical Annexes, p. 216.)

U.S.-Third World trade by and large followed an advantageous pattern. The United States exported heavy machinery, chemicals, and agricultural products to the developing countries in return for imports of lower-cost consumer goods and raw materials. In the 1970s, while U.S. GNP was growing at only 2.8 per cent a year, overall U.S. capital goods exports grew at 8.5 per cent a year, and exports to the developing countries grew even faster, at a rate of 11.7 per cent a year.

However, the experience of the last decade and a half demonstrates not only the benefits but also the risks of the new importance of the developing countries. The negative side of strengthened U.S.-Third World interdependence became apparent with the onset of global recession in the early 1980s. Driven by what an earlier ODC assessment in this series called "interlinked deterioration,"[3] growth rates in the industrial world plummeted, interest rates soared, and developing-country growth came to a screeching halt.

The negative impact of the economic downturn in the developing countries on the U.S. economy was direct and measureable: U.S. exports to all developing countries dropped from $88 billion in 1980 to $77 billion in 1985. If exports had grown in the first half of this decade at the same rate as in the 1970s, they would have totalled about $150 billion in current dollars. The impact on employment also was dramatic. The actual and potential employment loss (if exports had grown as they did in the 1970s) amounted to 1.7 million jobs—or nearly 21 per cent of total official unemployment in 1986. In addition, the global recession cast doubt on the ability of the middle-income debtor countries to make their debt-service payments to commercial banks in the industrial world.

## U.S. Economic Prospects and the Developing Countries

Given its own trade and budget deficits, and its growing level of foreign indebtedness, the United States cannot avoid eventual adjustment. The central questions are how well the adjustment process will be managed

## Figure 2. U.S. Exports to the Third World in the 1980s: Lost Opportunities ($ billions, constant 1980)

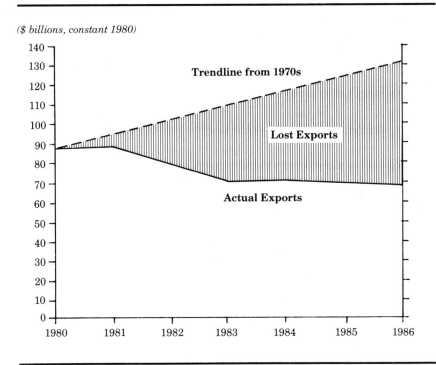

*($ billions, constant 1980)*

Source: ODC calculations from *U.S. Department of Commerce, Highlights of U.S. Export and Import Trade,* various December issues.

and whether or not policymakers can walk the narrow line between improving the position of the United States and avoiding throwing the world into a steep economic downturn.

Many of the measures that are widely considered a necessary part of this adjustment process fall outside the purview of this *Agenda.* Such measures include a political compromise to narrow the federal budget deficit by raising revenues and cutting expenditures, measures to increase real savings in this country, considerably improved coordination of economic policies among the OECD countries, and a continued willingness to let the value of the U.S. dollar drift further down. However, the adjustment process also requires attention to U.S. interests in Third World prosperity.

Conventional wisdom currently holds that the trade imbalance will be corrected by the depreciation of the dollar if Japan, Germany, and other industrial countries expand their economies. The role that could be played by the developing countries—or, more specifically, by the middle-income developing countries that are now important participants in the international economy—is virtually absent from current policy discussions.

The projections summarized in Table 2, prepared to illustrate a range of possible trajectories for the U.S. merchandise trade balance over the next four years, reveal the vital role that could be played by growth in developing countries. Scenario A projects what would happen if current trends remained unchanged. Three other scenarios illustrate what would happen if the industrial countries currently in surplus expanded their economies (Scenario B); if, in addition to this expansion, the import restraints on the debtor countries imposed by the debt crisis were released (Scenario C); and if, on top of this, the United States succeeded in improving its competitiveness in developing-country markets (Scenario D). Scenario E illustrates the possible consequences of a mild U.S. recession for the merchandise trade balance. (The assumptions underpinning each of the scenarios accompany Table 2.)

All six projections indicate that the trade deficit will not disappear quickly. *Scenario A* shows that if the trends evident at the beginning of 1987 were to continue, the U.S. merchandise trade deficit would be at roughly $200 billion in 1992. U.S. imports would continue to climb in proportion to U.S. gross national product, while U.S. merchandise exports, starting from a lower level, would lag. This projection does assume reasonably strong growth in industrial countries (2.9 per cent annually), as well as the continuation of the following pre-1987 trends: a) no change in the value of the dollar from its December 1986 value, b) no change in the import propensity (the use of income to buy imports) of industrial countries, c) no change in the U.S. market share of sales to industrial countries, d) a continuation of very weak income growth (2.8 per cent annually) in developing countries, e) a continuation of the currently restricted import propensity of developing countries (largely due to debt-servicing problems), and f) a stable U.S. market share of sales to the Third World.

Although a steady rise of the U.S. trade deficit toward $200 billion by the end of 1992 might conceivably be accepted by foreign creditors, most American politicians would not like to run in 1988 on a platform that promised such a gap. Even if the potential domestic political impact were ignored, the United States would remain dependent upon the good will of foreign investors and consequently would run the risk of losing its freedom to formulate its own international economic and political policies—in addition to yielding control over its own economic situation. Any prospect that foreigners might withdraw their funds from the United States because of a lower value of the dollar, or because of concern about the health of the U.S. economy, would push interest rates to unacceptable levels. Higher interest rates would in turn threaten U.S. and global economic growth. In short, a lingering trade deficit of nearly $200 billion, adding close to $1 trillion to U.S. foreign debt over the next five years, is politically unacceptable and probably economically unsustainable. Financial markets and Treasury officials of course realized this in 1987, and the dollar has been depreciating markedly, especially during the autumn of 1987.

*Scenario B*, which assumes high industrial-country growth and moderate growth in developing countries, shows the trade deficit declining toward a still-high $112 billion in 1992. The scenario assumes that Europe and Japan grow at a rate of 3.4 per cent annually—a very strong rate that is comparable to 1969–1978 performance and higher than the rate currently projected by most official forecasts. Scenario B also incorporates a fall of the dollar to well below its 1980 level; expanded import propensity by industrial countries; a recapturing of the U.S. market share in industrial countries that existed before the rise of the dollar in the 1980s; a pick-up in developing-country growth (to 4.7 per cent annually), but no change in management of developing-country debt or in Third World import propensities; and a stable U.S. share of Third World markets. Thus even a continuing devaluation of the dollar, combined with strong growth in industrial countries, would produce a relatively high deficit. A trade deficit of this magnitude would mean an increase of $650 billion in the U.S. foreign debt by 1992.

Scenario B, relying on resumed growth in the industrial countries and dollar depreciation, would result in a trade deficit lower than that projected in Scenario A. But this still might not be sufficient to blunt the economic pressures—such as the flight of foreign capital and consequent higher interest rates—that could push the U.S. economy into recession. Hence Scenario B is less likely to occur than the recession scenario. The recent drop in the value of the dollar has reduced the volume of U.S. imports, but this has been offset by higher import prices, leaving only a small effect on the overall import bill. Therefore any significant contraction of the U.S. import bill (relative to U.S. GNP) could only come from a recession.

*Scenario E* shows that a recession of the magnitude of 1981–82, followed by a reasonable recovery by 1992, might slice $40–50 billion from the trade deficit. However, the costs of a U.S. recession to U.S. economic and political interests, particularly in the developing world, would be considerable. A U.S. recession would inevitably spread to other countries and dampen already depressed export markets, and it would be disastrous for economic and political stability in many devel-

## Table 2.  Scenarios: U.S. Merchandise Trade and the U.S. Trade Deficit

| | U.S. Exports | 1992 U.S. Imports | Trade Balance |
|---|---|---|---|
| | | *($ billions, constant 1986)* | |
| **Growth Scenarios** | | | |
| **A:** Status quo trends from 1986 | 261 | 459 | −198 |
| **B:** High industrial-country growth | 347 | 459 | −112 |
| **C:** High global growth and improved debt management | 379 | 459 | −80 |
| **D:** High global growth, improved debt management, and marked U.S. competitive gain | 390 | 459 | −69 |
| **Recession Scenario** | | | |
| **E:** Mild U.S. recession | 261 | 423 | −162 |

### Scenario Assumptions

| Period Covered by Scenarios: 1989-1992[a] | A | B | C | D | E |
|---|---|---|---|---|---|
| | | | *(percentages)* | | |
| **U.S. Imports:** | | | | | |
| U.S. annual GNP growth rate | 3.1 | 3.1 | 3.1 | 3.1 | 1.0 |
| U.S. imports/U.S. GNP | 9.1 | 9.1 | 9.1 | 9.1 | [b] |
| **U.S. Exports:** | | | | | |
| Industrial-country GNP growth rate | 2.9 | 3.4 | 3.4 | 3.4 | 2.9 |
| Industrial-country import/GNP | 16.0 | 20.0[c] | 20.0[c] | 20.0[c] | 16.0 |
| U.S. share of industrial-country imports | 12.2 | 14.0 | 14.0 | 14.0 | 12.2 |
| Developing-country GDP growth rate | 2.8 | 4.7 | 6.1 | 6.1 | 2.8 |
| Developing-country import/GNP | 17.6 | 17.6 | 21.8[c] | 21.8[c] | 17.6 |
| U.S. share of developing-country imports | 15.7 | 15.7 | 15.7 | 17.0 | 15.7 |

[a] All scenarios start at the end of 1988 and use a common set of estimates for 1987 and 1988 data (IMF estimates): U.S. growth, 2.3% in 1987 and 3.1% in 1988; industrial-country growth, 2.3% in 1987 and 2.8% in 1988; developing-country growth, 3.0% in 1987 and 4.1% in 1988.
[b] 8.1% in 1989, 7.9% in 1990, 9.1% in 1991 and 1992.
[c] Arithmetic rise during 1988-1992 from the number listed in Scenario A to the number listed in this scenario.

Source: ODC projections, developed by Stuart K. Tucker, based on World Bank data for GNP and IMF and U.S. Department of Commerce data for trade.

# U.S. Trade Deficit

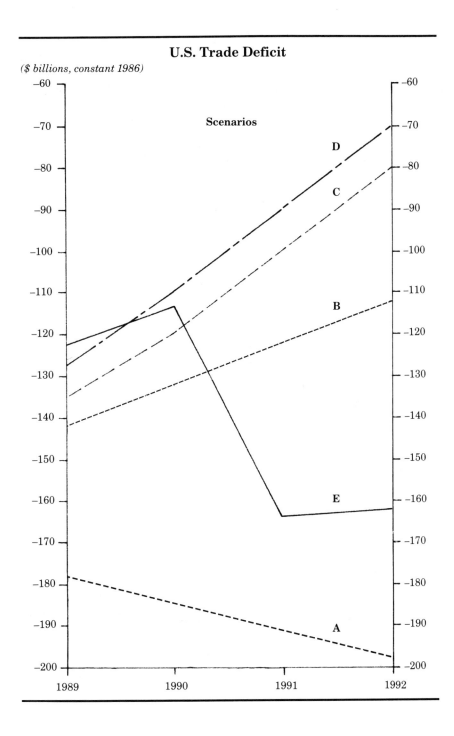

oping countries. The impact would be particularly sharp on the major debtors in Latin America.

The goal of U.S. policy therefore should be to narrow the trade deficit through export growth rather than through import compression and recession. Yet current policies hinging on resumed growth in the industrial world will not be sufficient. The only remaining untapped important source of global demand for U.S. exports are the middle-income developing countries. This possibility is illustrated by *Scenario C*, which relies upon growth rates in the developing world that approach the 6.1 per cent annual rate average of the 1970s and upon an increase in these countries of the propensity to use the increased income to buy imports. For that to happen, however, the net financial outflow from the Third World would have to be greatly diminished, whether due to resumed lending to developing countries or to some form of debt relief. In Scenario C, U.S export earnings in 1992 could be $32 billion higher than under the Scenario B projection of industrial-country growth alone, and the trade deficit also would decline to a more manageable $80 billion. The very optimistic *Scenario D*, in which the trade deficit drops below $70 billion, assumes that, due to a major national effort to improve U.S. competitiveness and to widen access to foreign markets, the U.S. share of developing-country imports increases above recent historical levels. (It should be noted that this probably unattainable change in the U.S. share adds only $11 billion to U.S. exports—a relatively small amount compared to the increases due to growth and better debt management.)

These projections show that resumed growth in the industrial countries will be necessary but not by itself sufficient to increase U.S. exports and reduce the U.S. trade deficit to manageable proportions. In addition, the current debt-induced net outflow of resources from the developing countries will have to be reversed to expand developing-country import capacity—and our own export potential. Contrary to the thrust of the current trade debate raging in this country, U.S. trade problems with the developing countries are far more due to their current debt predicament and weakened import capability than to either unfair trade practices or any fundamental decline in U.S. competitiveness.

The hard fact is that neither the U.S. merchandise trade account nor the current account is likely to be balanced even by the end of the next American president's first term. But sustained and rapid growth in the middle-income developing countries is a key element in making significant progress toward reducing the trade deficit without inducing a global recession. The essential question is how to support that growth—an issue that will be addressed in Part III of this overview chapter.

# II. The Technological Revolution: Opportunities for the United States, Problems for the Developing Countries

Improving the international economic position of the United States unquestionably deserves top priority on this country's policy agenda in the immediate future. And the interests of both the United States and the developing countries will be enhanced if adjustment is accomplished in a manner that does not throw the world into a global recession. This does not, however, mean—as some seem to assume—that if that task is accomplished, the world will revert to the *status quo ante*. Developments in science, technology, and industrial organization are rapidly changing the structure of the international economy, with profound implications for both the United States and the developing world. These changes, and their implications—taken up next in this overview—are, however, extraordinarily fluid. The pace of change, and the specific outcomes these changes will bring, are still very unclear and will not be determined by the technologies alone. The right policies can still make an enormous difference in outcomes; whether or not the scientific and technological revolution now under way works to the advantage of individual developed or developing countries still is open to choice.

The world is on the threshold of a technological revolution potentially comparable in magnitude to the introduction of the steam engine in the eighteenth century and the discovery of electricity in the nineteenth. The components of this Third Industrial Revolution include several virtually simultaneous developments:

- the introduction of new products and processes in microelectronics that are revolutionizing patterns of industrial production;
- leaps in communications technology—also an outgrowth of microelectronics—that are transforming global communications and have the potential to transform patterns of industrial organization;
- the rapid spread of new patterns of management that change decisions on industrial location;
- the development and use of new "advanced" materials that will replace many traditional raw materials in the production of many consumer and industrial goods; and
- advances in bioengineering that hold great promise for increasing industrial productivity as well as human well-being.

These developments have the potential to dramatically alter the relationships between developed and developing countries in ways that are only beginning to be perceived.

*The development and spread of microelectronics is changing methods of industrial production.* Microelectronics, "computers on chips," or the ability to process information electronically rather than manually, is revolutionizing industrial production throughout the world. Only ten years ago, the hand-held calculator was considered revolutionary, as it afforded dramatic savings in the cost of information processing. And, as virtually every office across the nation has experienced, the personal computer has literally revolutionized the activity of processing information in one short decade.

In addition to qualitative advances in information processing, microelectronics is also generating a qualitative transformation of product design and the production process. Computer-aided design (CAD), computer-aided manufacture (CAM), numerically controlled machine tools (NCMTs), industrial robots, automated transfer systems, and industrial process control systems are all automation technologies that have been widely introduced in the past decade. Collectively and individually, these systems afford engineers much greater flexibility and much lower costs in both the design and the production of goods. They also give rise to considerable savings of energy and materials in production, and they make small-scale production far more flexible and economical. Most important—especially for developing countries still planning to compete on the basis of plentiful, low-cost labor—the new technologies are generally labor-saving.

Automobile production in the industrial countries is currently at the forefront of industrial automation. Factories are increasingly being equipped with robots to perform repetitive and hazardous tasks such as welding and painting. Even such traditional manual processes as cutting fabric for clothing and assembling radios and televisions increasingly are being performed by robots. The direct effects of automation already are showing up in reduced labor costs. They are, for example, keeping the U.S. textile industry competitive with those of Third World countries. And the U.S. auto industry, which originally transferred production and jobs to offshore production facilities in order to maintain price competitiveness with lower-cost Japanese producers, has now begun to slow that transfer.

Another far-reaching implication of microelectronics technology is the eventual electronic linkage of design and production, which will drastically reduce the time lag from conception to production in the industrial process. Microchips should be viewed as electronic "building blocks" that can be combined together, allowing ever greater and more complex levels of integration of formerly separate processes. System-wide automation is possible because automation technologies share a common language of control. Only a very few factories in the world are today fully integrated and automated, but the development and spread of such factories—the linking up of previously discrete islands of auto-mation[4]—will generate greater qualitative gains in productivity and employ fewer people. Because these integrated systems are inherently far more complex to put into place than piecemeal automation, develop-ing countries will find it much more difficult to introduce these systems.

*The establishment of high-speed global communications networks enables virtually instantaneous communication worldwide, thereby in-tegrating markets and enabling centralized management of globally dispersed industries.* The advent of communications satellites and the development of high-speed communications equipment based on micro-chip technology enables industrial processes to be dispersed around the globe without loss of management control. Consequently, for many phases of the production process, physical location is no longer impor-tant. Communication technologies have begun to facilitate the disper-sal of manufacturing production around the world to take advantage of lower labor costs and access to markets and raw materials. They make the management of already dispersed facilities that much easier. Uni-sys, for instance, communicates directly by satellite with engineers in its Indian affiliate to develop new computer software; and simple data processing for U.S. firms is carried out by the educated work forces of nearby Caribbean islands. In addition, financial markets around the world are becoming integrated into a global network by means of these new technologies. As Jonathan Aronson discusses more fully in Chap-ter 2 of this volume, developing countries risk "being marginalized" unless they tie into the global telecommunications and information services network.

*New patterns of industrial organization are transforming producer/supplier relationships and patterns of industrial location.* New manage-ment and production techniques pioneered by the Japanese are an integral part of the process of industrial transformation now under way. "Just-in-time" (JIT) inventory practices; the emphasis on quality "no-defect" production; and the development of new, closer organiza-tional links between suppliers and producers are among the new or-ganizational techniques. The colossal success of Japanese industry in the past two decades is leading to the widespread adoption of these techniques in all industrial countries. The JIT inventory system, for example, saves the costs of idle stockpiles.

A decade ago, it was generally thought that industries in the developed world would increasingly shift production and assembly of components to low-wage areas in the developing countries. Many ana-lysts predicted that the automobile industry, for example, would do so. But as a result of the savings in labor, capital, and time afforded by new forms of industrial organization as well as industrial production, investment has instead increased dramatically in *developed* countries. The final outcome of this process and its effects on the developing nations lie in the future, but it is obvious that relationships have shifted. Industrial production throughout the world is in the midst of far-reaching change.

*New man-made "advanced" materials are increasingly important in industrial production.* In the decades ahead, the use of these synthetic materials will considerably affect the demand for traditional industrial raw materials. This shift is due in part to advances in the theoretical understanding of the structure of physical matter that now enable scientists to ". . . start with a need and then develop a material to meet it, atom by atom."[5]

The impact of these developments already can be seen in the communications field, where optical fibers (made from silicon) have virtually replaced copper in telephone cables. Similarly, lightweight plastics and new composites increasingly are being used in automobiles and aircraft to replace steel; General Motors now produces two lines of cars with plastic body panels, and some of the major control surfaces of new commercial airliners are being made of graphite-epoxy composites. Current research holds promise of auto and jet engines constructed of high-temperature ceramics in the next decade. In the area of bioengineering, new technological developments may well lead to the production—through the use of genetically engineered microorganisms—of an industrial glucose that will compete directly with sugar.

The development and use of these new materials in many cases has been speeded by the drive to conserve energy. Thus the average weight of an automobile produced in the United States was brought down more than 200 kilograms between 1975 to 1985, and iron and steel now account for only 69 per cent of the average vehicle, compared to 81 per cent of the much heavier vehicle of a decade ago.[6]

These new developments will reduce the demand for and prices of traditional raw materials such as copper and iron ore, and they will provide the opportunity for the emergence of new industrial supply sectors that will have a major impact on the economies of countries that can master the development, production, and utilization of these materials.

*Perhaps the most exciting new developments are taking place in biology; bioengineering, based on the vastly expanded understanding of genetics, holds promise of new ways to improve health and diminish hunger.* Advancements in bioengineering will bring about marked improvements in human well-being. In the field of preventive medicine, genetically engineered vaccines against malaria, typhoid fever, viral diarrhea, measles, and tetanus—all major killers in the Third World—could save millions of lives. Malaria alone annually affects some 200 million people and causes 2 million deaths.

Applications of biologically engineered products in increasing food production are also likely to expand rapidly in the 1990s, when genetic manipulation of plants can be used to increase resistance to insects and diseases and to improve yields with much lower use of expensive fertilizers and pesticides. For instance, it may be possible to place the genes of viruses and bacteria in plants, thereby enabling them to produce their own fertilizers or insecticides.

In the late 1990s, genetically engineered animals are also likely to become a commercial reality. Researchers are now developing a growth hormone that would permit existing breeds of cows to produce up to 40 per cent more milk. The prospects for improvement of existing breeds, and the possibility of developing animals that are less prone to disease and more able to cope with natural disasters such as drought, could have great impact on the agricultural sector not only in the developed world, but also in developing countries—where their effect could be even more significant in terms of advances in eliminating hunger.

# III. Laying the Groundwork for the 1990s

The severity of the present financial crisis and the tenacity of the U.S. trade deficit will be a continuing preoccupation of policymakers, but must not be allowed to obscure the simultaneous need to address the already emerging, longer-term challenge posed by massive technological change. Both problems require immediate policy attention if the United States and the Third World are to successfully cross from one era into the next.

The current U.S. trade predicament has focused political attention on the need to take policy action swiftly. To revitalize its economy and restore its ability to exercise international leadership, the United States must devise measures to support renewed global growth, including rapid growth in the developing countries. In the immediate future, financial measures will be of utmost importance to this effort.

Meanwhile, however, the longer-term economic trends driven by the technological revolution continue unabated. The kinds of policies needed to address these problems generally have longer lead times than the short-term financial measures that can stimulate growth, making it imperative to proceed on both fronts at the same time. Therefore the following policy recommendations, although separated out into measures to deal with the present economic crisis and measures to anticipate the now emerging, longer-term technological transformation, constitute a comprehensive action agenda for 1988.

## Managing the Short-Term Financial Crisis

The United States has a very strong interest in pursuing a short-term global economic strategy that emphasizes renewed global growth, particularly in the developing countries. Furthermore, if this growth is to have the necessary, positive impact on global trade imbalances, it is vital to design policy actions to help channel it into expanded trade. From the perspective of the United States as well as developing countries, these actions must pay particular attention to growth in developing countries. These policies will have to be developed and implemented in cooperation with other industrial countries and with the developing countries most concerned. In this setting, U.S. leadership remains pivotal. The policies described below can only be implemented if the United States, despite its current economic problems, takes an active role in designing and supporting them.

The central short-term issue for U.S. policymakers is to identify politically feasible new initiatives to help the developing countries resume and sustain economic growth. The imperatives of narrowing the U.S. budget deficit currently rule out any major expansion of resources for international programs designed to directly support economic expansion in the middle-income countries. And the commercial banks and private equity investors are highly unlikely to expand current lending levels or strengthen their investment position until growth resumes in those countries.

Renewed and sustained growth in the developing countries requires that these countries themselves adopt appropriate economic policies, and that the net transfer of resources to those countries once again be positive and at a level that supports growth. Currently, the reverse is true. In 1981, resource transfers to all developing countries were $35 billion. In 1986, however, interest payments and amortization of long-term debt by all developing countries surpassed new lending by about $29 billion. This pattern of negative resource flows is likely to continue well into the future unless specific steps are taken to change it. Moreover, the effect of negative resource transfers on the U.S. trade balance has been dramatic: The annual U.S. *trade* deficit with developing countries—in part due to the *net* drain of resources from the developing to the industrial world—now totals some $58 billion.

A globally coordinated, U.S.-led debt policy should be designed to reverse the net drain of resources from the debtor countries. Such a policy should allocate the costs of adjustment among banks, debtor countries, international institutions, and lending countries without

# Figure 3. Net Resource Transfers to the Third World ($ billions)

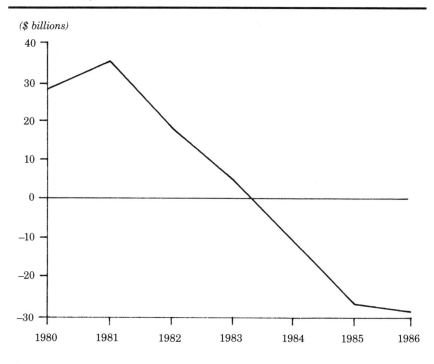

*($ billions)*

Note: Net resource transfer is equal to new lending minus payment of interest and principal in a given year.

Source: World Bank, *World Debt Tables, 1986-1987.*

destabilizing the international banking system. A central element of such a strategy would be the establishment of target figures, perhaps under the aegis of the World Bank and the International Monetary Fund, for individual debtor countries to reduce resource drains in ways supportive of more equitable economic growth. The strategy would include measures to both promote economic efficiency and protect particularly vulnerable groups of poor people within developing countries. Creditors—whether governments, international financial institutions, or commercial banks—would have discretion to decide to either extend new loans or cut debt-service requirements. A strategy containing these elements not only would spread the costs of adjustment more equitably but might also considerably improve the U.S. trade balance, enhance American leadership in international economic relations, and improve U.S. diplomatic relations with developing countries.[7] Such a strategy of course would not be costless. The commercial banks in industrial countries would suffer losses, and measures would need to be developed by regulatory and tax authorities to ensure the stability of the banks and that of the international financial system.

It can be argued that while debt relief would generate additional exports, it would also reduce the receipts of creditors, whether governments or private institutions. The benefit to the U.S. current-account balance would therefore be seemingly negligible. But a dollar lost in debt service cannot be equated to a dollar gained in trade. The money that a developing country uses not to service its debt but to pay for an equivalent amount of imports is money that stimulates income growth and increases the propensity to import. The imported commodities may, by relaxing supply bottlenecks, generate additional activity and imports. Over a period of several years, the gains for U.S. exports should outweigh the losses to U.S. creditors. In addition, resumed growth in the developing countries would have a positive effect on earnings from U.S. direct and portfolio investments overseas. During the global recession in the early 1980s, receipts from these investments in the developing world also fell sharply. For these reasons, the gains to the U.S. current-account balance that could be expected from a strong recovery in the developing world would substantially outweigh the potential lending losses.

Management of the debt crisis will be a central issue well into the 1990s. The key to resumed growth is a combination of tough policy choices by developing countries, an amelioration of the debt situation as discussed earlier, and a heretofore elusive degree of global macroeconomic coordination. Sustained economic growth in the developing countries will be necessary to expand world trade and long-term investment. Leaders of the developed countries will need to take coordinated action to avoid volatility in exchange rates and in interest rates, and to ensure that their macroeconomic policy choices provide an environment for global growth.

If this growth strategy is to happen, policymakers will need to design imaginative ways to stimulate the flow of additional public and private resources to the developing countries. Among the steps that need to be taken are the following:

**1. Increase transfers from countries in surplus.** Countries with large financial surpluses, most notably Japan, must begin to play a more important role in global finance. In 1986, Japan's current-account surplus was approximately $83 billion, and it is projected to be only slightly lower in 1987. Over the last few years, several detailed proposals recommended that Japan measurably increase its transfers to the developing countries. More recently, the Japanese government announced its intention to double its aid by 1992, but few details were given about how this commitment is to be implemented. Measured as a percentage of GNP, Japan's level of aid is already higher than that of the United States, and it is quite possible that Japan will join the United States in leading the world's aid donors in absolute terms by the end of the next decade. (See also Annex Table C-5, Statistical Annexes, p. 240.) But Japan has been reluctant to assume international economic leadership and generally has deferred to the United States. One of the creative challenges facing the OECD is to devise measures to encourage the Japanese and surplus countries in Western Europe to use their surpluses for restarting growth in the developing world. For both Japan and the United States, this task is not, however, without political problems. The Japanese surplus is largely in private hands, and measures will have to be devised to channel it to international purposes. The United States faces a different problem. The international financial institutions should have a major role to play in recycling these surpluses, but the United States would inevitably have to yield more of its voting power in these institutions to the Japanese and other new contributors.

**2. Generate new resources with minimal budgetary impact.** The exigencies of the current crisis should stimulate policymakers to look for nontraditional ways of providing capital to restore growth in the major debtor countries. The current crisis also calls for more imaginative use of guarantees to foster greater capital flows into the developing countries. For instance, the United States has agreed to an increase in the World Bank's capital to permit the Bank to borrow additional funds on private capital markets for lending to developing countries. Traditionally, Bank members have paid in a modest amount of capital as an earnest of their guarantee of repayment. Yet only a token paid-in contribution to capital is probably necessary to maintain the value of Bank bonds (previous capital increases have had as much as 10 per cent of capital paid in), and this budgetary cost can be diminished. A similar formula could be used for the next quota increase for the International Monetary Fund. And a special issuance of the Fund's Special Drawing Rights (SDRs) for allocation to developing countries under the aegis of the IBRD and the IMF is another potential source.

**3. Redirect resources available through the U.S. international affairs budget.** The United States should restructure its existing international affairs budget to respond to the challenges reviewed in this *Agenda*. During the first half of this decade, this budget (generally known as the "foreign aid" program) more than doubled, but all of the increase has gone to military and security aid—to the neglect of programs designed to foster American interests in the developing countries through economic growth and long-term development. Economic and developmental assistance has in fact declined. The imbalance between the military and the economic in current programs represents a misallocation of scarce resources that the United States can no longer afford in this period of budgetary stringency. U.S. interests in the developing world today by and large do not stem from concerns about military security; they are largely economic, political, and humanitarian. As currently structured, the U.S. foreign aid program has outlived its time. Even a modest reallocation of funds within the current budget—in the range of 10–20 per cent—could free a substantial amount of resources to support global growth in the developing countries.[8]

**4. Liberalize industrial-country trade to increase Third World exports.** A very important corollary of the financial measures outlined above is a strong effort to avoid further protectionist measures and thereby bolster world export earnings and buying power. It will not be possible for the developing countries to grow and service their debts if they are denied access to markets for their goods. Here, the trends are ominous. The United States already takes the lion's share of developing-country manufactured exports, and Europe and Japan have been very reluctant to expand imports. The United States seems bent upon a path of trade retaliation to force open foreign markets. Pending trade legislation makes "trade relief" for U.S. industry more likely, and administration efforts to avert such legislation have themselves been inherently protectionist. The likely outcome of this strategy is in fact the *reverse* of its intent. Few countries are willing to unilaterally dismantle their trade regimes. Most prefer the rewards of a multilaterally negotiated approach. U.S. bilateral actions therefore have little chance of opening up markets. In addition, as earlier analysis in this overview indicates, the major constraint on U.S. exports to developing countries is not trade barriers but lack of finance. These festering trade conflicts could explode at a moment's notice in response to certain economic circumstances—such as the beginning of a recession, or heightened and misdirected fluctuations in exchange rates. It is vital to sustain the commitment behind the current round of multilateral trade negotiations to reduce trade barriers and to resist protectionism.

**5. Avoid the recessionary impact of cutting the U.S. budget deficit.** The United States will have to pursue an expansionary, noninflationary monetary policy in conjunction with budget-cutting in order to avoid the recessionary impact of cutting the federal budget deficit. In today's internationalized economy, this requires the acquiescence of the central banks of the other major industrial countries. The dollar must fall significantly below its 1980 level if it is to assist in bringing about a reduction of trade imbalances. Should the industrial countries engage in competitive depreciations of their currencies, the likely effect would be a world trade contraction and disastrous financial movements.

There is still time to rectify this country's international imbalances, but doing so will not be easy, and the measures taken now will only be fully felt in the mid-1990s. By that time, the effects of the revolutionary changes now going on in science and technology will have established a markedly different setting for relations between developed and developing countries.

## The 1990s: Reaping the Benefits of the Technological Revolution

For both the United States and developing countries, a central requirement for success in the 1990s is an enhanced scientific and technological capacity to capitalize on the potential of the new technologies to promote economic growth and development in a highly competitive world. The changes in science and technology will open possibilities for new, mutually beneficial relationships between the United States and developing countries, but they also may lead to damaging conflicts over economic and political goals.

The last section of this overview outlines some of the longer-term implications of this technological revolution for policymakers in the areas of trade, employment, investment, development strategies, and international development assistance policies.

### Trade Policy

1. **Expand exports to developing countries.** Ensuring the continued growth of export markets in the developing countries will have to remain a central priority of U.S. foreign policy throughout the 1990s. The chapters in this *Agenda* make the persuasive case that in microelectronics-based manufacturing and in agriculture, American producers need to look to markets in the developing countries for future growth. In the case of microelectronics, Castells and Tyson argue that, "in the long run, the incorporation of the Third World into global technology markets, both as users and as producers of microelectronics innovations, will increase market demand and the range of applications for such innovations. For many years to come, the major markets will remain in the North. Only if new policies are designed now, however, will we be able to see a gradual expansion of demand in the Third World." In the case of agricultural exports, Robert Paarlberg points out that the world is not "awash in grain" due to increased agricultural production in the developing countries. Indeed, the experience of the 1970s indicates that the potential is great for mutually

beneficial market expansion through more rapid development in the developing countries.

**2. Establish new rules to govern international trade.** An open trading system is the key to export expansion, but a new intellectual framework of rules to promote cooperation and handle conflicts is urgently needed. The rules that govern the world's trading and financial systems have been remarkably successful, but they were put in place over four decades ago. They were a response to the experience of the 1930s, when many developing countries were not independent sovereign states, and to the immediate postwar period, when these countries were minor participants in the international economy. In the 1990s, it is essential that the developing countries participate in the design of a trading system that recognizes the benefits that uniform rules can have in promoting cooperation and brokering inevitable conflicts.

The technological changes described in this *Agenda* will give rise to two new issues in this regard: 1) accelerating differentiation among developing countries, and 2) conflicts that arise as governments seek to "create" comparative advantage.

The divergences that have arisen among developing countries in the last decade or two will undoubtedly widen; the traditional "North-South" divide is likely to attenuate and to be overshadowed by new divisions between countries that are and are not major participants in the emerging high-technology economy. The greatest beneficiaries of technological change will be countries that already are more advanced—in the first instance, the newly industrializing countries of Asia and Latin America, which are well down the path of industrialization and already have developed their own indigenous scientific and technological capability. On the other hand, the poorest countries, including most of Sub-Saharan Africa, will be particularly disadvantaged by the scale and pace of technological change. These countries are not major exporters of industrial products (they tend to depend heavily on exporting raw materials); they are not likely to attract much foreign investment; and they do not have an indigenous scientific and technological capacity. The exceptions among the low-income nations are the large but still poor countries with some capability in science and technology, particularly India and China. These two "giants" already have scientific establishments that have produced nuclear explosions and space satellites and increasingly sophisticated industries. In addition, they have a huge internal market for their own industries—a potential that is lacking in many equally poor countries.

Conflicts are likely to arise as both developed and developing countries increasingly seek to "create" comparative advantage in the global economy in the 1990s. The "lessons" of Japanese development and the successes of Korea and Taiwan have not been lost on decision-makers in other developing countries. But the lesson is not the beloved "magic of the marketplace" of industrial-country leaders. Instead, it is the success realized by these countries in using targeted government policies to create globally competitive industries in advanced sectors such as steel, shipbuilding, electronics, and automobiles. Other developing countries now seek to emulate this pattern, as indeed do a number of developed countries. Yet there are no accepted rules of the game about when such policies are legitimate and when they are "unfair" trade practices. The development of new rules to govern the conflicts and disputes that will inevitably result should be a policy priority in the period ahead.

New "rules" already are being proposed by the United States to govern trade in services and, most recently, to radically restructure the world's agricultural trading system. As Jonathan Aronson discusses in this volume, the negotiations on services are now under way. The present task is to arrive at agreements on new rules that reflect the impact of the telecommunications revolution on the interests of both developed and developing countries. Negotiations on agricultural policy pose a difficult challenge due to the political and economic importance of the agricultural sector in most countries. Among the policy measures needed are: the coordinated reduction of global agricultural subsidies (through GATT negotiations), the elimination of U.S. and EEC farm aid programs that encourage overproduction, and a policy of targeted income-support payments to overcome this sector's current crisis. In the long run, world farm trade will benefit from macroeconomic policies and debt management policies that step up growth in developing countries and increase their purchases of agricultural imports.[9]

The importance of formulating new rules for international trade to deal with the changes under way should lead policymakers to seek ways of fully integrating the developing countries into the current round of multilateral trade negotiations, rather than seeking side deals to pacify them.[10] And as trade barriers are major inhibitors of technology transfer and of growth in both developed and developing countries, a series of reciprocal agreements to roll them back in all countries should have high priority.

**3. Increase South-South cooperation.** Trade cooperation among developing countries should be encouraged as a complement to global trade liberalization. To the extent that developing countries find it increasingly difficult in the period ahead to compete in industrial-country markets—due to either technological change or trade barriers—their future growth will depend on trade with each other and on the growth of their own internal markets. New South-South production and trade links could serve to further the process of export specialization necessary for developing countries to maximize the potential benefits of the new industrial technologies and organization.

The potential, long-run importance of developing-country internal markets is very great. However, the size of most developing economies is still small relative to population size, and in most large-population developing countries, purchasing power remains very low or very inequitably distributed.

Greater regional cooperation among developing countries—despite its inevitable complexities—will now have to be pursued more vigorously in both production and trade, particularly by smaller countries. New exporters of manufactures in particular may find that markets will be easier to expand through regional arrangements than through attempting to penetrate less open industrial-country markets already preempted by the NICs. Regional cooperation and markets also may be one of the few available ways for smaller developing countries to attract foreign investment and to gain leverage to set foreign investment terms that favor their own development goals.

### Employment Creation

The current high levels of global unemployment, underemployment, and poverty are already very serious problems. Both developed and developing countries face important and potentially wrenching shifts in employment patterns as a result of the interaction of the new technologies and existing demographic trends. The nature of the challenges facing Northern and Southern policymakers is, however, quite different.

Employment problems in developing countries are particularly acute and likely to be make more difficult by the new microelectronic technologies that are even more "inappropriate" than older technologies for the resource endowments of these countries. As Ray Marshall points out in Chapter 5, unemployment and underemployment in developing countries now average 40 to 50 per cent, and many of those who are employed have very low incomes. Moreover, at least 600 million new jobs—more than the current total number of jobs in all the industrial market economies—will have to be created just to accommodate the new entrants into the labor force who are already alive today.

The United States, too, has an employment problem, despite the large number of jobs created in recent years. In the 1990s, both population and the work force will grow more slowly in the United States, and labor markets are likely to be much tighter (depending, of course, on the impact of technological change, migration, retraining of existing workers, and above all, economic growth). Many of the jobs that will be

# Figure 4. Increase in World Labor Force, 1985-2000 (millions)

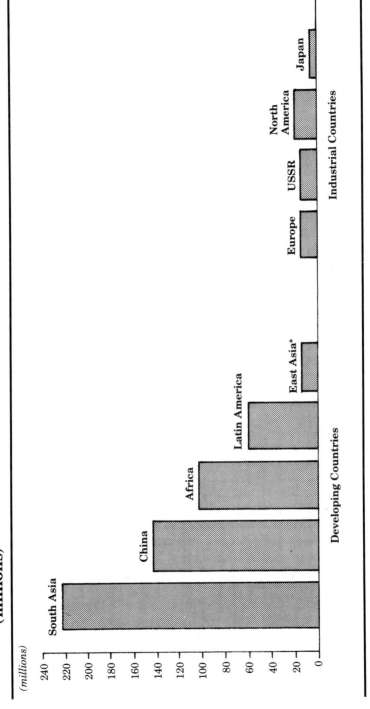

*(millions)*

[a]Excludes China and Japan.
Source: International Labor Office, *Economically Active Population Estimates, 1985.*

available will, moreover, require higher levels of education and skills. The central problem, therefore, is how to deal with deep pockets of structural unemployment (particularly among black and Hispanic youths) and with growing segments of the work force that lack the skills necessary for the new technologically sophisticated jobs.

Policy actions to increase jobs for Americans will be needed in five interrelated areas:

**1. Strengthen the U.S. work force and competitiveness.** The United States can seek to compete internationally either by lowering wages and the real income of Americans or by initiating *now* a major national effort to improve management and production systems, stimulate innovations in advanced technologies, revise outdated public policies that hamper international competition, and above all, to upgrade the skills of American workers through better education, job training, health care, and labor adjustment policies.[11]

**2. Encourage research and development.** U.S. expenditures on non-defense R & D have been low in the last 10 years, threatening to undermine the ability of U.S. business to be competitive in the new technolgical era. In the future, R & D will be a crucial determinant of a company's ability to expand and create jobs. Therefore, U.S. government tax incentives for non-defense R & D, both in the United States and overseas, merit expansion. The ability of universities and scientific research institutes to help expand U.S. and Third World technological capacity will also be necessary if enough skilled personnel are to be available for these R & D efforts.

**3. Reinforce the positive linkage of trade to jobs.** The link between U.S. exports to the Third World and U.S. jobs is important to future prosperity in this country. As summarized in Chapter 5, many recent studies demonstrate that, although employment in some industries has been adversely affected, the United States gains in overall employment from its trade with the developing countries. Programs of trade adjustment therefore need to be considerably improved and specifically linked to the new initiatives that will be needed to retrain workers for jobs in the new technologically sophisticated industries.

**4. Incorporate international labor rights into trade policy.** If workers in developing countries are to benefit from the gains from trade, internationally accepted labor standards need to be a part of trade policy. The goal is not to equalize wages, nor to promote disguised protectionism, but to reach international agreement on issues such as freedom of association and collective bargaining, a prohibition of forced labor, a minimum age for employment, and occupational health and safety guidelines. Labor standards, along with the rising wages that would result, could enable developing countries to become a growing source of aggregate global demand to stimulate the world economy.

**Table 3.   U.S. Highly Skilled Service Jobs: A Large and Growing Share of Total U.S. Employment, 1986 (millions jobs and percentages)**

| | Total Service Jobs (millions jobs) | Share of Total U.S. Employment (per cent) | Expected Growth |
|---|---|---|---|
| **Service jobs, by category:** | | | |
| Managerial and professional specialties | 26.5 | 24.5% | rapid |
| Executive, administrative,  and managerial | 12.6 | 11.7 | rapid |
| Professional specialties | 13.9 | 12.8 | rapid |
| Technical sales and administrative support | 34.3 | 31.7 | average |
| Technicians and related support | 3.4 | 3.1 | n.a. |
| Sales occupations | 13.2 | 12.2 | average |
| Administrative support, including clerical | 17.7 | 16.4 | slow |
| Service occupations, including food preparation, cleaning, and personal services | 13.6 | 12.6 | slow |

n.a. = not available.

Source: U.S. Department of Labor, Bureau of Labor Statistics, *Occupational Outlook Handbook, 1986* and unpublished data.

**5. Reassess immigration policies.** Labor markets have become internationalized, and immigration into the United States, particularly from Mexico, is likely to continue despite efforts to control the flows. Migration could help to alleviate the twin problems of labor surplus in developing countries and the potential shortages of labor in the United States. Care must be taken, however, to ensure that these flows are legal and carefully regulated to prevent adverse impact on low-wage American workers, who are the principal losers from immigration—and whose employment prospects already are not bright.

### International Investment

**1. Avoid conflict over incentives for multinational investment.** In the world of the 1990s, investment will be a very central issue. Much of the new technology has been developed and is owned by private firms and will only be available through them. In addition, as highlighted earlier, the large multinational firms are likely to be an increasingly critical source of new investment capital; until current debt burdens are eased and global growth is restored, commercial banks will be very cautious about their exposure in many developing countries, and economic conditions in developed countries will make it very difficult to increase development assistance levels to meet acute developing-country needs.

Current technological trends in some cases lead toward more investment in the industrial world and in other cases toward more in the developing countries. The new industrial technologies and patterns of organization will lead to expansion of industries in the developed countries to service their own markets. This trend already is apparent in the auto industry and has been reinforced by growing protectionism in the industrial world. Moreover, the threat of being closed out of lucrative industrial-country markets, together with the emergence of technologies in which labor is a less important cost factor, already has led investors to locate new production facilities within industrial rather than developing countries. Thus Hong Kong apparel manufacturers now are investing in the British Midlands—in part to avoid European trade barriers.

At the same time, developing countries also possess some advantages for attracting multinational investment. Firms are likely to invest overseas in the 1990s for several new reasons. First, investors will seek to capitalize on *existing* investments in developing countries. They also will want access to large markets of actual and potential significance. And they will need to tap skilled but relatively lower-cost labor—for example, microchip designers and computer programmers. Thus India, for example, already is serving as a source of skills for U.S.

computer firms, and geographic proximity to the U.S. market and existing transportation infrastructure make Mexico's border areas and the Caribbean attractive to U.S. firms. Competition with industrial-country firms for market access will also drive investment decisions. Finally, firms will invest in particular developing-country locations in order to improve coordination of worldwide production and marketing; thus Singapore, for example, is now seeking to become the financial capital of the Far East.

In this setting, incentives to attract multinational investment will become a major policy issue. A recent ODC study identified more than forty different kinds of incentives designed by developing countries to attract private investment.[12] Similar measures have been adopted by the European Community and over twenty-five U.S. states. When such measures are and are not "fair" is, however, a very contentious issue. As in the trade field, the need for generally accepted international rules governing investment incentives will loom larger in the decade of the 1990s.

**2. Protect intellectual property.** As Castells and Tyson point out in this volume, perhaps no other trade issue will be as significant in the future as the protection of intellectual property. The value of proprietary technology is greatly increasing as higher technology moves to the fore. As a result, innovative concepts are becoming as important as goods themselves in international trade competition. The battle over patents and copyrights already is joined. The current dispute between Brazil and the United States over the protection of computer software is just one harbinger of this trend. Developments in biotechnology also will bring a series of problems stemming from the fact that much of the research being carried out in these technologies is owned by private firms. A major developing-country concern is that the granting of patents will allow firms in the industrial world to dominate the biotechnology field. Similarly, many have expressed the fear that products to meet Third World needs will get lower priority because their market in the foreseeable future is much smaller and poorer.[13] The technological revolution will certainly multiply these conflicts and concerns. One of the key issues of the decade ahead consequently will be the development of new rules for the legitimate protection of intellectual property that are acceptable to both developed and developing countries.

**3. Expand investment insurance and guarantee schemes.** Bilateral and especially multilateral investment guarantee mechanisms (such as the Overseas Private Investment Corporation, the Inter-American Investment Corporation, and the Multilateral Investment Guarantee Agency) should seek to promote investments that enhance technology transfer, scientific education, and Third World research and development capacity. Such guarantees could foster greater mutual benefits for U.S. investors and Third World countries by establishing a more favorable Third World investment climate centered on the dynamic, leading-edge industries and services.

### Development Strategies and Technological Change

In the 1980s, thinking about development strategies has undergone considerable evolution.[14] Development strategies in developing countries and multilateral institutions now need to include policy prescriptions concerning the new microelectronics-based technologies. The new industrial technologies will considerably slow the dispersal of previously labor-intensive industries to developing countries other than the current NICs.[15] The fact that labor accounts for a much smaller part of the costs of manufacturing with these new technologies, and that a trained and educated work force is necessary for their utilization, means that many developing countries will not be able to reap their benefits.

The net effect will be a considerable increase in the difficulties encountered by "new entrants." Traditionally, development planners have assumed that countries would gradually shift to greater reliance on industrial production, usually for export. But one of the important results of the new technologies may be to virtually rule out that option for countries that want to follow the path of industry-led development blazed by the NICs. The prospects for new entrants are diminished rather than enhanced by the changes outlined earlier, simply because they lack the trained personnel to assimilate the new technologies and do not already participate in established patterns of foreign investment. The "second-tier" NICs, including countries such as Malaysia, Thailand, the Philippines, and perhaps some Caribbean countries—and certainly many of the poorer countries with similar aspirations—are likely to suffer as a result.

**1. Build national scientific and technological capacity.** Development success will in the future depend heavily on whether countries already have or can rapidly develop their own scientific and technological capacity. As one of the best case studies of the experience of developing countries in this area concludes, "The costs of attaining international competitiveness . . . are the costs of acquiring technological capability."[16] However, this is precisely where most of the developing world is severely disadvantaged. Although educational levels in most developing countries are much higher than they were three decades ago, only about 10 per cent of the scientists and engineers engaged in research and development in 1980 were in the developing countries, and over 94 per cent of all R & D expenditures were made by the industrial countries. A further problem is that the R & D that is conducted in the developing world is very unevenly distributed among countries; much of it is in the fast-growing Asian NICs and India. In many cases, moreover, developing-country research is not linked to domestic industrial structures.[17]

**2. Limit dependence on raw material exports.** The low-income countries must be helped to reduce their economic dependence on exports of industrial raw materials. Many developing countries already have done so. But, as Raymond Mikesell shows in this *Agenda*, in 17 developing countries, raw materials still account for more than 50 per cent of export earnings, and in an additional 30 countries, raw materials remain very important to foreign trade, accounting for over 15 per cent of export earnings. The countries that continue to be most heavily dependent on exporting raw materials are also among the poorest, with the worst development prospects. Yet the demand for and real prices of raw materials are unlikely to increase over the next decade—in good part due to technological change and the introduction of new synthetic materials. Unless countries have high-quality ore, or a raw material of strategic importance, such as uranium, their continued dependence on exports of industrial raw materials will be a dead end.

**3. Acknowledge a role for the state in the technological revolution.** The new technologies will force reconsideration of the role of the state. Governments will assume a greater role in planning the direction of economic development in order to adapt to the new technological environment. The activities of Korea's and Taiwan's buoyant private sectors have obscured the fact that the success of these countries' development models was *heavily dependent* on the skilled guidance of their governments.[18] But if developing countries are to manage the adaptation to these new industrial technologies, their governments will play a crucial role, particularly in creating the proper set of economic signals, and in making the necessary investments in education and training to participate in these new processes. Governments will also surely play a major role in attracting the investment that brings with it access to these new technologies.

### Development Assistance Policies

Multilateral and bilateral aid policies will need to be radically re-designed to take account of the technological revolution and to ensure that its benefits do not bypass low-income countries and poor people. As discussed earlier, countries that do not already have an industrial base and do not already export to the industrialized countries will find it increasingly difficult to compete in world markets unless they have some particular resource—material, human, or geographic—that will

## Figure 5. Non-Oil Commodities: Real Prices

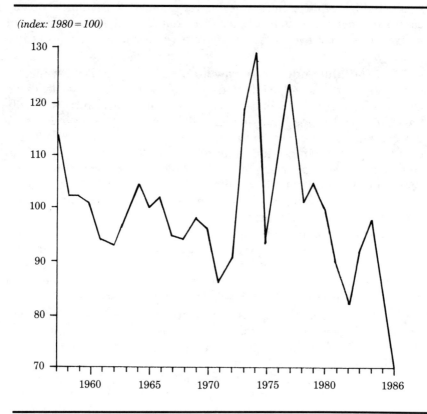

*(index: 1980 = 100)*

Source: IMF, Commodities Division, unpublished data.

give them an edge. Low-income countries by and large will not be able to reap the benefits of the new industrial technology. In addition, past experience with dramatic technological innovations—most notably, some of the lessons learned in the introduction of the successful "green revolution" crops—illustrates that such innovations must be very carefully launched so as to avoid increasing social inequity.

**1. Strengthen national capacity to utilize the new technologies.** Aid programs should focus on assisting developing countries, particularly the poorer countries, to equip themselves to use the new technologies. Manuel Castells and Laura Tyson conclude in this *Agenda* that "the major policy concerns are how to acquire technological know-how and how to use it for national development purposes." To do so, aid progams will need to train men and women to understand and utilize the new technologies. In addition, countries will need the indigenous capacity to assimilate, adapt, and eventually create technologies to meet their own particular needs. The issue of adapting technological advances to domestic economic circumstances is particularly important, since many of the new industrial technologies and techniques are labor-saving, while most developing countries must create jobs for the large number of people who will enter their work forces in the next decade.

Again, the crucial issue is not only the development of scientific and technological personnel, but the effective linkage of basic research to productive processes. Due to the high costs of research, developing countries have to be quite selective in their efforts. Most studies conclude that they should focus on assimilating and adapting existing technologies with as little time lag as possible if they are to compete on a global basis.

The level of skills that will be needed by developing countries to assimilate and adapt the new technologies is already changing. Obviously scientific and management skills will be crucial to run complex industries and to compete on a global basis. In addition, higher-level skills will be needed to maintain and service microelectronic based equipment (although the increasing use of modular components that are self-diagnosing and that can be replaced with "plug-in" parts may help in this area). In contrast, the skills required for the many fewer employees needed to operate the automated equipment are probably lower, as computer programming takes over choices previously made by people.

**2. Buffer the human impact of the new technologies.** Care must be taken to ensure that the impact of the new technologies on global poverty and on the well-being of individuals will not be adverse. The technological revolution now under way will not automatically or necessarily ameliorate the human condition. Herein lies a dilemma of considerable proportions.

The precise impact of the new technologies is still very difficult to predict; they are not yet in widespread use in developing countries, and their potential for improving human well-being through applications to health, education, and agriculture is far from fully understood. There is, moreover, a strong possibility that at least some of their side-effects will be adverse, especially in the near term. The reason lies in the nature of the technology. Fewer new jobs will be created, and those that are will be at a higher skill level—for which the majority of people in the developing world will not be qualified. As a result, in countries that achieve competitiveness, middle-class workers benefiting from the new technologies are likely to form "islands of prosperity," with a resulting aggravation of income disparities within the country.[19]

On the other hand, the potential of the new technologies for vastly improving human well-being is also great. As Castells and Tyson point out, the microelectronics technology can be applied to development problems in even the poorest countries. For instance, remote sensing by satellites can be used for identifying resources, demographic planning, and early warning of drought. Personal computers can have a great impact on government planning and data collection, as is already the case in Nigeria and Kenya. The new telecommunications technologies make remote areas more accessible, permitting village-level education to spread widely and inexpensively. The new developments in biotechnology have vast potential for improving human welfare. As mentioned earlier, these include a range of new agricultural products, vaccines and medicines, and new sources of energy. Many potential biotechnology applications are of great significance for developing countries because they are "relatively less capital-intensive, less energy-demanding, and less sophisticated than most of the current physical-chemical industrial methods."[20]

**3. Increase aid to low-income countries.** If the low-income countries are to benefit from technological change, their share of overall aid flows must increase. The measures outlined earlier in this *Agenda* to promote renewed growth clearly will help to support development in the middle-income countries. But they will not necessarily do much for the low-income countries that are not now major participants in the world's trade and financial systems.

Currently only 40 per cent of all aid from the OECD countries goes to the low-income countries; the U.S. share going to lower-income countries is 24 per cent. (See also Annex Table C-6, Statistical Annexes, p. 241.) In most industrial countries, budgetary resources for development will be scarce, and the acute needs of the low-income countries make it imperative that concessional assistance be directed to them. The need for this shift is analogous to the importance of preserving a domestic "safety net" for disadvantaged groups in our own society, even in the face of economic adversity.

**4. Support export diversification.** The reduction of low-income country dependence upon earnings from raw materials will require finance for diversification. In the last decade, a great deal of attention was paid to commodity programs designed to buffer countries against swings in raw material prices. Despite their theoretical attractions, these schemes have proven to be very costly and very difficult to manage. Yet even when prices drop, poor countries with an acute need for foreign exchange have little choice but to continue production. In the near term, as Raymond Mikesell indicates, some form of compensatory financing will be needed; over the longer term, countries dependent on raw material exports need support in diversifying their economies.[21]

Most industrial countries view funds for compensatory financing as a trade-off with other uses of concessional resources. If the *low-income* countries are to make any development progress, they will urgently need sustained flows of concessional aid well into the next decade. Their already bleak prospects will worsen in the absence of concerted action by the industrial countries, and particularly the United States, on the concessional assistance front.

**5. Redirect U.S. aid programs.** No one set of policies will be applicable to the entire range of increasingly differentiated developing countries in the new economic environment of the 1990s. Long-standing programs of development assistance will have little relevance for middle-income countries that are major commercial partners of the United States. The importance to U.S. interests of continued growth and development in the middle-income countries should lead to a comprehensive rethinking of how trade, financial, and commercial policies can be coordinated to support those interests along the lines suggested earlier in this overview. The poorer countries, however, will certainly continue to need assistance that can *only* be provided by bilateral and multilateral development programs.

In the decade ahead, U.S. aid programs therefore should be targeted predominantly at the poorer countries, and on programs that will help developing countries utilize the new technologies to stimulate equitable economic growth and to enable their citizens to lead vastly better lives. These are precisely the areas in which the United States has a comparative advantage in the aid business. And as it adapts its own economy to the Third Industrial Revolution, this country should also have valuable new experience to share with the developing countries.

The United States clearly is entering a new era. Policymakers cannot ignore the constraints that the changed international economic position of the United States imposes on a broad range of its foreign policy choices without causing a further long-term erosion of this country's international position—or without condemning future generations of Americans to paying off an unprecedented level of foreign debt. If the United States successfully overcomes its immediate economic problems and takes advantage of the technological opportunities now on the horizon, it can emerge in a stronger international economic position than at any time in the recent past. The majority of developing countries, however, because they have fewer assets and much less wealth than the industrialized countries, face a far more difficult task if they are to realize the potential benefits of the technological revolution.

This overview has taken the essentially optimistic view that the changes now under way open up opportunities for the United States to promote its own long-term economic and political interests as well as those of the developing countries. But whether this country can take advantage of those opportunities is an open question. More than ever, U.S. prosperity is inextricably linked to the achievement of global development. Yet many still believe that "our own" economic problems must have priority, and that other countries must play a greater role in the international economy. This *Agenda* argues the opposite. Even in a world in which the United States is only first among equals, its international leadership is essential, and in the 1990s this country can be in a position to provide it. The United States of course has a choice. It can pursue a purely reactive policy, and thereby make itself a hostage to the all-too-likely financial and political disorders of the developing world. Or it can take the lead in designing and supporting international solutions for the urgent problems of the developing world. That choice lies with the administration that takes office next year.

## Notes

[1] These analysts of course differ among themselves as to how this should be done. See, for example, Martin Feldstein, "Correcting the Trade Deficit," *Foreign Affairs*, Vol. 65, No. 4 (Spring 1987); Robert Z. Lawrence, *Can America Compete?* (Washington, D.C.: The Brookings Institution, 1984).

[2] See, for example, Stephen S. Cohen and John Zysman, *Why Manufacturing Matters: The Myth of the Post-Industrial Economy* (New York: Basic Books, 1987); or Lester Thurow, *The Zero-Sum Solution: Building a World Class American Economy* (New York: Simon and Schuster, 1985).

[3] John P. Lewis and Valeriana Kallab, eds., *U.S. Foreign Policy and the Third World: Agenda 1983* (New York: Praeger Publishers for the Overseas Development Council, 1983).

[4] Kurt Hoffman, "Technological and Organizational Transformation in Industry: The Role of TNCs and Implications for Developing Countries" (Paper prepared for the Policy Analysis and Research Division, United Nations Center on Transnational Corporations, September 1987), p. 16.

[5] Joel P. Clark and Merton C. Flemings, "Advanced Materials and the Economy," *Scientific American* (October 1986), p. 51.

[6] Eric D. Larson, Marc H. Ross, and Robert Williams, "Beyond the Era of Materials," *Scientific American* (June 1986).

[7] Richard E. Feinberg, "An Open Letter to the World Bank's New President," in Richard E. Feinberg and contributors, *Between Two Worlds: The World Bank's Next Decade* (New Brunswick, N.J.: Transaction Books for the Overseas Development Council, 1986).

[8] John W. Sewell and Christine E. Contee, "Foreign Aid and Gramm-Rudman," *Foreign Affairs*, Vol. 65, No. 5 (Summer 1987).

[9] Stuart K. Tucker, "Reforming U.S. Agricultural Trade Policy," ODC *Policy Focus* No. 5, 1987.

[10] Ernest H. Preeg, ed., *Hard Bargaining Ahead: U.S. Trade Policy and Developing Countries* (New Brunswick, N.J.: Transaction Books for the Overseas Development Council, 1985).

[11] The report of the President's Commission on Industrial Competitiveness, released in 1985, provides a number of creative policy recommendations in this area. See also *Reversing America's Declining Competitiveness* (Report of the 74th American Assembly, November 1987).

[12] Stephen Guisinger, "Host-Country Policies to Attract and Control Foreign Investment," in Theodore H. Moran and contributors, *Investing in Development: New Roles for Private Capital?* (New Brunswick: N.J.: Transaction Books for the Overseas Development Council, 1986).

[13] John Elkington, *Double Dividends? U.S. Biotechnology and Third World Development* (Washington, D.C.: World Resources Institute, 1986). For example, the U.S. firm Merck & Co. has developed a drug known as ivermectin that prevents or halts the disease "river blindness," which affects 18 million people; Merck has made it available free of charge to programs worldwide.

[14] John P. Lewis and Valeriana Kallab, eds., *Development Strategies Reconsidered* (New Brunswick, N.J.: Transaction Books for the Overseas Development Council, 1986).

[15] See James P. Womack, "Prospects for the U.S.-Mexican Relationship in the Motor Vehicle Sector," in Cathryn L. Thorup and contributors, *The United States and Mexico: Face to Face with New Technology* (New Brunswick, N.J.: Transaction Books for the Overseas Development Council, 1987), p. 107.

[16] Howard Pack and Larry E. Westphal, "Industrial Strategy and Technological Change: Theory vs. Reality," *Journal of Development Economics*, Vol. 22, No. 1, p. 106.

[17] Carl J. Dahlman and Claudio R. Frischtak, "Technological Change and Industrial Competitiveness in Semi-Industrialized Countries" (Industrial Strategy and Policy Division, Industry Department, World Bank, October 1986, mimeo.).

[18] Colin I. Bradford, Jr., "East Asian 'Models': Myths and Lessons," in *Development Strategies Reconsidered*, op. cit.

[19] This conclusion is suggested by one of the few quantitative studies of this question, summarized in Sam Cole, "The Global Impact of Information Technology," *World Development*, Vol. 14, No. 10/11 (1986).

[20] Arnoldo K. Ventura, "Biotechnologies and Their Implications for Third World Development," *Technology and Society*, Vol. 4, No. 2, 1982.

[21] John D.A. Cuddy, "Commodity Trade," in *Hard Bargaining Ahead*, op. cit. See also the special issue of *World Development* on "Primary Commodities in the World Economy: Problems and Policies," Vol. 15, No. 5 (May 1987).

# Summaries of Chapter Recommendations

## 1. High-Technology Choices Ahead: Restructuring Interdependence (Manuel Castells and Laura D'Andrea Tyson)

The new microelectronics-based technologies are widely perceived to have profound implications for the developing countries, but there is deep disagreement about exactly what those implications are and how they will affect the development prospects of individual countries. To some, the new technologies hold out the hope of solutions to pressing problems of nutrition, health, education, and industrialization in the Third World. To others, they raise the specter of greater Third World dependence on multinationals, greater differentiation of income both within and among Third World countries, and the marginalization of much of the Third World in international trading and production patterns in which the availability of unskilled labor becomes increasingly irrelevant. Evidence from a variety of industries, including the automobile and electronics industries examined in this paper, indicates that reality is more complicated and more uncertain than either the optimistic or pessimistic perspective suggests. What is certain is that policy choices by the developing countries themselves and by the developed countries will play a critical role in determining the outcomes.

The impact of the microelectronics revolution on a particular developing country depends on its access to technological know-how and on its "technological capacity," or the ability to harness such know-how for its developmental objectives. The more developed among the developing countries, especially some of the NICs, are in a better position than the poorer ones on both counts. They are better able to acquire technological know-how through joint ventures, foreign direct investment, and the like, and better able to diffuse it effectively. Therefore, in the absence of policy interventions, the new technologies are likely to afford a handful of developing countries the opportunity to jump to the technological frontier while the majority of them fall still farther behind.

The developing countries themselves, either individually or in regional or other groupings, can formulate policies to improve their acquisition and use of the new technologies. Developing-country governments must be flexible in their negotiations and regulations on foreign technology transfer, using different strategies (including tax and legal incentives) with different foreign producers and for different types of technologies. Efforts to acquire technology should emphasize arrangements that include nationally or regionally based R & D facilities and training programs. Intra-regional cooperation among a group of countries to finance the development of a regional pool of talent by establishing a cooperative training program is a sensible strategy. Such a program might be combined with an R & D program focusing on the applications of microelectronics technologies to regional problems. Intra-regional cooperation for these purposes might also lower the cost of acquiring the needed technology from foreign suppliers and attract foreign direct investment on favorable terms to a region that might otherwise have been overlooked. It also might attract external support from multilateral agencies or from foreign producers with an interest in potential markets for their technologies. Such efforts should focus on blending microelectronics technologies with traditional economic activity and with developing new applications of the technology suitable for regional economic and social needs.

The ability of Third World countries to mobilize the new technologies for economic development will be significantly influenced by the policies of the advanced industrial countries, especially the United States. The present worldwide insufficiency of global demand, reflected in individual sectors, especially those in which the new technologies provide the foundation for rapid increases in output, has already brought about competitive clashes—such as those between the United States and other developing as well as developed supplier nations in the cases of autos and electronics.

It is in the fundamental economic interest of the United States and its leading economic sectors to foster a process of technological development in the Third World that *stimulates demand* for microelectronic products. What is now needed is a major, U.S.-led, international technological initiative that will provide the means to finance the utilization of the new microelectronics technologies for more rapid economic growth in the Third World to the benefit of *both* developing and developed countries. Without such a large-scale strategy, encompassing policy measures by both the developing and the developed countries, the pessimistic view of the longer-term effects of the microelectronics revolution on the developing world is likely to become a reality.

## 2. The Service Industries: Growth, Trade, and Development Prospects (Jonathan D. Aronson)

The revolution in services technology, coupled with changing regulatory philosophies, requires industrial and developing countries to consider the role of services in their economies and to agree on how to manage the international exchange of services.

The United States and other industrial countries should give more priority to creating more efficient and competitive service industries in order to boost their economies. A more robust service sector would help agriculture and manufacturing sectors thrive, and it would promote jobs and growth. Special attention should be paid to creating efficient domestic telecommunications and information industries. This sector is critical to the productivity and competitiveness of finance, insurance, education, and other service sectors, and it will also improve manufacturing productivity.

Developing countries also need to promote greater efficiency of their service sectors. Technological service innovations in industrial countries make it possible to transfer new technology to developing countries and to tie their industries more closely into the world economy. This promises to promote short-term growth in developing countries—but at the cost of some control over sovereign decisions.

Developing countries thus need to walk a tightrope between control and openness. They can try to build their own service industries by adopting infant-industry strategies, by stimulating their domestic economies through the modernization of telecommunications, finance, and other high-technology service sectors—or they can try to do so by introducing more competition and experimentation with privatization.

The cost of creating a domestic service industry in isolation from competition is probably too high for all but the largest developing countries. Moreover, infant-industry strategies are unproven for high-technology services. Developing countries should increase their investment in modernizing their high-technology service industries, such as telecommunications and finance—converting these sectors from sources of revenue for the treasury into engines of development. Profits need to be reinvested in these sectors. Developing countries should also experiment with increasing competition in the provision of services. This can be done in many ways, and each country must decide what path best suits its needs. The options include: a) licensing *new* domestic service suppliers, b) allowing foreign firms to enter into joint ventures with domestic service providers, c) permitting foreign competitors into the domestic market, d) permitting competition in the provision of international service while maintaining national control over the provision of domestic services. Whether or not increased competition is allowed, developing countries should consider the appropriateness of partial or total privatization. Sale of government monopolies can promote efficiency and raise revenues.

The goal of the Uruguay Round of multilateral negotiations is to begin to overhaul the rules and principles used to manage the world economy. An agreement on trade in services is critical to this effort. Industrial and developing countries therefore should try to depoliticize the negotiations.

Industrial countries should encourage and assist developing countries to undertake more careful analysis of the role of their own service sectors. The industrial world should also accept that the exclusion of labor-intensive service sectors and immigration from the negotiations will require that developing countries be compensated for an agreed period of time in the form of special and differential treatment.

The negotiations hold out some real opportuntities for developing countries if they all engage in the give and take. If some of them continue to oppose the negotiations altogether, however, this is likely to prompt industrial countries to work out an arrangement among themselves.

## 3. U.S. Agriculture and the Developing World: Opportunities for Joint Gains (Robert L. Paarlberg)

Between 1981 and 1986, agricultural production in developing countries increased while U.S. agricultural exports to the developing world suddenly declined by 30 per cent. This led some vocal observers to mistakenly conclude that U.S. farmers lost out because farmers in poor countries were suddenly doing better and to argue that the United States should protect its own farmers by stopping development assistance for Third World agriculture.

A careful examination of recent production trends shows this line of thinking to be largely unfounded. There has been no *sudden* surge in developing-country agricultural production. During the first half of the 1980s, agricultural production in developing countries (excluding China) grew at almost exactly the same average annual rate (2.76 per cent) that was recorded over the preceding decade of the 1970's (2.74 per cent). It was not a change in agricultural production performance, but instead a change in developing-country economic growth rates, foreign debt service burdens, and U.S. competitiveness (high dollar exchange rates between 1981 and 1985 made U.S. farm products less attractive) that caused developing countries to reduce their farm purchases from the United States.

If the developing countries in fact were to achieve sudden above-trend gains in their own agricultural production, the consequences might not be all bad for U.S. farmers. Agricultural success in developing countries could lead to broadly based income growth, dietary enrichment, and hence, to *larger* food import demand. The paradoxical result could then be a larger rather than a smaller volume of agricultural imports—a result that is most visible in the agriculturally successful and rapidly developing countries of East Asia. South Korea and Taiwan import more wheat and coarse grain every year than all of the hungry but poor (and agriculturally unsuccessful) countries of Sub-Saharan Africa combined.

The policy steps necessary to stimulate the kind of agricultural success in developing countries that will lead to broadly based income growth, to dietary enrichment, and hence to expanded world farm trade include a mix of measures—both farm-policy and non-farm policy measures—not only in the developing world but also in the United States and other developed countries.

In the developing world, "urban-biased" national policies that overtax the farm sector—such as low farm commodity-price policies, lagging public investments in rural extension and infrastructure, overvalued exchange rates, marketing restrictions, and monopoly marketing boards—must be replaced by policies that promote productive employment and income growth in the countryside. To ensure broadly based results, these policies must be designed to weaken rather than reinforce rural concentrations of land ownership, wealth, social status, and political power.

In developed countries such as the United States, the most important policy steps waiting to be taken are not in the agricultural sector itself, but in the larger arena of international trade, financial, monetary, and development assistance policy. Protectionist trade policies must be avoided, debt policies must stress future growth, discipline must be reimposed on U.S. fiscal policy (so as to make room for less stringent monetary policy), and the trend away from generous U.S. support for bilateral and multilateral agricultural development must be reversed. U.S. farm interest groups hoping to revive their export sales to the developing world should be leading the fight to set these policies in place.

## 4. The Changing Demand for Raw Materials (Raymond F. Mikesell)

The decline in raw materials prices during the 1980s has been caused by a *combination of structural changes*, including: a fall in the rate of growth of world consumption of raw materials; overcapacity, especially in the metal mining industries; competition from synthetic products; and a reduction in real costs of production achieved through technological advances. The decreases in real raw materials prices are unlikely to be reversed in the foreseeable future, and for some raw materials, real prices may be lower at the end of the century than they were the mid-1980s.

Although most developing countries have reduced their dependence on raw material exports over the past decade, a number of very poor countries remain heavily dependent on one or two raw materials for their foreign exchange income. These countries are the principal victims of declining raw material prices, and remedial action should be taken to reduce the impact on their economies.

The author makes the following recommendations:

1. Development strategies should be designed to diversify the export earnings of poor countries that are heavily dependent on a few raw materials by promoting exports of primary commodities with favorable market prospects and exports of processed commodities, manufactures, and services. This does not suggest that traditional raw material exports should be reduced. On the contrary, efforts should be made to increase productivity in the raw material industries and to adapt the products to changes in world demand.

2. In the case of very poor countries, development programs should be directed to expanding the production of food and other essentials for domestic consumption. If their costs can be reduced through increased productivity, some of these products will be able to find markets in other developing countries in the same region or in world trade.

3. International commodity agreements are of doubtful usefulness in modifying price fluctuations arising from cyclical causes, and such arrangements may even be counterproductive in dealing with a long-term or secular decline in commodity prices. International assistance for dealing with the problems arising from declining raw material prices can be made more effective by promoting the development objectives outlined in the preceding two recommendations than by artificially supporting raw material prices.

4. Industrial countries should eliminate their restrictions on imports of raw materials and of processed and manufactured goods from developing countries. This will promote the diversification of their exports, especially since tariffs and other trade restrictions tend to be

concentrated on processed commodities and on labor-intensive manufactures such as textiles.

5. Foreign direct investment should play a larger role in financing mineral resource development in Third World countries. This will require changes in the foreign investment policies of the developing countries themselves as well as new initiatives by both industrial-country governments and multinational agencies to encourage direct private investment—particularly in manufacturing and processing that contribute to export diversification.

## 5. Jobs: The Shifting Structure of Global Employment (Ray Marshall)

In most countries, workers—as well as producers and governments—are encountering problems generated by major, worldwide changes in production and employment patterns. The most fundamental of these are internationalization of the world economy, demographic and labor-market changes, and the spread of technological innovations, especially information technologies. These new working conditions also present public policymakers with new problems.

Developing-country employment problems are particularly grim, with unemployment and underemployment on the order of 40-50 per cent. Furthermore, at least 600 million jobs must be created over the next 20 years just to keep joblessness from rising. Industrial countries face a different problem—that of deep pockets of structural unemployment and an increasingly bifurcated work force.

Employment concerns are important political issues in all countries, and trade policy is bearing the burden of recent efforts to buffer domestic sectors from external shocks. Yet the evidence clearly shows that North-South trade in fact results in *net job gains*. Therefore policymakers need to develop strategies for increasing North-South trade while at the same time ameliorating the localized dislocations, thus maximizing the overall gain for the United States and the developing countries.

U.S. policies should pursue three broad goals:

*1. U.S.-Third World Policies.* U.S. economic strategies should give greater attention to North-South relations, especially in the areas of immigration, technology transfer, trade, and development. These relations can be boosted in a way that helps both the United States and developing countries by recognizing and acting upon their common interests in the following two areas:

a) Migration could overcome the labor surplus situation in the Third World and alleviate future labor shortages in the United States, and

b) Strengthened international labor rights could ensure the equitable distribution of the gains from (and therefore a sustained support for) direct foreign investment in the Third World.

*2. U.S. Official and Public Support for a Global Strategy.* High priority should be given to building a national consensus for an employment-oriented global development strategy—that is, for taking advantage of the internationalization of the global economy and adjusting the U.S. economy to enhance the benefits of interdependence. Three elements are vital if the United States is to successfully pursue such an approach. First, unilateral action must give way to greater international cooperation in institution building. Second, the U.S. should put its own economic house in order through a realignment of its macroeconomic policy. Third, U.S. human resources need to be enhanced through better education, health care, job training, and an adequate labor adjustment program.

*3. U.S. Competitiveness.* In order to avoid a painful compression of U.S. wages, U.S. competitiveness must be improved through three other mechanisms. First, management systems need to be altered to reflect the transformation of U.S. production into more sophisticated systems, with greater employee involvement in production decisions. Second, the United States should vigorously pursue innovations in advanced technologies. Third, obsolete public policies can be updated to avoid major legal conflicts in business relations and instead create a stable economic environment built on more rational macroeconomic and investment policies.

# Growth, Exports, and Jobs in a Changing World Economy

# Chapter 1

# High-Technology Choices Ahead: Restructuring Interdependence

Manuel Castells and Laura D'Andrea Tyson

## The Microelectronics Revolution

The microelectronics-based revolution, although widely discussed, is still in its infancy. This is nowhere more true than in discussions of the impact of the new technologies on the Third World. While there is widespread agreement that such technologies have profound implications for developing countries, disagreement and uncertainty abound as to exactly what these implications are and how they will affect the development prospects of individual countries. To some, the new technologies hold out the hope of solutions to pressing problems of nutrition, health, education, and industrialization in the Third World.[1] To others, they raise the specter of greater Third World dependence on multinational corporations, greater differentiation of income both within and among Third World countries, and the marginalization of much of the Third World in international trading and production patterns in which the availability of cheap unskilled labor is increasingly irrelevant.[2]

Reality is more complicated and more uncertain than either the optimistic or the pessimistic scenario suggests. The new technologies present both constraints and opportunities for the countries of the Third World, and the outcome in individual cases will not be technologically determined. Indeed, flexibility is a critical feature of the new technologies.[3] Machinery formerly designed to perform a single task can now be designed to perform a wide variety of tasks. Product and process innovations that earlier required substantial retooling can now be realized by the reconfiguration of existing machinery on the

55

shop floor. Production tasks that once needed to be spatially contiguous can now be dispersed around the globe and linked together by new communications and transportation technologies.[4] The remote-sensing technologies whose primary application is currently in the military sphere have great potential for agricultural and demographic planning as well as for the prediction and management of ecological disasters.

As with past technological revolutions, such as the introduction of the steam engine in the eighteenth century and of electricity in the nineteenth, the microelectronics revolution will provide an impetus for the industrialization and development of some developing countries that currently lag behind the technological frontier.[5] Many other countries, however, will fall still farther behind as the technological frontier moves rapidly outward while they stagnate.[6] Countries that are best able to acquire and use the new technologies will benefit the most. Not surprisingly, this suggests that the more developed countries of the Third World, particularly the newly industrializing countries (NICs)— which are in a better position to acquire technology through trade, joint ventures, and foreign direct investment and to diffuse it through their manufacturing base—stand to benefit the most from the new technologies. Indeed, some of these countries may be able to use the new techniques to leapfrog to the technological frontier.[7] In contrast, the poorest countries, which cannot afford expensive technological imports, cannot attract foreign investment, and lack the educational and infrastructural base required for the diffusion of modern technology, are certain to fall still farther behind. In individual countries, the outcome will be largely the result of political, social, economic, and historical factors that traditionally influence development. Technology will be a powerful tool mediating the effects of such fundamental structural factors.

The outcome of the microelectronics revolution for developing countries will also depend on how it changes relationships between them and the developed countries.[8] The new technologies constitute the material infrastructure for the internationalization of the economy in all its dimensions: production, management, distribution, marketing, and finance. They allow for new patterns in the international division of labor and in the dispersion of economic activity, both across firms and across countries. The access of the developing countries to new microelectronics technology will depend on how these patterns develop, and this in turn will depend on the decisions of consumers, producers, and governments in the developed countries.

As in the past, but with even more force in the integrated world economy made possible by the technological revolution, development prospects in the Third World will be shaped largely by economic and political decisions taken in the *developed* world. At the same time, however, the pace and form of technological development in the Third World will affect the prospects for the expansion of high-technology industries in advanced countries as well as for the equilibrium of the overall process of development worldwide.

This paper explores some of the implications of new micro-electronics-based technologies for North-South relationships, aiming at understanding the process from a global perspective—the only one appropriate to the realities of the world of our time. We first examine the effects of the new technologies on two major industries: electronics, both a producer and a user of such technologies; and automobiles, the manufacturing industry in which the application of microelectronics-based technologies in production has proceeded the farthest. After reviewing some evidence on these particular industries, we consider the impact of the new technologies on specific Third World countries. We argue that because of country differences in the ability to obtain and use them, such technologies are likely to result in growing economic *differentiation* within the Third World. We conclude by discussing some policy options for promoting development and moderating this differentiation through more effective diffusion and more appropriate applications of the new technologies throughout the Third World. We examine policy choices from the point of view of the North, from the position of the South, and from a global perspective.

# Implications for Developing Countries: Electronics and Automobiles

The new microelectronics technologies are changing international economic relationships among countries of the North as well as between them and the countries of the South in two principal ways.[9] First, the industrial sectors producing these technologies are among the fastest growing in the world. Between 1965 and 1985, the global output of the electronics complex grew by over 13 per cent per annum in real terms, and by 1985 it equaled the global output of the automobile industry and surpassed the global output of the steel industry.[10] Ability to compete in the electronics industries is an increasingly critical factor in a nation's ability to win a share of growing world markets. Second, microelectronics technologies are changing the competitive dynamics of downstream industries by changing their production techniques and locational patterns.[11] Producers with access to the newest technologies in industries as diverse as automobiles, textiles, and machine tools are defining new production frontiers that give them an absolute cost advantage over competitors relying on older technologies. The new production techniques also allow for the introduction of new products with which traditional suppliers often are unable to compete. An absolute cost advantage or a product innovation advantage conferred by superior technological know-how is a major determinant of trade flows among the advanced industrial countries, and it is becoming increasingly so for trade flows between them and the developing countries.[12] This is not to deny that traditional comparative cost arguments still explain a large share of Third World trade with developed countries. However, developing countries that compete on the basis of their labor-cost advantage in producing traditional products with traditional techniques are increasingly likely to find themselves with stagnant export markets and deteriorating terms of trade in the future.[13]

Even if one adopts a standard comparative advantage explanation of international trade flows, the new technologies would seem to pose a threat to the competitive position of the developing countries. Until recently, it was thought that the developing countries, especially the NICs, would gradually take over the production of mass-produced, standardized goods, leaving the production of advanced-technique, high value-added goods to the developed countries. The developing countries that succeeded in building productive capacity for standardized goods—either by promoting the growth of indigenous industry or by attracting multinationals with low-cost labor and supportive policies—were expected to find attractive export markets for such goods in the developed countries. This product-cycle view of trade and production patterns was consistent with the experience of the 1970s in sectors such as consumer electronics, semiconductors, and automobile components.

The new manufacturing techniques allow for labor-saving automation on a large scale, while upgrading product quality and the reliability of the production process. These techniques reduce the influence of low-skill labor-cost considerations on production location decisions in favor of such considerations as closeness to market and the availability of relatively cheap engineering and scientific talent. In principle, such techniques can be applied to almost all products and production processes.

These characteristics of the new technologies have engendered speculation about the possibility of a "comparative advantage reversal" in which the traditional comparative advantage of developing countries in labor-intensive activities becomes a comparative advantage of the developed countries as a result of labor-saving automation. In its extreme form, the comparative-advantage-reversal argument predicts "relocation back to the North"—that is, the migration of production from locations in developing countries back to developed countries.[14]

As an illustration, Susan Walsh Sanderson has evaluated the potential impact of automated manufacturing on the "offshoring" of the U.S. electronics industry in Mexico.[15] According to her estimates, 45 per cent of U.S. electronics exports from Mexico are component fabrications and board assemblies, two manufacturing processes expected to be automated between 1986 and 1990. By 1990, roughly 40 per cent of the revenue and employment Mexico currently derives from offshore assembly could be affected by the automation of these processes. This kind of analysis, applied to other countries and to other industries, underlies speculation about possible comparative advantage reversal.

To date, there is little evidence of such a reversal on a significant scale. Comparative advantage reversal on a major scale is likely only if automation possibilities are fully implemented across a wide range of activities and only if they take place solely in the developed countries. As Sanderson writes in her analysis of U.S.-Mexican relationships: "How quickly these new manufacturing technologies will be adopted depends not only on the availability of the new technology, but also on a number of other macro- and microeconomic factors."[16]

The likely implications of changing production techniques on the competitive position of the developing countries is suggested by evidence from two industries: electronics and automobiles. In both industries, foreign direct investment and other forms of technology transfer, such as licensing and joint ventures, have been critical to the acquisition of technology by the developing countries. In both industries, the new production techniques made possible by microelectronics have the same general characteristics. First, production can be made much less labor-intensive than before. Better quality and less labor-intensive goods can now be produced with the use of computer-aided design and computer-aided manufacturing systems and industrial robots. Second, although the introduction of such techniques increases the capital costs and the capital intensity of production, it also makes production more flexible. Different specifications can now be incorporated in the same production line. Although a firm may need to produce in large volume to defray the huge initial set-up costs of the new techniques, it can produce several batches of different products in small quantities. In other words, the new techniques may increase the economies of scale of a firm but decrease the economies of scale of a particular product. Third, with microelectronics innovations in communications and information, the different stages of production can be linked in one single information system. Better information coordination enhances the gains from forward and backward linkages with suppliers and customers and makes the just-in-time inventory system more attractive.

How are these technological tendencies reflected in the new distribution of industrial production across the world? Let us consider evidence from both manufacturing sectors.

## The Electronics Industry

Starting in the early 1960s, the electronics industry experienced a process of decentralization of low-skilled manufacturing activities from the North to new production sites in the South.[17] This decentralization was driven by the worldwide sourcing requirements of the multinationals, especially U.S. firms, searching for low-cost labor. Geographically, the result was the concentration of electronics production in a few key locations in the Third World, mainly in Southeast Asia, as indicated by the data in Tables 1 and 2.[18] The dramatic success of the electronics industries in Southeast Asia would not have occurred without the infusion of investment and technology from the multinationals, although government programs played a major role in upgrading the technological level of output, particularly in South Korea.[19]

In the mid-1970s, signs of a possible change in the locational patterns of the electronics industry, especially in semiconductors, began to develop. After 1975, the bulk of international investment in semiconductor manufacturing was directed to locations within the developed member countries of the Organization for Economic Cooperation and Development (OECD).[20] This reflected both the growth potential of OECD markets, particularly in Western Europe, and more recently the threat of protectionism in the United States. However, the growing share of intra-OECD investment flows in semiconductors did not mean that investment in Third World sites stopped. Although there was a slowdown in the *growth* of foreign direct investment in semiconductors and other electronics in Southeast Asia between the late 1970s and the early 1980s, the *level* of investment did not fall, and new firms and production sites entered the picture.[21] As Table 1 indicates, exports of electronics products from the major production sites in the developing countries continued to rise in value terms and as a share of world exports and of total exports from these countries. During the late 1970s and early 1980s, the first signs of greater complementarity among the Southeast Asian producers became apparent as multinationals redirected assembly investment to new low-cost production sites in countries such as the Philippines, Thailand, and Malaysia, and the more developed East Asian NICs began to move into more sophisticated products, such as industrial electronics.[22]

In early 1983, with the sharp cyclical upturn in the demand for many electronic products, foreign direct investment in electronics—particularly in offshore chip assembly—began to gain momentum. Significantly, this occurred even though many multinationals had built or were building automated plants at home. Moreover, there is evidence that many offshore production sites were themselves becoming quite capital-intensive. While a few firms, such as Fairchild, did move some

# Table 1. Electronics Exports and Imports of Major Trading Economies[a]

## A. AUTOMATIC DATA PROCESSING EQUIPMENT (SITC 752)[b]

### IMPORTS

| | Value ($ millions) | | | Per Cent of World Total | | | Per Cent of Area's Imports[c] |
|---|---|---|---|---|---|---|---|
| | 1978 | 1981 | 1984 | 1978 | 1981 | 1984 | 1984 |
| WORLD[b] | 7,729 | 14,340 | 24,888 | 100 | 100 | 100 | 1.25 |
| United States | 397 | 722 | 3,630 | 5 | 5 | 15 | 1.1 |
| Japan | 396 | 681 | 925 | 5 | 5 | 4 | 0.7 |
| E.E.C. | 4,220 | 7,385 | 11,200 | 55 | 51 | 45 | 2.0 |
| Subtotal | | | | 65 | 61 | 64 | |
| Hong Kong | 18 | 85 | 384 | 0.2 | 0.6 | 1.5 | 1.3 |
| Singapore | 25 | 102 | 309 | 0.3 | 0.7 | 1.2 | 1.1 |
| Rep. of Korea | 43 | 110 | 247 | 0.6 | 0.8 | 1.0 | 0.8 |
| Saudi Arabia | 24 | 87 | 210 | 0.3 | 0.6 | 0.8 | 0.6 |
| Mexico | 60 | 235 | 204 | 0.8 | 1.6 | 0.8 | 1.8 |
| Argentina | 44 | 117 | 119 | 0.6 | 0.8 | 0.5 | 2.6 |
| Venezuela | 51 | 82 | 87 | 0.7 | 0.6 | 0.4 | 1.3 |
| Subtotal | | | | 3.5 | 5.7 | 6.2 | |
| Taiwan[d] | — | 61 | 235 | — | 0.4 | 0.9 | |

### EXPORTS

| | Value ($ millions) | | | Per Cent of World Total | | | Per Cent of Area's Imports[c] |
|---|---|---|---|---|---|---|---|
| | 1978 | 1981 | 1984 | 1978 | 1981 | 1984 | 1984 |
| WORLD[b] | 7,102 | 13,128 | 24,206 | 100 | 100 | 100 | 1.27 |
| United States | 2,688 | 5,043 | 7,230 | 38 | 38 | 30 | 3.3 |
| Japan | 339 | 873 | 4,566 | 5 | 7 | 19 | 2.7 |
| E.E.C. | 3,193 | 5,246 | 7,908 | 45 | 40 | 33 | 1.3 |
| Subtotal | | | | 88 | 85 | 82 | |
| Singapore | 3 | 18 | 638 | 0 | 0.1 | 2.6 | 2.6 |
| Hong Kong | 2 | 35 | 363 | 0 | 0.3 | 1.5 | 1.3 |
| Rep. of Korea | 2 | 15 | 261 | 0 | 0.1 | 1.1 | 0.9 |
| Brazil | 67 | 199 | 201 | 0.9 | 1.5 | 0.8 | 0.7 |
| Argentina | 21 | 53 | 130 | 0.3 | 0.4 | 0.5 | 1.6 |
| Mexico | 0 | 30 | 34 | 0 | 0.2 | 0.1 | 0.1 |
| Malaysia | 1 | 0 | 15 | 0 | 0 | 0.1 | 0.1 |
| Subtotal | | | | 1.2 | 2.6 | 6.7 | |
| Taiwan[d] | — | 7 | 988 | — | 0.1 | 4.1 | — |

(continued)

## B. TELECOMMUNICATION EQUIPMENT AND PARTS (SITC 764)[b]

### IMPORTS

| | Value ($ millions) | | | Per Cent of World Total | | | Per Cent of Area's Imports[c] |
|---|---|---|---|---|---|---|---|
| | 1978 | 1981 | 1984 | 1978 | 1981 | 1984 | |
| WORLD[b] | 11,051 | 17,348 | 22,708 | 100 | 100 | 100 | 1.14 |
| United States | 2,326 | 4,096 | 7,606 | 21 | 24 | 33 | 2.2 |
| Japan | 268 | 346 | 443 | 2 | 2 | 2 | 0.3 |
| E.E.C. | 3,535 | 4,817 | 4,399 | 32 | 28 | 19 | 0.8 |
| Subtotal | | | | 55 | 54 | 54 | |
| Hong Kong | 255 | 491 | 615 | 2.3 | 2.8 | 2.7 | 2.2 |
| Rep. of Korea | 237 | 482 | 614 | 2.1 | 2.8 | 2.7 | 2.0 |
| Saudi Arabia | 398 | 461 | 564 | 3.6 | 2.7 | 2.5 | 1.7 |
| Singapore | 80 | 393 | 472 | 0.7 | 2.3 | 2.1 | 1.6 |
| Mexico | 76 | 450 | 421 | 0.7 | 2.6 | 1.9 | 3.7 |
| Iraq | 94 | 307 | 350 | 0.9 | 1.8 | 1.5 | n.a. |
| Egypt | 74 | 41 | 317 | 0.7 | 0.2 | 1.4 | n.a. |
| Subtotal | | | | 11.0 | 15.2 | 14.8 | |

### EXPORTS

| | Value ($ millions) | | | Per Cent of World Total | | | Per Cent of Area's Imports[c] |
|---|---|---|---|---|---|---|---|
| | 1978 | 1981 | 1984 | 1978 | 1981 | 1984 | |
| WORLD[b] | 12,947 | 19,449 | 22,802 | 100 | 100 | 100 | 1.2 |
| United States | 2,190 | 3,135 | 3,634 | 17 | 16 | 16 | 1.7 |
| Japan | 2,876 | 4,923 | 6,639 | 22 | 25 | 29 | 3.9 |
| E.E.C. | 5,766 | 6,802 | 6,332 | 45 | 35 | 28 | 1.1 |
| Subtotal | | | | 84 | 76 | 73 | |
| Hong Kong | 103 | 280 | 903 | 0.8 | 1.4 | 4.0 | 3.2 |
| Mexico | 4 | 786 | 776 | 0 | 4.0 | 3.4 | 3.3 |
| Singapore | 28 | 334 | 476 | 0.2 | 1.7 | 2.1 | 2.0 |
| Rep. of Korea | 208 | 282 | 457 | 1.6 | 1.4 | 2.0 | 1.6 |
| Malaysia | 24 | 51 | 172 | 0.2 | 0.3 | 0.8 | 1.1 |
| Brazil | 25 | 39 | 58 | 0.2 | 0.2 | 0.3 | 0.2 |
| Philippines | 2 | 10 | 13 | 0 | 0 | 0.1 | 0.2 |
| Subtotal | | | | 3.0 | 9.0 | 12.7 | |

## C. TRANSISTORS, VALVES, ETC. (SITC 776)[b]

### IMPORTS

| | Value ($ millions) | | | Per Cent of World Total | | | Per Cent of Area's Imports[c] |
|---|---|---|---|---|---|---|---|
| | 1978 | 1981 | 1984 | 1978 | 1981 | 1984 | 1984 |
| WORLD[b] | 9,162 | 15,666 | 27,760 | 100 | 100 | 100 | 1.4 |
| United States | 1,972 | 4,014 | 8,323 | 22 | 26 | 30 | 2.4 |
| Japan | 435 | 713 | 1,293 | 5 | 5 | 5 | 0.9 |
| E.E.C. | 3,449 | 5,274 | 6,659 | 38 | 34 | 24 | 1.2 |
| Subtotal | | | | 64 | 64 | 59 | |
| Malaysia | 364 | 985 | 1,854 | 4.0 | 6.3 | 6.7 | 13.2 |
| Singapore | 704 | 1,325 | 1,768 | 7.7 | 8.5 | 6.4 | 6.2 |
| Hong Kong | 404 | 787 | 1,603 | 4.4 | 5.0 | 5.8 | 5.6 |
| Rep. of Korea | 386 | 611 | 1,295 | 4.2 | 3.9 | 4.7 | 4.2 |
| Philippines | 24 | 61 | 880 | 0.3 | 0.4 | 1.5 | 14.4 |
| Mexico | 29 | 278 | 406 | 0.3 | 1.8 | 1.5 | 3.6 |
| Brazil | 175 | 220 | 181 | 1.9 | 1.4 | 0.7 | 1.2 |
| Subtotal | | | | 23 | 27 | 27 | |

### EXPORTS

| | Value ($ millions) | | | Per Cent of World Total | | | Per Cent of Area's Imports[c] |
|---|---|---|---|---|---|---|---|
| | 1978 | 1981 | 1984 | 1978 | 1981 | 1984 | 1984 |
| WORLD[b] | 8,625 | 14,400 | 26,206 | 100 | 100 | 100 | 1.38 |
| United States | 2,313 | 4,179 | 6,432 | 27 | 29 | 25 | 3.0 |
| Japan | 1,269 | 2,662 | 5,816 | 15 | 18 | 22 | 3.4 |
| E.E.C. | 2,629 | 3,148 | 4,757 | 30 | 22 | 18 | 0.8 |
| Subtotal | | | | 72 | 69 | 65 | |
| Malaysia | 526 | 1,091 | 2,414 | 6.1 | 7.6 | 9.2 | 14.9 |
| Singapore | 792 | 1,093 | 1,662 | 9.2 | 7.6 | 6.3 | 6.9 |
| Rep. of Korea | 372 | 525 | 1,338 | 4.3 | 3.6 | 5.1 | 4.6 |
| Philippines | 13 | 77 | 1,110 | 0.2 | 0.5 | 4.2 | 21.0 |
| Hong Kong | 300 | 627 | 1,007 | 3.5 | 4.4 | 3.8 | 3.6 |
| Mexico | 24 | 236 | 228 | 0.3 | 1.6 | 0.9 | 1.0 |
| Indonesia | 23 | 58 | 118 | 0.3 | 0.4 | 0.4 | 0.5 |
| Subtotal | | | | 24 | 26 | 30 | |

Note: SITC = Standard International Trade Classification. Developing-country importers and exporters are listed in the order of the 1984 value of their imports or exports.
[a]United States, Japan, the ten EEC countries, and the seven largest trading Third World countries.
[b]The world economy excluding the socialist economies.
[c]Share of the SITC sector in the area's 1984 total imports (exports).
[d]Taiwan data are from national sources (see below) and may not be completely comparable to data for other countries.
Sources: Calculated from the *U.N. Yearbook of International Trade Statistics,* 1982, 1984; Taiwan statistics from Inspectorate General of Customs, Republic of China, cited in Jia-Shen Wu, "Projections of Manpower Demand of Informatics Industry in Taiwan," in *Bank of Taiwan Quarterly,* Vol. 37, No. 4 (December 1986).

## Table 2. U.S.-Owned Semiconductor Assembly Plants in Asia and U.S. Semiconductor Imports Under Sections 806.30/807.00 of the U.S. Tariff Schedule

*(number of plants)*

| | Hong Kong | Rep. of Korea | Taiwan | Singapore | Malaysia | Philippines | Thailand | Indonesia | Total of the Asia 8 |
|---|---|---|---|---|---|---|---|---|---|
| 1964 | 1 | 1 | — | — | — | — | — | — | 2 |
| 1974 | 8 | 9 | 11 | 2 | 1 | 9 | 3 | 1 | 44 |
| 1985 | 8 | 5 | 14 | 2 | 11 | 11 | 8 | 4 | 63 |

*(U.S. 806.30/807.00 imports from country, as per cent of total from Asia 8)*

| | Hong Kong | Korea | Taiwan | Singapore | Malaysia | Philippines | Thailand | Indonesia | Total U.S. imports from the Asia 8 in 1983 dollars *($ millions)* | As percentage of total 806.30/807.00 imports |
|---|---|---|---|---|---|---|---|---|---|---|
| 1969 | 49.2 | 22.9 | 14.8 | 9.8 | — | — | — | — | 77 | 60.0 |
| 1970 | 44.6 | 23.2 | 8.9 | 17.9 | — | — | — | — | 90 | 56.3 |
| 1971 | 32.7 | 30.9 | 12.7 | 23.6 | — | — | — | — | 98 | 55.1 |
| 1972 | 25.4 | 26.9 | 10.4 | 37.3 | — | — | — | — | 170 | 66.9 |
| 1973 | 19.4 | 23.6 | 12.5 | 33.3 | 8.3 | 1.4 | — | — | 297 | 71.9 |
| 1974 | 17.1 | 22.9 | 12.9 | 22.9 | 21.4 | 2.9 | — | — | 479 | 70.0 |
| 1975 | 11.8 | 17.1 | 7.9 | 26.3 | 30.3 | 5.3 | — | — | 469 | 76.0 |
| 1976 | 13.1 | 20.7 | 7.3 | 28.0 | 25.6 | 7.3 | — | — | 721 | 82.0 |
| 1977 | 8.0 | 21.8 | 9.2 | 24.1 | 27.6 | 6.9 | 1.1 | 1.1 | 974 | 87.0 |
| 1978 | 6.8 | 17.0 | 5.7 | 22.7 | 34.1 | 9.1 | 3.4 | 1.1 | 1,300 | 88.0 |
| 1979 | 4.6 | 13.8 | 4.6 | 23.0 | 33.3 | 11.5 | 2.3 | 2.3 | 1,667 | 87.0 |
| 1980 | 4.5 | 10.2 | 4.5 | 25.0 | 34.1 | 15.9 | 3.4 | 2.3 | 2,205 | 88.0 |
| 1981 | 3.4 | 9.2 | 4.6 | 23.0 | 34.5 | 18.4 | 4.6 | 2.3 | 2,458 | 87.0 |
| 1982 | 3.4 | 8.9 | 4.5 | 19.1 | 36.0 | 20.2 | 3.4 | 2.2 | 2,787 | 89.0 |
| 1983 | 1.2 | 16.5 | 4.7 | 12.9 | 36.5 | 21.2 | 4.7 | 2.4 | 2,876 | 85.0 |

Source: A.J. Scott and D.P. Angel, *Global Assembly Operations of U.S. Semiconductor Firms: A Geographical Analysis*, Working Paper, Department of Geography, Simon Fraser University (Burnaby, British Columbia), March 1987, pp. 21–24.

of their production back to automated factories in the United States, most multinationals planned to automate and upgrade their facilities in Asia.

Overall, the evidence does *not* indicate a comparative advantage reversal in the electronics industry to any significant extent for several reasons:

1. As Dieter Ernst argues: "Any change in the current pattern of manufacturing and sourcing would involve substantial production costs, both in terms of closing down plants, reshuffling supply and market networks, and in terms of benefits foregone that could be reaped from achieving even higher stages of internationalization. Thus, the mobility of capital invested during previous rounds of internationalization of electronics manufacturing is likely to be much lower than originally expected."[23] Those countries that attracted investment and built production capacity in the past now benefit from significant scale economies as well as from expanding regional markets.

2. Many developing countries, especially those in Southeast Asia, remain attractive as a result of government support in the form of infrastructure, tax incentives, relaxed regulation, and political backing.

3. Such sites also continue to offer significant labor-cost advantages in the engineering manpower required by new production techniques.

4. Since 1986–87, the rising value of the yen, rising production costs in Japan, and the need to diversify production sites in order to overcome trade barriers have led Japanese electronics companies to join their American counterparts in a major move to offshore manufacturing facilities in Southeast Asia (mainly Singapore and Malaysia) and in the OECD countries. The Japanese strategy encourages consolidation of the electronics complex in Southeast Asia and an extension of the forward and backward linkages of the industry in the region.

5. Most of the developing countries that already have a significant presence in the electronics industry—including the countries of East and Southeast Asia—and other developing countries with large potential markets—notably China, Brazil, India, and Mexico—will remain attractive locations for investment and production. In the future, locational patterns in electronics are likely to be driven more by considerations of market access than by considerations of unskilled labor costs both because of the threat of protectionism and because the new technologies allow for a market access location strategy.

6. Some developing countries will keep a share of the global electronics industry even with a lesser role played by multinational corporations. The East Asian NICs, especially South Korea and Taiwan, have been able to upgrade their technological and industrial ca-

pabilities, and they now represent a force to reckon with in the international arena. Other countries, for example Brazil, India, and China, are engaged in vast government-supported, import-substitution programs to promote domestic electronics industry for their own purposes.[24] Their potential markets also enable them to bargain for the acquisition of know-how in exchange for shares of their markets.

The available evidence suggests that despite automation possibilities, electronics production will continue to be important in a variety of Third World countries for a variety of reasons. On the one hand, automation is likely to reduce the diffusion of investment and production for new ventures originating in the multinationals of the developed countries. But several developing countries that benefited from past decentralization under earlier technological conditions are likely to consolidate and expand on their own, eventually penetrating the markets of the OECD. In addition, new countries, based on the potential of their domestic markets and with the support of their governments, are also building new electronics complexes. Under the new technological conditions, however, the majority of Third World countries will most likely be unable to attract foreign investment by multinationals or to mount a domestic effort to build production capacity in the electronics industry. Thus the new technologies are likely to result in increasing differentiation among Third World countries and between them and the OECD countries.

### The Automobile Industry

In the automobile assembly and components industry, changes in technology and market conditions are also likely to affect the prospects of the developing countries.[25] To understand how, it is necessary to begin with an overview of the automobile industry in these countries. Although automobile production in developing countries grew rapidly in the 1970s, it nevertheless accounted for only 4–5 per cent of total world production by 1983, and the bulk of production in the developing world was concentrated in only a few countries: Brazil, Argentina, Mexico, Yugoslavia, and South Korea (see Table 3). Most production in the developing countries was devoted to domestic markets, and the developing countries as a group satisfied about 60 per cent of their own demand by the early 1980s, up from 40 per cent in 1970.[26] As Table 4 indicates, in 1984 the seven largest developing-country exporters of motor vehicles accounted for only 1.4 per cent of world exports, up from 0.4 per cent in 1976. In parts and accessories, the comparable figure was 2.8 per cent in 1984, up from 1.5 per cent in 1976. Exports of completed vehicles from the developing countries were principally directed to other developing countries, with the exception of exports from South Korea and Yugoslavia, which were directed to the United States.

## Table 3. Passenger Cars: Production (thousands)

| Country | 1970 | 1975 | 1980 | 1983 |
|---|---|---|---|---|
| Brazil | 255 | 525 | 652 | 685 |
| Mexico | 136 | 262 | 316 | 214 |
| Yugoslavia | 63 | 132 | 186 | 168 |
| Argentina | 169 | 185 | 218 | 132 |
| Republic of Korea | — | 19 | 57 | 128 |
| India | 45 | 23 | 30 | 45 |
| China | — | — | 5 | — |
| Subtotal | 668 | 1,146 | 1,464 | 1,372 |
| Japan[a] | 3,179 | 4,568 | 7,038 | 7,152 |
| United States[a] | 6,642 | 6,914 | 6,376 | 6,781 |
| West Germany | 3,528 | 2,905 | 3,530 | 3,875 |
| France | 2,458 | 2,951 | 3,488 | 3,228 |
| Italy | 1,720 | 1,349 | 1,445 | 1,395 |
| Spain | 455 | 711 | 1,048 | 1,136 |
| United Kingdom | 1,641 | 1,268 | 924 | 1,045 |
| Canada | 923 | 1,045 | 847 | 971 |
| Australia | 391 | 361 | 399 | 363 |
| Sweden | 272 | 336 | 268 | 281 |
| Austria, Finland, and the Netherlands | 76 | 85 | 110 | 146 |
| Subtotal | 21,285 | 22,493 | 25,473 | 26,373 |
| Socialist Bloc | 711 | 1,792 | 2,142 | 2,055 |
| Total | 22,664 | 25,431 | 29,079 | 29,800 |

[a]Production by location, not by nationality of firm.
Source: United Nations, *Statistical Yearbook*, 1986.

# Table 4. Automobile Industry Exports and Imports of Major Trading Economies[a]

## A. PASSENGER MOTOR VEHICLES, EXCLUDING BUSES (SITC 781)

### IMPORTS

| | Value ($ millions) | | | Per Cent of World Total | | | Per Cent of Area's Imports[c] |
|---|---|---|---|---|---|---|---|
| | 1978 | 1981 | 1984 | 1978 | 1981 | 1984 | |
| WORLD[b] | 30,939 | 59,723 | 71,772 | 100 | 100 | 100 | 3.61 |
| United States | 9,477 | 18,017 | 31,191 | 31 | 30 | 43 | 9.1 |
| Japan | 222 | 452 | 456 | 0.7 | 0.8 | 0.6 | 0.3 |
| E.E.C. | 10,464 | 22,370 | 20,164 | 34 | 37 | 28 | 3.5 |
| Subtotal | | | | 66 | 68 | 72 | |
| Saudi Arabia | 253 | 1,340 | 1,338 | 0.8 | 2.2 | 1.9 | 4 |
| Malaysia | 152 | 396 | 459 | 0.5 | 0.7 | 0.6 | 3.3 |
| Kuwait | 211 | 428 | 446 | 0.7 | 0.7 | 0.6 | 5.8 |
| Nigeria | 416 | 613 | 345 | 1.3 | 1.0 | 0.5 | n.a. |
| Oman | 52 | 210 | 289 | 0.2 | 0.4 | 0.4 | 10.5 |
| Algeria | 18 | 61 | 277 | 0.1 | 0.1 | 0.4 | 2.7 |
| Indonesia | 89 | 165 | 255 | 0.3 | 0.3 | 0.4 | 1.8 |
| Subtotal | | | | 3.9 | 5.4 | 4.8 | |

### EXPORTS

| | Value ($ millions) | | | Per Cent of World Total | | | Per Cent of Area's Imports[c] |
|---|---|---|---|---|---|---|---|
| | 1978 | 1981 | 1984 | 1978 | 1981 | 1984 | |
| WORLD[b] | 31,678 | 59,080 | 72,272 | 100 | 100 | 100 | 3.79 |
| United States | 3,284 | 4,031 | 5,077 | 10 | 7 | 7 | 2.3 |
| Japan | 6,056 | 16,114 | 21,899 | 19 | 27 | 30 | 12.9 |
| E.E.C. | 17,243 | 30,901 | 28,912 | 54 | 52 | 40 | 4.9 |
| Subtotal | | | | 83 | 86 | 77 | |
| Brazil | 48 | 327 | 317 | 0.2 | 0.6 | 0.4 | 1.2 |
| Rep. of Korea | 2 | 50 | 174 | 0.0 | 0.1 | 0.2 | 0.6 |
| Oman | n.a. | 67 | 152 | n.a. | 0.1 | 0.2 | n.a. |
| Yugoslavia | 21 | 118 | 127 | 0.1 | 0.2 | 0.2 | 1.3 |
| Mexico | 0.3 | 31 | 119 | 0.0 | 0.1 | 0.2 | 0.5 |
| Singapore | 35 | 89 | 79 | 0.1 | 0.2 | 0.1 | 0.3 |
| Hong Kong | 5 | 1 | 61 | 0.0 | 0.0 | 0.1 | 0.3 |
| Subtotal | | | | 0.4 | 1.3 | 1.4 | |

# B. MOTOR VEHICLE PARTS AND ACCESSORIES (SITC 781)

## IMPORTS

| | Value ($ millions) | | | Per Cent of World Total | | | Per Cent of Area's Imports[c] |
|---|---|---|---|---|---|---|---|
| | 1978 | 1981 | 1984 | 1978 | 1981 | 1984 | 1984 |
| WORLD[b] | 20,365 | 33,575 | 40,057 | 100 | 100 | 100 | 2.01 |
| United States | 3,730 | 5,510 | 10,169 | 18 | 16 | 25 | 3.0 |
| Japan | 58 | 101 | 192 | 0.3 | 0.3 | 0.5 | 0.1 |
| E.E.C. | 5,894 | 11,381 | 9,972 | 29 | 34 | 25 | 1.7 |
| Subtotal | | | | 47 | 50 | 51 | |
| Mexico | 628 | 1,450 | 475 | 3.1 | 4.3 | 1.2 | 4.2 |
| Venezuela | 112 | 170 | 453 | 0.5 | 0.5 | 1.1 | 6.8 |
| Saudi Arabia | 185 | 604 | 433 | 0.9 | 1.8 | 1.1 | 1.3 |
| Iran | 452 | 300 | 450 | 2.2 | 0.9 | 1.1 | n.a. |
| Algeria | 76 | 331 | 347 | 0.4 | 1.0 | 0.9 | 3.4 |
| Thailand | 144 | 232 | 339 | 0.7 | 0.7 | 0.8 | 3.3 |
| Argentina | 78 | 218 | 267 | 0.4 | 0.6 | 0.7 | 5.8 |
| Subtotal | | | | 8.2 | 9.8 | 6.9 | |

## EXPORTS

| | Value ($ millions) | | | Per Cent of World Total | | | Per Cent of Area's Imports[c] |
|---|---|---|---|---|---|---|---|
| | 1978 | 1981 | 1984 | 1978 | 1981 | 1984 | 1984 |
| WORLD[b] | 17,988 | 32,882 | 39,133 | 100 | 100 | 100 | 2.05 |
| United States | 5,097 | 7,572 | 10,446 | 28 | 23 | 27 | 4.8 |
| Japan | 887 | 2,168 | 4,716 | 5 | 7 | 12 | 2.8 |
| E.E.C. | 8,334 | 17,215 | 14,423 | 46 | 52 | 37 | 2.4 |
| Subtotal | | | | 79 | 82 | 76 | |
| Brazil | 81 | 252 | 361 | 0.5 | 0.8 | 0.9 | 1.3 |
| Mexico | 24 | 244 | 317 | 0.1 | 0.7 | 0.8 | 1.3 |
| Yugoslavia | 81 | 220 | 225 | 0.5 | 0.7 | 0.6 | 2.3 |
| Singapore | 45 | 83 | 84 | 0.3 | 0.3 | 0.2 | 0.3 |
| Rep. of Korea | 3 | 20 | 52 | 0.0 | 0.1 | 0.1 | 0.2 |
| Hong Kong | 4 | 1 | 45 | 0.0 | 0.0 | 0.1 | 0.2 |
| India | 33 | 72 | 29 | 0.2 | 0.2 | 0.1 | 0.3 |
| Subtotal | | | | 1.6 | 2.8 | 2.8 | |

Note: SITC = Standard International Trade Classification. Developing-country importerrs and exports are listed in the order of the 1984 value of their imports or exports.
[a] United States, Japan, the EEC countries (nine in 1976, ten in 1980, 1984, and the seven largest trading Third World countries.)
[b] The world economy excluding the socialist economies.
[c] Share of the SITC sector in the area's 1984 total imports (exports).
Source: Calculated from United Nations, *Yearbook of International Trade Statistics*, 1980, 1984.

Most of the exports of parts and accessories came from Brazil and Mexico and were directed from multinational production bases in these countries to the U.S. market.

During the 1970s, as world trade in autos and auto parts grew rapidly, and as interest in a "world-car strategy"—involving world sourcing of components—intensified, it appeared that traditional product-cycle considerations might improve the competitive position of developing countries in auto production and export. Labor costs in the developing countries were considerably lower than in the developed countries, and demand for autos was growing faster in many developing countries than in the developed ones. Under these conditions and given substantial protectionist barriers to auto imports in large developing-country markets, it seemed likely that there would be a substantial infusion of foreign direct investment into developing-country locations and that the share of these locations in world production would increase. In addition, the possibility of an export-platform strategy (using production bases in Third World locations for export to developed-country markets) in auto components by the major multinationals, especially the U.S. firms, seemed a very real one.

Two factors operated against these expected outcomes. First, Japanese organizational and process innovations "pulled the rug out from under the feet of the developing countries."[27] As a result of such innovations, by 1980 even the South Koreans with a wage rate of $1 per hour could not produce a comparable vehicle for the same cost as the Japanese with a wage rate of $7 per hour. Japan's dramatically growing share of the world auto market was not based on offshoring components and assembly to low labor-cost sites, but on organizational and process innovations that called into question the wisdom of the offshoring strategy of U.S. producers.

Second, since the late 1970s, new automated techniques have diffused rapidly into auto assembly in the developed countries.[28] These techniques have reduced the importance of the labor-cost advantages of developing-country locations. The competitive position of the developing countries in the production of mechanical components also has been adversely affected because the production of such components is best suited to automation. Furthermore, the new technologies are changing the relationship between car assemblers and components suppliers.[29] Car assemblers are tending to specialize more in assembly, to withdraw from components production, and to rely more on components producers for R & D and design innovations. As a result of these trends, it is likely that there will be a reconcentration of the production of major components around each major assembly location. Indeed, this is inevitable if the just-in-time inventory system is to be put into operation. For all of these reasons, the new technologies seem to undermine the basis for a world-car strategy based on the old product-cycle logic. Under the new technological conditions, "only a small advantage can be gained through sourcing in low-wage areas, and the number of components on which costs can be saved is likely to decline as OECD factories are more highly automated and OECD production systems are more tightly centralized."[30]

In automobile parts, as in electronics, diffusion of the new technologies into production undermines the product-cycle arguments in favor of a gradual shift in the location of production to the developing countries. As in electronics, however, this argument does not mean that there will be a relocation of production away from the few developing countries that have already succeeded in building a production capability in autos and auto parts. Brazil and Mexico, for example, have been involved in encouraging auto-related production for a quarter of a century, and they are now firmly incorporated in international supply networks, mainly through U.S. multinationals. Both countries offer the promise of large domestic markets, and both provide substantial policy incentives to foreign producers. Thus the multinational firms already active there are likely to remain, along with new ones, such as the Japanese firms attracted to Mexico as a source of components for U.S.-based sales and production. Indeed, despite sharp contractions in domestic demand in Brazil and Mexico in the early 1980s, multinational firms increased investment in auto capacity in these production locations as part of their worldwide competitive strategy.[31]

What about the rest of the developing world? First, it seems unlikely that many other developing countries will be able to pursue the Brazilian or Mexican strategy of becoming a major link in the international supply network. The new technological conditions argue for the increasing concentration of auto and component production near the point of sale. Under these conditions, the real options for most developing countries are to import autos and parts to satisfy domestic demand, or to set up domestic production capabilities on the basis of imported technology via licenses, joint ventures, and foreign direct investment. In a few large developing countries, like India and China, the lure of a large potential market is likely to be an effective tool for bargaining with OECD multinationals for access to technology on attractive terms, especially if, as seems likely, these multinationals face a significant amount of excess supply in OECD markets by the early 1990s.[32] For some other countries with smaller market potential, an import-substitution strategy in autos may have been made more attractive by the fact that the new production techniques reduce the scale requirements for efficient production. Thus countries traditionally thought too small to support an auto industry might be able to do so in the new technological environment. It is unlikely that production for the domestic market in most developing countries will find export opportunities. In other words, the Korean and Yugoslav strategy of producing for a market niche in the OECD is unlikely to be successful for many other developing countries, especially since projected excess capacity in OECD markets is likely to lead to greater protectionist barriers.

### What Prospects for Other Industries?

How applicable are our analyses of the electronics and automobile industries to other key industries in the Third World? It is impossible in a single paper to provide an across-the-board evaluation of current tendencies for the entire economic structure. However, we believe that there is some consistency between our sectoral conclusions and available evidence for other industries.

For instance, if we take the garment industry, which accounts for about 21 per cent of all manufactured exports from the Third World, the thorough study by Kurt Hoffman demonstrates that: a) trade restrictions rather than technology are the main sources of concern for the continued expansion of garment production in and export by developing countries; and b) "given the central importance of the assembly stage, the limited impact of microelectronics on sewing technology means by definition that automation has had little measurable impact on international trade patterns in the clothing sector at the aggregate level."[33] In the 1990s, however, several technological initiatives in the OECD countries will come to maturity and will restructure the technological and economic bases of the garment industries. These initiatives are designed to strengthen the competitive position of domestic garment producers by further automation of labor-intensive parts of the production process. If successful, these restructuring and automation efforts will work to the disadvantage of Third World garment-producing countries unless they, too, take measures to upgrade their productive capabilities.

This is precisely what some developing countries are doing, according to our own recent research in Southeast Asia.[34] Let us take the case of the Hong Kong garment industry. On the one hand, firms are automating as much as possible, very often at levels similar to those in OECD countries. On the other hand, they are decentralizing and subcontracting production to other low-cost areas, mainly to China, to offset recent increases in domestic wages. Finally, they are trying to bypass protectionist barriers through two different tactics: a) diversifying production locations within the same network of firms to several countries, including Sri Lanka, Indonesia, Thailand, and China, to avoid the national export quotas set for individual countries by bilateral and multilateral trade agreements; and b) investing in production within the OECD countries, particularly in Portugal, Ireland, and Britain. (There is obviously some historical irony to the fact that Hong Kong industrialists are taking over the ailing textile industry of the English Midlands.)

Current trends in the garment industry point in similar directions to those we analyzed in the electronics and automobile industries. The new technologies are reducing the importance of labor costs as a competitive factor and are putting pressure on Third World producers to upgrade their own production processes. Technological developments will gradually change the dynamics of world competition in the garment industry, but the process will be a slow one—slower than in automobiles or electronics, and will leave more room for adjustment by Third World countries. Successful adjustment, however, will depend on the ability of Third World producers to acquire and assimilate the new technologies, and for the poorer Third World countries, this ability will be limited. The result of asymmetric adjustment in the Third World will be greater differentiation between the haves and the have-nots.

To summarize, the microelectronics revolution has several implications for the developing countries.

*First*, traditional product-cycle forces favoring the gradual relocation of production from high-wage, developed-country locations to low-wage, developing-country locations have been significantly weakened.

*Second*, in automobiles and electronics, the new technologies seem to favor the development of concentrations of production near major markets, or "key growth poles." This trend will benefit the larger, more developed countries of the Third World, notably Brazil, Argentina, Mexico, China, and India, which will be able to use access to their markets to bargain for access to technological know-how. Smaller, less developed countries will have little to offer in exchange for technology and will have to rely on exports of traditional products for foreign exchange to either import the technologically advanced products or import the technology required to produce them at home.

*Third*, because the new technologies necessitate adding complementary scientific and engineering manpower to assure their effective utilization while economizing on unskilled labor requirements, they are even more "inappropriate" than earlier technologies to the resource endowments of most developing countries. As the technological frontier moves outward, developing countries face an even more adverse trade-off between resorting to the best practices available and using those with the greatest employment and other spillover effects on the domestic economy.

This does not mean, however, that there is any simple relationship between the new technologies and overall employment levels in the developing countries. A variety of factors, including macroeconomic policies, industrial structure, and international competition, mediate the relationship between technology and employment at both the firm and national levels. As an illustration, the introduction of robots in welding and painting in an automobile factory may displace jobs on the assembly line, but the resulting productivity gains may enhance the company's competitive position, thus actually increasing its total employment. A worldwide recession would reduce employment levels in the auto industry, regardless of the production techniques in use. The link between technology and employment becomes even more uncertain when one takes into consideration the multiplier effects of productivity gains in the national and international economy, particularly over long periods of time. The available evidence, summarized by Kaplinsky,[35] underscores the necessity of examining the interplay between technology, world economic conditions, and the institutional environment to predict the effects of new production technologies on employment levels in the long run. What is certain is that these technologies are inevitably changing the types of jobs, the skill requirements of the work force, and the characteristics of the work process in both developed and developing countries.[36]

A *fourth* conclusion that emerges from the electronics and automobile cases is that those developing countries previously tied into the international supplier network as major production and export sites under older technological conditions are likely to continue to occupy such positions under the new conditions. And countries that were left out of these networks before will find it harder to break in now. Recent history will play a role in how the technological revolution affects individual countries.

*Fifth*, intensifying competitive pressures on producers in the developed countries, especially in the United States, may lead to greater protectionism that will redirect investment flows to protected developed-country locations, limiting the export prospects of the developing countries. Since the United States has been a major market for exports of electronics, automobiles and parts, and clothing from the Third World, greater protection of the U.S. market or slower U.S. growth would have particularly deleterious effects on such prospects.

*Finally*, we can point to a positive trend in the relationship between new technologies and Third World development. The acceleration of technological change and greater competition among producers in the developed countries could benefit certain Third World countries by reducing the price of imported know-how. But developing countries will benefit from potentially cheaper access to technology transfer only if they have the ability to use technology as an instrument to promote development. And this ability is itself a function of the position of each country in the structure of the world economy.

# Growing Differentiation Among Developing Countries

The impact of the microelectronics revolution on a particular developing country will depend on its access to technological know-how and its ability to use it. This ability can be thought of as a country's technological capacity, and it depends on several factors, including: its *human infrastructure*—that is, the educational, scientific, and skill characteristics of its labor force; its *basic infrastructure*, in particular its communications network; its *ability to finance and organize R & D efforts* to modify or diffuse imported know-how for its particular needs; and its *industrial base*—since microelectronics technologies have diffused at quite different rates in different industrial sectors worldwide. All of these factors are positively associated with a country's level of economic development. In other words, the more developed a developing country is, all other things equal, the greater its technological capacity. The more advanced developing countries are more likely to have eliminated the barriers to technological learning and to have the resources required for such learning. In the vocabulary of the literature on technological diffusion, such countries have the absorptive capacity required to diffuse innovations more rapidly.[37]

In most developing countries, technological capacity in the sense defined here is quite limited, and barriers to the diffusion of microelectronics innovations are substantial. As a result, such innovations have the potential of increasing differentiation within the Third World. The impact of current technological changes on individual Third World countries will depend on the above-mentioned determinants of national technological capacity and on each country's potential as a future market—either because of the size of its population (as in the case of China), or because of its purchasing power (as in the case of Saudi Arabia). However, a nation's capability to assimilate and use new technologies on a large scale—a capability that depends on social and institutional organization (rather than on ethnic and cultural characteristics, as some have asserted)—affects its potential as a future high-technology market. Thus Nigeria's large population and oil resources are not enough to make it an important prospective market for high-technology products; the country's lack of the requisite social and institutional organization is undermining its bargaining power in the process of technology transfer. A similar argument could be made for some oil-rich countries; in Iran, for example, the all-powerful theocratic state is unlikely to use technology transfer as an instrument of economic development.

If we combine the factors of technological capacity with the market potential of each country—into what might be thought of as the supply and demand factors of technological development—we can distinguish five different categories into which most developing countries fall. Table 5 contains some comparative data on individual countries in these different categories. It is our hypothesis that the new technologies will have different effects on these different groups of countries and will increase differentiation among them.

1. *The East Asian NICs are in the best position to benefit from the microelectronics revolution.* They are already part of the global electronics network both as suppliers and, increasingly, as demanders, and they are likely to be able to continue to upgrade their technological base by means of licenses, joint ventures, and foreign direct investment on favorable terms. They have also achieved high enough development levels to be able to support nationally financed R & D programs for technological breakthroughs of their own. Perhaps most important, they are best suited among all of the developing countries to diffuse microelectronics technology through their production base because they have achieved the scientific, educational, and experience levels required to do so. Moreover, their human resources are available at a cost significantly lower than that in the developed countries. For this group of developing countries, the possibility of using new technologies to leapfrog to the technological frontier in a variety of sectors is very real.[38] It is not surprising that surveys of business leaders in the advanced countries frequently identify the East Asian NICs as the major competitive challenge in the near future.

2. *Countries with large potential markets, including China, India, Brazil, Argentina, and Mexico, are in a good position to acquire microelectronics technologies.* Brazil, Argentina, and Mexico benefit from their relatively high development levels and their large potential markets. Mexico also enjoys a locational advantage relative to U.S. markets. China and India have great market potential because of their sheer size. In addition, India has a significant reserve of scientific and engineering talent available at low cost, and China is developing such a reserve. Brazil, Mexico, and Argentina have achieved higher overall educational and skill standards than China or India and are better equipped with telephones—a key component of the infrastructural base required for the successful application of many microelectronics technologies (see Table 5). Because these three countries have made a strong commitment to build up local computer industries and because they have relatively strong auto industries, they appear to have taken

up the new technologies more rapidly than any other Third World country outside the four East Asian NICs.[39]

Both China and India have introduced new programs to help them catch up with the new computer and telecommunications technologies, but it is still too early to judge the success of such programs, although China already has 1,300,000 workers in electronics, and India has one of the largest domestic electronics industries in the developing world.[40] Until quite recently, however, the insulation of both the domestic manufacturing base and the indigenous electronics industry in India dampened incentives for technological upgrading and diffusion. As this example suggests, the incentives motivating economic agents are a key determinant of how and whether a country's technological capacity is utilized. In China, an ambitious new computerization program has also been stymied by poor management, personnel shortages, and an underdeveloped telecommunications system. As a result, there are reports that by the end of 1985, more than 18,000 microcomputers were gathering dust in warehouses, and the utilization rate of installed microcomputers was only 26 per cent in Beijing and even lower in the rest of the country.[41]

Even in Brazil, Mexico, and India, the most developed countries that fall into this group, the diffusion of microelectronics technology has been quite limited. Most of the applications have occurred in foreign subsidiaries or in government services and the military.

3. *The so-called "second-tier" or "peripheral" NICs,[42]—Malaysia, the Philippines, Thailand, and perhaps some countries of the Caribbean—have probably suffered as a result of the change in techniques made possible by the microelectronics revolution.* In the 1970s, these countries strongly benefited from the traditional labor-cost and product-cycle forces that have been weakened by the new techniques. Thus their ability to acquire technological know-how either through foreign exchange earnings as an export platform or through inflows of foreign direct investment have been adversely affected. Nonetheless, those countries that already had attracted substantial investment in the past, such as Malaysia, are not likely to lose it now. Malaysia and other member states of the Association of South East Asian Nations (ASEAN) are in fact likely to continue to benefit from growing regional specialization in electronics.[43] Because of their lower development levels, however, their technological capacities are very limited, and the spillover effects of foreign direct investment or joint ventures on their domestic economies are likely to remain small.

4. *Depending on what happens to the price of oil, the oil-exporting countries, especially those of the Middle East, will have the ability to acquire microelectronics technology with their oil revenues.* Indeed, the Middle East is a major potential market for such technology, in the

## Table 5. Indicators of Technological Capacity of Various Countries

| Country | Number of Telephones per 100 Persons | School Enrollment as Percentage of Age Group | | | Scientists and Engineers | | Per Capita GNP | | 1983 Population (millions) |
|---|---|---|---|---|---|---|---|---|---|
| | | Primary | Secondary | Higher | Total (thousands) | Per million population | 1983 Value ($US) | 1965–83 Rate of Growth (percentage) | |
| **Industrial Market Economies** | | | | | | | | | |
| United States | 76.0e | 100 | 97 | 58 | 702e | 2,994 | 14,110 | 1.7 | 235 |
| Japan | 53.5 | 100 | 92 | 30 | 496f | 4,159 | 10,120 | 4.8 | 119 |
| West Germany | 59.9 | 100 | 50 | 30 | 128d | 2,087 | 11,430 | 2.8 | 61 |
| Spain | 36.0 | 110 | 88 | 24 | 6b | 157 | 4,780 | 3.0 | 38 |
| **East European Centrally Planned Economies** | | | | | | | | | |
| Soviet Union | 9.8e | 106 | 97 | 21 | 1,431e | 5,254 | — | — | 273 |
| East Germany | 21.1 | 94 | 88 | 30 | 121 | 7,251 | — | — | 17 |
| Poland | 10.9 | 100 | 75 | 18 | 79e | 2,153 | — | — | 37 |
| Hungary | 13.4 | 100 | 73 | 14 | 22e | 2,053 | 2,150 | 6.4 | 11 |
| **East Asian Newly Industrializing Countries** | | | | | | | | | |
| Rep. of Korea | 17.3 | 100 | 89 | 24 | 28e | 711 | 2,010 | 6.7 | 40 |
| Taiwan | 20.9 | 100 | 85 | 12 | — | — | 2,740 | 6.8 | 19 |
| Hong Kong | 40.3 | 105 | 67 | 11 | — | — | 6,000 | 6.2 | 5 |
| Singapore | 39.4 | 108 | 66 | 11 | 5d | 2,058 | 6,620 | 7.8 | 2 |
| **Latin American Middle-Income Countries** | | | | | | | | | |
| Brazil | 8.0 | 96 | 32 | 12 | 33e | 251 | 1,880 | 5.0 | 130 |

| | | | | | | | | | |
|---|---|---|---|---|---|---|---|---|---|
| **Mexico** | 9.1 | 121 | 54 | 15 | — | — | 2,240 | 3.2 | 75 |
| **Argentina** | 10.4f | 119 | 59 | 25 | 10c | 321 | 2,070 | 0.5 | 30 |
| **Venezuela** | 7.8 | 105 | 40 | 22 | 4c | 212 | 3,840 | 1.5 | 17 |
| **Middle East Oil Exporters** | | | | | | | | | |
| Saudi Arabia | 14.6f | 67 | 32 | 9 | — | — | 12,230 | 6.7 | 10 |
| Iran | 4.3f | 109 | 59 | 10 | — | — | — | — | 15 |
| Iraq | 5.3 | 97 | 40 | 4 | — | — | — | — | 43 |
| **Second-Tier Newly Industrializing Countries** | | | | | | | | | |
| Malaysia | 7.5 | 92 | 49 | 5 | — | — | 1,860 | 4.5 | 15 |
| Philippines | 1.5 | 106 | 64 | 27 | 5e | 99 | 760 | 2.9 | 52 |
| Thailand | 1.4 | 96 | 29 | 22 | — | — | 820 | 4.3 | 49 |
| **Large Protected Economies** | | | | | | | | | |
| China | 0.5 | 110 | 35 | 1 | — | — | 300 | 4.4 | 1,019 |
| India | 0.4 | 79 | 30 | 9 | — | — | 260 | 1.5 | 733 |
| Indonesia | 0.4e | 120 | 33 | 4 | 21e | 132 | 560 | 5.0 | 156 |
| **Low-Income Stagnant Economies** | | | | | | | | | |
| Afghanistan | 0.2c | 35 | 12 | 1 | — | — | — | 0.5 | 17 |
| Bangladesh | 0.1a | 60 | 15 | 4 | — | — | 130 | 0.5 | 96 |
| Sudan | 0.3c | 52 | 18 | 2 | 4b | 183 | 400 | 1.3 | 41 |

Note: All figures are for 1984 unless otherwise noted.
[a]1975.
[b]1976.
[c]1980.
[d]1981.
[e]1982.
[f]1983.

Sources: World Bank, *World Development Report*, 1985; United Nations, *U.N. Statistical Yearbook*, 1986.

form of both military hardware and telecommunications equipment and some industrial equipment. These countries, however, have only limited technological capacity to diffuse imported technology beyond a few applications with minimal spillover effects on the rest of the economy. They are likely to be consumers rather than producers of the new technologies.

5. *Finally, most of the developing countries are likely to be consumers—and very limited ones—of microelectronics technology in the near future.*[44] The microelectronics revolution increases the gap between these countries and the technological frontier and makes their main resource—a surplus of cheap labor—increasingly irrelevant in the production of manufactured goods. It also makes their successful catching up more dependent on the resource they lack most acutely: scientific and technical knowledge. For these countries, selective use of microelectronics technology in such areas as warfare, telecommunications, government functions, and banking may mean closer linkage with an interdependent world from which, ironically, the bulk of their populations will be even more disconnected than before.

Overall, in the absence of significant new policy initiatives by both developed and developing countries, it seems likely that the microelectronics revolution will increase the gap between the haves and the have-nots in the world economy. This outcome is not inevitable, however, since the new technologies can be used in a variety of ways to promote economic development in even the poorest countries of the world. Indeed, the capital-saving nature of these technologies represents a boon to developing countries that are short of capital and foreign exchange. And the savings on energy use and other scarce material inputs made possible by these technologies are a boon to developing and developed countries alike.

Several isolated examples indicate how new microelectronics techniques can be applied to pressing development problems in the poorest countries of the world. Satellite-based remote-sensing devices, which are heavily dependent on microelectronics technology and are primarily used for military purposes by the superpowers, can be used to observe ground-level resources in great detail and thus have vast potential for agricultural and demographic planning in the Third World. India is at the leading edge in such applications of this technology, and the U.N. Food and Agriculture Organization is also fostering its use in a variety of countries to plan irrigation, manage and predict harvests, and estimate forest cover. Electronic load-controllers are sophisticated electronic devices that adjust alternator speed automatically as use of electricity is switched on and off. The result is a significant reduction in the feasible scale of hydroelectric power that permits the development of local power-generating sites using very small streams. Colombia, Sri Lanka, and Thailand have introduced hydroelectric projects made possible by incorporating the new loader systems. Microcomputers can be used to improve rural planning, previously hampered by information and literacy constraints. Nigeria, for example, has installed microcomputers to record and process data in agronomic and household surveys used in rural planning, and Nepal is using microcomputers in family planning and maternal health programs. Finally, sophisticated telecommunications devices can provide new channels of information and education to rural areas. Compared to the older cabling system, microwave and satellite technologies radically reduce the cost of installing telecommunications links with rural areas.[45] China is currently making a major effort to build a national telecommunications network based on these new technologies.[46] Examples such as these, however, remain exceptions to the general rule that most applications are driven by product and process considerations in the *industrial* world. On the product side, this means consumer applications appropriate to high-income societies and military applications. On the process side, it means applications that economize on labor, the resource most abundant in the Third World, and that are biased toward manufacturing and away from agriculture and raw material extraction.

Nevertheless, how the new technologies affect individual countries or groups of countries will ultimately depend on policy actions taken by the developing countries themselves as well as the developed countries. And in the North, these policy actions will be influenced not only by considerations of development prospects in the South, but more significantly by national reactions to the competitive pressures that the microelectronics revolution has unleashed among the advanced countries.

# U.S. Policy Considerations

During the last seven years, the U.S. trade deficit increased dramatically. The deterioration in the U.S. trade position was broadly based, occurring in all major product groups—even those high-technology products in which the United States traditionally ran a surplus—and with all major trading partners. The primary causes of the growing trade deficit were macroeconomic conditions in the United States and the rest of the world. Macroeconomic conditions caused the dramatic appreciation of the dollar that reduced the price competitiveness of U.S. products on world markets between 1981 and 1986. Macroeconomic forces also resulted in the rapid growth of the U.S. market and stagnant growth in foreign markets—especially Third World markets, which were increasingly important to U.S. exporters during the 1970s.

These macroeconomic trends were superimposed on longer-term trends of relatively low U.S. productivity growth and the gradual disappearance of America's technological lead in a number of indus-tries. In many industries important to the economic strength of the developed countries, especially the United States, competition has in-tensified. Industries that were once considered stable, such as auto-mobiles, have entered a new phase of instability, and relatively new industries, such as semiconductors and computers, have seen an inten-sification of competition as a result of the rise of Japan and of the new East Asian producers.

In the United States, the growing competitive challenge from foreign producers in industries only recently thought to have been obvious sources of American economic strength has coincided with the emergence of the huge trade imbalance. To a large extent, the im-balance is the result not of this competitive challenge but of the mac-roeconomic forces noted above.[47] Nonetheless, long-run changes in the competitive position of U.S. producers have played a role in key man-ufacturing industries, and awareness of this has stimulated interest in a number of policies to restore or improve long-run competitiveness, especially in the so-called "high-tech" industries.[48] Three basic types of policy initiatives are under consideration: (1) *general policies to en-hance U.S. competitiveness*, such as policies to improve the educational base and to increase funding for R & D in commercial areas; (2) *promo-tional policies targeted at specific industries or technologies*, such as the proposed Sematech program for the semiconductor industry or pro-posed programs to foster research on commercial applications of super-conductivity; and (3) *trade policy measures designed to force greater openness of protected foreign markets*, including those in developing countries such as Brazil, Korea, and Taiwan, *and to close beleaguered U.S. markets at least temporarily.*

Of these policy measures, by far the most threatening to countries of the developing world are protectionist trade policies. The United States is the major market for manufactured goods from the Third World.[49] Indeed, during the first half of the 1980s, when demand declined and then stagnated in the other developed countries, the United States became the buyer of last resort and was a major impetus to growth for the developing countries. If U.S. markets become less open, or if, as seems inevitable, they become less buoyant as the U.S. trade imbalance adjusts, developing countries will face sharply re-duced market prospects for their manufactured exports.

There are a variety of ways in which trade policy measures in the United States may affect developing countries in the new technology area. An obvious example is the impact of Sections 806.30 and 807.00 of the U.S. Tariff Schedule on the offshoring decisions of U.S. semiconductor firms. Under these rules, imports of assembled goods are dutiable only to the extent of the value added to the goods at offshore plants. Lured by low-cost labor and encouraged by these rules, U.S. semiconductor firms invested heavily in foreign facilities in several East Asian developing countries in the 1970s (see Table 2). By 1980, the United States imported $2.3 billion from offshore semiconductor plants located in these countries.

A more recent illustration of the effects of U.S. trade legislation on the developing countries comes from the U.S.-Japan semiconductor trade agreement, one objective of which is an increase in the price of semiconductors in all third-country markets. This acts to the advantage of a third-country producer like Korea, but to the disadvantage of third-country consumers like Brazil and India. In response to large trade deficits in electronics with Korea, anti-dumping duties have been imposed on color televisions. In addition, the United States has threatened to withdraw favorable treatment under the Generalized System of Preferences to induce export restraint by developing countries that run large trade surpluses with the United States. The new proposed trade legislation underscores growing support for the use of trade retaliation against developing countries that discriminate against U.S. producers in critical high-tech markets.

In the high-tech area, perhaps no trade issue is as significant as that of intellectual property. With steeper learning curves and shortened product cycles, the value of proprietary technology has increased, and this has resulted in increased efforts to protect property rights over such technology. The United States is pursuing bilateral negotiations with its trading partners to strengthen intellectual property protection. Bilateral pressure has been brought to bear on a number of countries including Singapore, Korea, Japan, Taiwan, Brazil, and China. Korea is the object of an action filed by Texas Instruments with the International Trade Commission seeking relief from injury due to patent infringement; and National Semiconductor is suing a Taiwanese company for patent infringement.[50]

If intellectual protection did become more effective—despite the great difficulties involved in enforcing appropriability over microelectronics innovations—this would tend to increase the price of technology imports in developing countries and to reduce their access to the latest generation technology. There is little doubt that at least some developing countries, especially the East Asian NICs, have benefited from their ability to copy innovations of U.S. companies and to earn a substantial fraction of the rents resulting from such innovations because of their competitive manufacturing capabilities. According to

Soete,[51] the failure of the international patent system to provide effective protection for innovations in electronics has meant that imitation and the competing away of innovation/monopoly rents have proceeded much more rapidly both nationally and internationally.

In addition to stimulating political interest in policy measures to improve the competitive position of the U.S. economy, the changing world economy has stimulated new responses by American producers themselves. The current period is one of intense technological competition among the technological leaders of the developed countries, and this competition has reduced the rate of *return* on innovation, while the *cost* of innovation has increased. Producers in the developed countries are scurrying to find new strategies to shore up their position. Many of these strategies have implications—some disadvantageous, others advantageous—for the developing countries. It is too early to assess their net effects.

On the *negative* side, multinational producers are trying even harder to limit access to frontier technology by potential competitors in both developed and developing countries. Their efforts show up in reduced willingness to license state-of-the-art technology and a decision to press intellectual property rights to the "absolute limit." Limitations on access to frontier technology are likely to be especially harmful to the East Asian NICs, which may have the human and basic infrastructure to jump to the technological frontier if such technology is available to them.

Also potentially disadvantageous to the developing countries are the forces encouraging an increase in intra-OECD investment flows in such important industries as automobiles and semiconductors. As noted earlier, current competitive dynamics in both industries—along with the features of microelectronics technology—encourage a strategy of locating close to major markets, and in both sectors the major markets remain overwhelmingly in the developed countries. In addition, actual or threatened protectionist barriers in the United States and the sharp drop in the dollar have attracted and will continue to attract new investment flows into the United States in both industries. Because of the way technological know-how flows in social networks and is embodied in individuals, there is also often a strategic advantage to locating in an area with a high concentration of high-tech production. In part this explains the interest of European, Japanese, and Korean firms in setting up joint ventures or production locations in U.S. high-tech communities.

On the *positive* side, competition among producers from the developed countries encourages a scramble among them for new markets. This scramble, along with the rapid pace of technological breakthrough, has caused dramatic declines in the prices of semiconductors, computers, and other electronic equipment to the benefit of all users, including those in developing countries. Moreover, market pressure makes it difficult for firms to avoid the temptation of licensing their best technologies in order to gain an edge over their competitors. Thus even as producers struggle to enforce intellectual property rights and to increase royalties, they seem willing to make deals that could be advantageous for developing countries with large potential markets, such as China, and for producers in developing countries, especially those in East Asia.[52]

Finally, as a result of competition among producers in the developed countries, locating production in certain NICs continues to be an attractive competitive strategy. Such locations offer cheap engineering talent; cheap components; a supportive infrastructure, tax, and regulatory environment; and the possibility of outmaneuvering Northern competitors from third-country platforms.

## Developing-Country Policy Considerations

For developing countries, the major policy concerns are how to acquire technological know-how and how to use it for national development purposes. In the acquisition of microelectronics technology, developing countries must depend on foreign suppliers, in particular on large multinational firms from the developed countries. In this sense, the growing significance of such technology in world production and trade patterns increases the dependence of the Third World on the North. But, as the cases of Japan and the East Asian NICs demonstrate, under some conditions such dependence can be turned into a gradual competitive advantage against the very firms that initially supplied the technology. And, as at least a few NICs—Korea, Brazil, Taiwan, Singapore, and India—develop their own technological base, there will be greater possibilities for developing countries to purchase technology from one another.

In principle, developing countries can acquire foreign technology in a variety of ways: by importing products and copying the embodied technology to produce at home, by licensing, by establishing joint ventures with foreign producers, and by attracting wholly owned foreign direct investment. Each of these routes has potential advantages as well as limitations. Allowing wholly owned foreign direct investment may not provide enough inducement to foreign firms to share their technology with local entrepreneurs, but the foreign firms may employ and train local personnel who may develop know-how and spin off their own enterprises. Licensing may give local entrepreneurs a greater degree of control over technology transfer, but it may not induce foreign producers to supply first-generation technology. Joint ventures are an attractive compromise, since they encourage the transfer of managerial and organizational know-how, but they are often difficult to negotiate because of differences in the objectives of the country and the firms involved.[53] Given these trade-offs, developing-country governments must be flexible in their policies toward foreign technology transfer, using different strategies with different foreign producers and for different types of technology. Since the spillover effects of the new microelectronics technologies are likely to be smaller than those of traditional technologies, policies to acquire technology should emphasize arrangements that include nationally based R & D facilities and training for national personnel.[54]

The developing countries must take care to avoid overgenerous tax and other concessions for foreign suppliers. All too often, such concessions are offered without serious consideration of their effects on the economy as a whole. Developing countries frequently engage in competitive bidding to attract multinationals, with the result that the concessions offered are sometimes very high.[55] Intra-regional cooperation among several developing countries on the package of incentives offered to foreign investors in the region could lower the cost of attracting such investors for individual countries. This is only one of several ways in which intra-regional cooperation could help developing countries acquire technology at a more attractive price. Since market access is a key magnet for foreign producers, the establishment of a common regional market among a number of smaller developing countries might draw investors to a region that might otherwise be overlooked.

Government policy, whether exercised by a single state or a number of states acting collectively, is critical to the development of technological capacity in the developing countries. Microelectronics technology differs fundamentally from technical advances in both the process industries and the mechanical-electrical industries in terms of its closer reliance on scientific knowledge and technical/educational learning.[56] A pool of highly trained scientific, engineering, and technical personnel is a *sine qua non* of successful diffusion of the new technologies and their adaptations to new purposes in the Third World. The creation of such a pool of talent represents a substantial challenge for most developing countries. The developing world's aggregate share of scientists and engineers is about 13 per cent,[57] and this share is concentrated in a small number of countries—mainly the East Asian NICs, Brazil, India, and Mexico. The same countries also account for the lion's share of spending on R & D in science and technology in the developing countries, which together account for only 3–5 per cent of total world spending for such purposes.[58]

To realize the skilled personnel base required for the new technologies, developing countries will have to rely on two strategies. First, they will have to send large numbers of national engineers and scientists to be trained in the universities of the advanced countries. Second, a large number of scientific and technical personnel will have to be trained in the developing countries themselves. The poorest countries will find it difficult to meet these challenges. For them, providing a modicum of elementary education for the largely rural population is a more pressing problem. Intra-regional cooperation among a group of such countries to finance the development of a regional pool of talent by establishing a cooperative training program would be a sensible strategy. Such a program might be combined with an R & D program focusing on the application of microelectronics technologies to regional problems.

A cooperative effort to establish an intra-regional training and R & D center for several developing countries might attract external support from multilateral agencies, such as the World Bank or the United Nations Development Programme, or from foreign producers with an interest in the region as a potential market for their technologies.[59] Such an effort should focus on blending microelectronics technologies with traditional economic activity in the region and with developing new applications of the technology suitable to the region's economic and social needs. As illustrations, there are many promising applications in the areas of telecommunicated health and educational programs based on expert systems and in the development of new agricultural techniques. As noted earlier, some experiments in applications such as these exist in a few countries and regions, but by far the largest use of microelectronics technologies in the South continues to be in government offices and multinational subsidiaries and in the military. Such applications have limited spillover effects on the rest of the economy and tend to create a technical and bureaucratic elite divorced from the largely rural population, with the result of increasing differentiation *within* individual developing countries as well as among them.

In addition to providing the necessary educational infrastructure and supportive R & D activities, governments dedicated to the development of a domestic capacity in the production and application of new microelectronics products will have to rely, at least temporarily, on a host of promotional and protectionist measures. Such policies have been a critical element in the competitive success of Japan and most of the East Asian NICs in high-technology industries.[60] Their experience suggests that state-led strategies rather than free-market forces are required for domestic economic development based on the acquisition and diffusion of the new technologies.[61] This is not surprising given the nature of global competition in high-technology sectors, where increasing returns based on scale economies, learning curve effects, and other first-entry advantages are the rule rather than the exception, and where the existence of significant technological spillover effects calls into question the optimality of pure market forces. An equally significant lesson from the experience of the successful developing countries is that while protection and promotion of domestic producers are both necessary, they are not in themselves sufficient to secure the development of a competitive domestic capability in high-technology industries. Contrasting the difficulties of Brazil and India with the successes of Korea and Taiwan suggests that intervention should have an outward orientation—that is, it should encourage domestic producers to concentrate on production and process strategies that have competitive potential in the world economy.[62]

# Policy Choices Ahead:
# Need for Global Perspective

The world economy is in a period of macroeconomic imbalance and volatility. The economies of the North, and particularly that of the United States, face the problem of stimulating global demand in a sustained way in a context darkened simultaneously by the U.S. trade imbalance and debt and by the financial limitations of the developing countries.[63] For the developing countries, the preconditions for successful development—rapid growth of world trade and access to finance—are not likely to be realized without coordinated action by the developed countries. The U.S. market can no longer serve, as it did in the first half of the 1980s, as the engine of growth for the developing countries. Nor can the United States alone afford to bear the total burden of debt relief required to address the debt crisis that remains unresolved in much of the Third World. Coordinated macroeconomic expansion in the North, especially in Europe and Japan, is essential to stimulating demand in the global economy. And protectionist barriers to Third World exports must be reduced if the developing countries are to benefit fully from growing demand in the developed countries.

The current insufficiency of global demand at the macroeconomic level is reflected in individual sectors, especially those in which the new technologies provide the foundation for rapid growth on the supply side.[64] Demand potential is not keeping pace with supply potential in key industrial sectors, such as autos and electronics, and this is partly the result of demand limitations in the Third World. Thus any serious discussion of the new relationship between technological development and economic growth from a global perspective must include the potential role of the Third World economies in overcoming the demand crisis that threatens both the producers and the users of the new technologies.

Under these conditions, policies to spur the acquisition and diffusion of these technologies for economic development objectives in the Third World could become a key area in international relations over the next several years—an area in which a global strategy based on the respective interests of both North and South could yield beneficial results for both groups of countries.

It is easy to understand why the South could benefit from the international coordination of policies to support its technological development. The new technologies hold great promise for solving many pressing developmental problems in education, energy use, power generation, agriculture, raw material extraction, communications, transportation, and health. In addition, as argued earlier, the new production technologies are an increasingly important determinant of a nation's competitive position in the most rapidly growing world markets.

In principle, it is less clear why the North in general, and the United States in particular, should be interested in creating the conditions for technological advancement in less developed and often hostile Third World environments. One could make a humanitarian argument in favor of such a strategy, but in a time of slow growth and economic difficulty in the North, humanitarian values are not likely to hold much sway over policy initiatives toward the Third World. Alternatively, one could make the argument that an increasing gap in income and well-being between the haves and the have-nots in the world economy carries the threat of greater social and political disruption that the North and especially the United States might wish to avoid for security reasons. However, the experience of the last several decades indicates that there is no simple causal relationship between economic conditions and political and social order in a given national context. Thus political and security concerns are not likely to be a solid foundation for generous economic and technology policies financed and supported by the North to spur technology-based development in the South.

In our opinion, only the economic self-interest of the North—and of the United States in particular—can motivate a vigorous new policy of technology transfer to the Third World. Taking such a perspective, we think that policies to promote technological development in the Third World could be an important mechanism for averting the recessionary demand conditions that are likely to confront the U.S. high-technology industries in the coming years.

The 1984–86 slump of the electronics industry in the United States signaled some of the dangers ahead. Three factors played a role in this slump and will continue to play a role in market developments in the future:[65]

(1) Increasing international competition from Japan and the NICs, sometimes reinforced by unfair trade practices, particularly by Japan.

(2) A process of global restructuring, with a shifting from producer firms to system firms, leading to strategic alliances and cutthroat competition in a market that offers limited expansion opportunities to an increasing number of players.

(3) A developing gap between the supply capabilities of the high-technology microelectronics industries and the demand for their products. Despite the growth in military demand for such products in the United States, market potential has failed to keep pace with the supply potential made possible by product and process innovations.

Add to these three factors a likely slowdown in overall levels of world demand, production, and trade stemming from macroeconomic conditions in the developed countries during the next several years, and a demand-induced slowdown in U.S. high-technology industries seems even more probable. Over the longer run, even if a cyclical crisis can be averted, global demand for the products of the microelectronics industries confronts two types of bottlenecks:

(1) Cultural, institutional, and budgetary obstacles in the North that limit civilian applications of the new microelectronics technologies and encourage the producers of such technologies to concentrate on a limited number of increasingly standardized products, in which U.S. firms are relatively most disadvantaged in international competition.

(2) The absence, by and large, of the Third World as a major world market for the products and processes made feasible by the new technologies.

In the long run, the incorporation of the Third World into global technology markets, both as users and as producers of microelectronics innovations, will increase market demand and the range of applications for such innovations. For many years to come, the major markets will remain in the North. Only if new policies are designed now, however, will we be able to see a gradual expansion of demand in the Third World. Beyond moral reasons and political strategies, it is in the fundamental *economic* interest of the United States and its leading industrial sectors to promote a process of technological development in the Third World that fosters growing demand for microelectronics innovations.

Several measures can be taken by the countries of the North, including the United States, to encourage such a process. Such actions—which can be taken by individual countries or groups of countries, often in conjunction with the multinational institutions such as the World Bank, the IMF, and the United Nations—include:

(a) Measures that provide financial and technical assistance for the deployment of microelectronics technologies in Third World development programs aimed at social and economic needs in such areas as communication, transportation, health, education, energy and raw material use, and agriculture.

(b) Measures to support the formation of internationally sponsored regional centers for scientific and engineering training and R & D in the Third World, with an emphasis on encouraging new applications of microelectronics technologies for the specific developmental needs of different regions.

(c) Tax and legal incentives to encourage multinational corporations to engage in technology transfer to the Third World.

(d) Measures to increase financial aid and organizational facilities for access by Third World students to technical-scientific schools in the advanced countries.

Some may continue to argue against such measures on the grounds that if the United States promotes the diffusion of new technologies to the developing countries, its already dwindling technological lead will erode still further and its competitive difficulties will only get worse. But this argument overlooks the fact that the growth of the U.S. economy increasingly depends on the growth of world demand for the output of its high-technology industries and related services.

From a global perspective, what is now required is a major, U.S.-led international technology initiative that will benefit the Third World and U.S. industries at the same time. Furthermore, the acceleration of technological development in the Third World will not undermine the U.S. competitive position because science-based development is a cumulative process in which the innovative capacity of U.S. institutions and corporations will continue to support a technological edge, provided industrial growth keeps pace with scientific discovery. Thus the more rapid the adoption and diffusion of new microelectronics technologies in the world economy, the stronger the relative competitive position of the United States is likely to be. In this sense it is true that the strategy suggested here is unlikely to modify the relative disparity of wealth and competitive position between the North and South to any significant extent. Yet the absolute levels of development and well-being could rise dramatically for both North and South. The successful deployment of the new technologies to aid Third World development would result in a more affluent, more balanced, integrated, secure, and humane world, in which the technological and institutional capacities of the United States would still assure the nation a strong competitive position in the international economy.

In the absence of the necessary policy measures, the pessimistic scenario about the effects of the microelectronics revolution on the developing world is likely to become a reality. In the current social and economic circumstances, the new technologies threaten to cause: greater dependence of Third World countries on foreign companies with limited spillover effects on national development; greater differentiation of income both within and among Third World countries; the marginalization of most developing countries in new international trade and production patterns; and a growing gap between supply potential and demand potential ushering in an era of instability in world technology markets.

## Notes

[1] Carlota Perez, "Microelectronics, Long Waves and World Structural Change: New Perspectives for Developing Countries," in *World Development*, Vol. 13, No. 3, March 1985, pp. 441–463; Nathan Rosenberg and Claudio Frischtak, eds., *International Technology Transfer: Concepts, Measures and Comparisons* (New York: Praeger Publishers, 1985).

[2] See, for example, Dieter Ernst, ed., *The New International Division of Labor, Technology, and Underdevelopment: Consequences for the Third World* (Frankfurt: Campus Verlag, 1980); Tagi Sagafi-Hejad, Richard W. Moxon, and Howard V. Perlmutter, eds., *Controlling International Technology Transfer: Issues, Perspectives and Policy Implications* (New York: Pergamon Press, 1981); Frances Stewart and Jeffrey James, eds., *The Economics of New Technology in Developing Countries* (Boulder: Westview Press, 1982).

[3] See Bruce Guile, ed., *Information Technologies and Social Transformation* (Washington, D.C.: National Academy Press, 1985).

[4] Manuel Castells, *Information Technology, Economic Restructuring, and Urban Development* (Oxford: Basil Blackwell, 1988).

[5] Edward K. Y. Chen, "Industrial Development, Foreign Direct Investment and Economic Cooperation: A Study of the Electronics Industry in the Asian Pacific" (Paper delivered at the Seminar on Economic Cooperation through Foreign Investment among Asian and Pacific Countries, Bangkok, May 19–22, 1987).

[6] Dieter Ernst, "Automation and the Worldwide Restructuring of the Electronics Industry: Strategic Implications for Developing Countries," *World Development*, Vol. 13, No. 3, March 1985.

[7] Luc Soete, "International Diffusion of Technology; Industrial Development, and Technological Leapfrogging," *World Development*, Vol. 13, No. 3 (March 1985).

[8] UNCTAD, *New and Emerging Technologies: Some Economic, Commercial and Developmental Aspects*, Report by the UNCTAD Secretariat, Trade and Development Board, TD/B/C/ 6/120 (Geneva: August 1984).

[9] See Dieter Ernst, *The Global Race in Microelectronics* (Frankfurt: Campus Verlag, 1983).

[10] See Bruce R. Guile and Harvey Brooks, eds., *Technology and Global Industry, Companies and Nations in the World Economy* (Washington, D.C.: National Academy Press, 1987).

[11] Allen J. Scott and Michael Storper, eds., *Production, Work, Territory* (London: Allen and Unwin, 1986).

[12] Giovanni Dosi and Luc Soete, "Technology Gaps and Cost-Based Adjustment: Some Explorations on the Determinants of International Competitiveness," *Metroeconomica*, Vol. XXXV, October 1983, pp. 197–222.

[13] Jagdish N. Bhagwati, *The New International Economic Order: The North-South Debate* (Cambridge: MIT Press, 1977); "Industrial Policies and Manufacturing Exports," *World Bank Staff Paper* (Washington, D.C.: 1982); Anne O. Krueger and Constantine Michalopoulos, "Developing Country Trade Policies and the International Economic System," in Ernest H. Preeg, ed., *Hard Bargaining Ahead: U.S. Trade Policy and Developing Countries* (New Brunswick, N.J.: Transaction Books for the Overseas Development Council, 1985), pp. 39–58.

[14] Juan F. Rada, *The Impact of Microelectronics* (Geneva: International Labor Office, 1982).

[15] Susan Walsh Sanderson, "Automated Manufacturing and Offshore Assembly in Mexico," in Cathryn L. Thorup, ed., *The United States and Mexico: Face to Face with New Technology* (New Brunswick, N.J.: Transaction Books for the Overseas Development Council, 1987).

[16] Ibid., p. 136.

[17] Dieter Ernst, *Innovation, Industrial Structure and Global Competition: The Changing Economics of Internationalization* (Frankfurt: Campus Verlag, 1987).

[18] There is no consistent data series that breaks down production on employment in electronics by country. Table 1 uses country shares in world imports and exports of specific electronics products as an imperfect indication of country shares in world production. For recent evidence on the role of Southeast Asian countries in world semiconductor production, see also Allen Scott and D.P. Angel, "The Global Assembly Operations of U.S. Semiconductor Firms: A Geographical Analysis" (Discussion paper, The Simon Frazier University, Burnaby, B.C., March 1987).

[19] For more on the role of government in the Korean electronics industry, see Chen, "Industrial Development, Foreign Direct Investment and Economic Cooperation," op. cit., and Ashoka Mody, "Recent Evolution of Microelectronics in Korea and Taiwan: An Institutional Approach to Comparative Advantage" (Unpublished research paper, AT&T Bell Labs, December 1986).

[20] For more on changes in foreign direct investment in industry after 1975, see Ernst, "Automation and the Worldwide Restructuring of the Electronics Industry," op. cit.

[21] See Ernst, *Innovation, Industrial Structure and Global Competition*, op. cit.; Peter W. Schulze, "Shifts in the World Economy and the Restructuring of Economic Sectors: Increasing Competition and Strategic Alliances in Information Technologies," in Richard C. Gordon and Linda Kimball, eds., *The Future of Silicon Valley* (Santa Cruz: University of California, Silicon Valley Research Group, forthcoming).

[22] See Ernst, *Innovation, Industrial Structure and Global Competition*, op. cit.; Chen, "Industrial Development, Foreign Direct Investment and Economic Cooperation," op. cit.

[23] Dieter Ernst, "Automation and Worldwide Restructuring of the Electronics Industry," op. cit.

[24] See Francis W. Rushing and Carole Ganz Brown, eds., *National Policies for Developing High Technology Industries: International Comparisons* (Boulder: Westview Press, 1986); Fabio Stefano Erber, "The Development of the 'Electronics Complex' and Government Policies in Brazil," *World Development*, Vol. 13, No. 3, March 1985; Manuel Castells, "The Developmental City-State in an Open World Economy: The Singapore Experience," *BRIE Working Paper*, University of California, December 1987; and U.S. Congress, Office of Technology Assessment, *Technology Transfer to China* (Washington, D.C.: 1987).

[25] U.N. Industrial Development Organization, Global and Conceptual Studies Branch, Division for Industrial Studies, *International Industrial Restructuring and the International Division of Labor in the Automobile Industry* (Vienna: UNIDO, 1984).

[26] Daniel T. Jones and James P. Womack. "Developing Countries and the Future of the Automobile Industry," *World Development*, Vol. 13, No. 3, March 1985, pp. 393–411.

[27] Ibid.

[28] Alan Altshuler, Martin Anderson, Daniel Jones, Daniel Roos, and James Womack, *The Future of the Automobile* (Cambridge: MIT Press, 1984).

[29] Cecilia Castano, *Cambio Tecnologico y Mercado de Trabajo en la Industria del Automobil* (Madrid: Editorial IELSS, 1985); Dennis P. Quinn, "Dynamic Markets and Mutating Firms: The Changing Organization of Production in Automotive Firms," *BRIE Working Paper*, University of California at Berkeley, July 1987.

[30] Jones and Womack, "Developing Countries and the Future of the Automobile Industry," op. cit., p. 403.

[31] Automobile production in Mexico jumped from 67,000 finished vehicles in 1965 to 597,000 in 1981, falling to a level of 398,000 in 1985, of which about 14.6 per cent were exported. But engine production for export dramatically increased in the last five years, mainly on the basis of "maquila" operations of U.S. firms. However, Womack argues that the main focus of U.S. automobile producers in Mexico in the future will be Mexico's large domestic market. See James P. Womack, "Prospects for the U.S.-Mexican Relationship in the Motor Vehicle Sector," in Cathryn L. Thorup, ed., *The United States and Mexico*, op. cit., pp. 101–126.

[32] At a recent meeting at the Harvard Business School, several automobile industry experts agreed that there would be 50-per-cent overcapacity in the auto industry by the early 1990s.

[33] Kurt Hoffman, "Clothing, Chips and Competitive Advantage: The Impact of Microelectronics on Trade and Production in the Garment Industry," *World Development*, Vol. 13, No. 3, March 1985, pp. 371–396.

[34] The analysis of developments in the garment industry in Hong Kong is based on research by Manuel Castells in Hong Kong during the summer of 1987. The results of this research are contained in Manuel Castells, *State Intervention in the Economy and the Hong Kong Model* (Berkeley: University of California, Institute of International Studies, forthcoming).

[35] Raphael Kaplinsky, *Microelectronics and Employment Revisited: A Review* (Report prepared for International Labor Organization World Employment Program, Institute of Development Studies, University of Sussex, February 1986).

[36] For further discussion of the relationship between the new technologies and employment, see Manuel Castells, *High Technology, World Development, and Structural Transformation*," in Saul H. Mendlovitz and R. B. J. Walker, eds., *Towards a Just World Peace* (London: Butterworths, 1987), particularly pp. 97–109.

[37] See Mario Cimoli, Giovanni Dosi, and Luc Soete, "Innovation Diffusion, Institutional Differences and Patterns of Trade: A North-South Model" (Paper delivered at a Conference on Innovation Diffusion, Venice, March 17–22, 1986).

[38] Edward K. Y. Chen, *The Newly Industrializing Countries in Asia: Growth Experience and Prospects* (Hong Kong: University of Hong Kong, Center for Asian Studies, 1985).

[39] Brazil has 75 per cent of the computer industry in Latin America and 59 per cent of the industry in all developing countries. It is in third place, after the United States and Japan, in its ability to supply its own computing needs. See Kaplinsky, *Microelectronics and Employment Revisited*, op. cit.

[40] Office of Technology Assessment, *Technology Transfer to China*, op. cit.; Ashok V. Desal, "Achievements and Limitations of India's Technological Capability," in Martin Fransman and Kenneth King, eds., *Technological Capability in the Third World* (London: MacMillan, 1984), pp. 245–261.

[41] See Denis Fred Simon, "China's Computer Strategy," *The China Business Review*, November-December 1986, pp. 44–50.

[42] See C. Y. Ng, R. Hirono, and Narongchai Akrasanee, *Industrial Restructuring in ASEAN and Japan: An Overview* (Singapore: Institute of Southeast Asian Studies, 1987).

[43] See Kamal Salih and Mei Ling Young, "Social Forces, the State and the International Division of Labor: The Case of Malaysia," in Jeff Henderson and Manuel Castells, eds., *Global Restructuring and Territorial Development* (London: Sage, 1987), pp. 168–202.

[44] See Raphael Kaplinsky, *Comparative Advantage and Development* (London: Frances Pinter, 1982).

[45] The examples in the text are taken from evidence in Kaplinsky, *Microelectronics and Employment Revisited*, op. cit., and International Labour Office, *Technological Change: The Tripartite Response, 1982–1985* (Geneva: 1985).

[46] Carolyn Dowling, "Fiber Optics: Chinese Fascination and American Frustration," *The China Business Review*, March-April 1987, pp. 6–11.

[47] See Laura Tyson, "The U.S. and the World Economy in Transition," *BRIE Working Paper*, University of California at Berkeley, July 1986.

[48] See Michael G. Borrus, *Chips of State: Microelectronics and American Autonomy* (Cambridge: Ballinger Publishing Co., forthcoming).

[49] American buyers took a whopping 85 per cent of the increase in developing-country exports between 1981 and 1984. During this period, U.S. imports of manufactured goods from developing countries more than doubled, from $34 billion to $70 billion, while Japanese imports rose by only $2 billion and European imports actually declined. By 1985, the United States was buying 62 per cent of the developing countries' exports of manufactured goods to industrialized countries. See Lester Thurow and Laura D'Andrea Tyson, "The Economic Black Hole," *Foreign Policy* (June 1987). For evidence on the role of U.S. markets in the export surge from ASEAN countries, see Lawrence Krause, "Economic Trends in the U.S. and their Implications for ASEAN" (Paper presented at University of California Pacific Rim Conference, Davis, California, May 1987).

[50] Ashoka Mody, "Information Industries: The Changing Role of the Newly Industrializing Countries" (Paper delivered at a conference on technology and government policy in telecommunications and computers, Brookings Institution, Washington, D.C., August 1987).

[51] Soete, "International Diffusion of Technology, Industrial Development and Technological Leapfrogging," op. cit.

[52] China, for example, has been able to buy advanced program-controlled exchange systems for several major cities from several major foreign suppliers, all on concessionary finance terms. The Chinese strategy is to install model long-distance fiber optics links using foreign equipment while simultaneously contracting for the transfer of technology for some of the equipment.

[53] David C. O'Connor, "The Computer Industry in the Third World: Policy Options and Constraints," *World Development*, Vol. 13, No. 3, March 1985.

[54] United Nations, *Technology and Science for Development* (Report of the Intergovernmental Committee on Science and Technology for Development, Seventh Session of the Economic and Social Council, E/1985-L.43, July 1, 1985).

[55] Staffan Jacobsson and Jon Sigurdson, eds., *Technological Trends and Challenges in Electronics: Dominance of the Industrialized World and Responses in the Third World* (Lund, Sweden: University of Lund, Research Policy Institute, 1983).

[56] Soete, "International Diffusion of Technology, Industrial Development and Technological Leapfrogging," op. cit.

[57] Ann Johnston and Albert Sasson, *New Technologies and Development* (Paris: UNESCO, 1986).

[58] Ibid.

[59] For example, the World Bank provided an education loan to China in 1982 to spearhead computer equipment purchases and the introduction of higher-level computer courses in school.

[60] Mody, "Recent Evolution of Microelectronics in Korea and Taiwan," op. cit., and Laura D'Andrea Tyson and John Zysman, "Politics and Productivity: Developmental Strategy and Production Innovation in Japan," in a book on the Japanese economy edited by Chalmers Johnson (Cambridge: Ballinger Publishing Co., forthcoming).

[61] Nigel Harris, *The End of the Third World: Newly Industrializing Countries and the Decline of a Ideology* (London: Penguin Books, 1986).

[62] Outward orientation in this sense differs from the notion of outward orientation developed by Bela Balassa and others at the World Bank. According to Balassa's formulation, outward orientation characterizes a development strategy that is guided by market forces with limited state intervention. As the cases of Japan and the successful East Asian NICs demonstrate, successful development strategies often involve a large extent of state intervention, including the promotion of important industries closely tied to world market conditions. Such strategies are outwardly-oriented in the sense used in the text. For more on the Balassa formulation, see *Development Strategies in Semi-Industrial Countries* (Baltimore: Johns Hopkins University Press, 1982).

[63] See Thurow and Tyson, "The Economic Black Hole," op. cit.

[64] See, for example, the forecast of a few years ago by Bro Uttal, "The Coming Glut of Semiconductors," *Fortune*, March 19, 1984, pp. 125–128.

[65] Manuel Castells, "The Real Crisis of Silicon Valley," in Richard C. Gordon and Linda Kimball, eds., *The Future of Silicon Valley* (Santa Cruz: University of California, Silicon Valley Research Group, forthcoming).

Chapter 2

# The Service Industries: Growth, Trade, and Development Prospects

Jonathan D. Aronson

Like the air around us, services are everywhere and usually invisible. They are hard to define and even harder to measure. In national and international statistics, services generally are treated as a residual category—as whatever is not agriculture, natural resources, or goods. The following selective list illustrates the range of activities falling into this category: transportation, tourism, accounting, advertising, education, repairs and maintenance, construction, engineering, telecommunications, information, data processing, broadcasting and motion-pictures, financial services, insurance, employment services, hospital management, wholesaling, and retailing—as well as income derived from foreign investment, licensing, and workers' remittances.[1]

By 1982, the contribution of the service sector to the gross domestic product exceeded the contributions of agriculture, mining, and manufacturing in most countries. It is estimated that in developing countries services average 48 per cent of the gross domestic product and 18 per cent of employment, while in industrial countries the corresponding figures are 66 and 67 per cent.[2] More important, services account for growing numbers of jobs and increasing economic output in almost all developed and developing countries.

As this trend becomes more evident, services are becoming the focus of intensive study and debate in many countries. Trade in services is also a source of controversy. Some hail services as a panacea for creating new jobs and as the instrument of the next boost in prosperity and competitiveness. Others worry that if industrial countries promote service sectors at the expense of manufacturing, the result could be disastrous. Developing countries wonder how to treat their domestic service industries and whether they can risk opening their relatively weak service sectors to possible domination by large, sophisticated service providers from abroad.

To begin clarifying some of these questions, this chapter mainly focuses on knowledge-intensive services, particularly finance and telecommunications, because they are at the core of the changes under way. Labor-intensive services such as construction, education, and personal services are treated only in passing. The general themes are straightforward: (1) A technological revolution in the service industries is transforming national economies and the global economy. (2) Efficient service industries promote growth, jobs, and competitiveness in both developed and developing countries. (3) On balance, freer trade in services would benefit both developed and developing countries. Overall, although the services revolution will create some important problems, its benefits will outweigh its costs.

This chapter highlights the impact of technological and regulatory changes on service industries, assesses the importance of services for U.S. competitiveness and prosperity, and explores the link between services and development. It also examines the prospects for, and implications of, freer trade in services, and suggests the implications of reaching agreement on services for the management of the world economy.

## The Revolution in Services

For decades, the system for managing knowledge-based services domestically and internationally functioned quite smoothly because the technology on which services were based was changing relatively slowly, because the same services were for the most part available everywhere, and because these services were easily distinguishable from each other (for example, there was little overlap between computer and communications services). The same basic range of services was provided in all countries and was offered under similar regulatory conditions. All this has changed.[3]

In the past two decades, technological breakthroughs—particularly in the telecommunications and information arena—have stimulated the emergence of a world information economy. These breakthroughs led to fundamental changes in the telecommunications, finance, transportation, and other service sectors as well as in manufacturing and agriculture. One consequence of these technological changes was the erosion of boundaries within and among service sectors. For example, communications, computer, and broadcast technologies increasingly overlap, and once discrete financial services are all being offered in new financial supermarkets. At the same time, firms that once were just manufacturers now depend on services for an increasing portion of their revenues. Similarly, the service component of manufactured goods is rising. The adoption of new technologies has also permitted some countries to offer a wide array of new and different services and products. Indeed, production processes have changed so dramatically that many firms are rethinking their global financial, trade, and investment strategies as well as their relationships with corporate allies and competitors.

In the case of trade in services, Jagdish Bhagwati has distinguished between services requiring "physical proximity" and "long-distance services." Physical proximity is essential to three categories of services. First, some services require the provider to go to the user. For example, to build a dam or highway, the construction company must bring workers to the site. Second, sometimes the users have to go to the provider. To get a Harvard education, the student must travel to Cambridge. Heart transplant patients go to the surgeon, equipment, and support team, not vice versa. Third, in some cases either the service provider or user can move. Haircutting, tailoring, and lecturing are three examples. For "long-distance services," in contrast, physical proximity between providers and users may be useful but it is not necessary. Banking, insurance, telecommunications, and data processing can always be sold from a distance.[4]

The difficulty of providing services where physical proximity was required tended to hold down the international exchange of services. Still, although the official figures are almost certainly understated, it is estimated that between 1970 and 1980, trade in services increased by an average of 18.8 per cent annually, reaching $436 billion in 1980. Even if the global recession of the early 1980s holds this decade's increase to half that rate, trade in services nevertheless will shortly total $1 trillion annually.

Moreover, the technological innovations of the past twenty years have removed the necessity of proximity to trade of some services; enhanced the ability to trade some long-distance services; and created new, tradeable services. For example, new transportation technology may allow some workers to stay home. Giant oil rigs and even whole factories can now be built in one country and floated to another. In addition, new telecommunications and information technologies make it possible to supply services such as accounting, advertising, consulting, design, education, law, and health care with much less need for physical proximity. For example, the Open University in the United Kingdom broadcasts all its lectures. Similarly, it is now practical for skilled medical specialists to diagnose and treat illnesses and even supervise certain surgical operations from afar. Finally, new value-added and information services, such as videotext services, can be traded as easily as goods.

Proximity also matters less because the relationship between distance and the cost of providing a service (not the price that is charged) is breaking down. For example, telephone authorities typically subsidize local calls by charging higher rates to long-distance users; international callers are forced to pay a premium to subsidize domestic users. Technological and regulatory changes, however, are pushing telephone authorities to rebalance the rates. Technological advances have made the cost of providing international services practically the same as providing domestic services; consider that a call that uses a satellite must travel more than 44,000 miles up and down regardless of whether the sender and receiver are one hundred, one thousand, or ten thousand miles apart. New international facilities (satellites and fiber optic cables) promise to create excess capacity and force down international rates.

Two trends in this realm have particularly important and conflicting implications. First, skilled, knowledge-intensive services are far more likely to be transacted "long-distance" than labor-intensive services. Developing countries—which in 1980 accounted for only 13.5 per cent of services exports and 17.5 per cent of services imports—fear that if trade in services is liberalized, they will import more skilled services but will be unable to increase their exports of labor-intensive services, in which they may have a comparative advantage. Developing countries worry that their growth, jobs, and balances of payments could be adversely affected. This is one reason why many developing countries have been reluctant to liberalize trade in services.

Second, the globalization of service industries, particularly at the telecommunications/finance nexus, is fundamentally revolutionizing the way the world economy works. In the wake of deregulation, controls on interest rates and international capital flows were relaxed, allowing new players to enter the financial services arena. These new entrants now offer innovative products that were unimaginable only a few years ago on a global basis.[5] The global financial market relies on the immediate availability of information and the ability to transfer funds electronically anywhere in the world in an instant. The technology made possible the introduction of new services and financial instruments. It also meant that to be competitive, players must be able to operate on a global basis. At the very least, access to Europe, North America, and Japan is imperative.[6]

What is emerging is a global "green belt" that connects the principal financial centers of the world: London, New York, and Tokyo. This money belt has established a 24-hour-a-day financial market in which there is substantial freedom in financial transactions, which in turn has created strong incentives for the unification of related services. It is no accident that the most sweeping changes in the regulation of telecommunications and information services have come in the three countries that host the major financial markets of the world. These countries are also likely to lead the way to increasing competition in transportation and other vital support services. All other countries, including developing countries, must decide how to respond to the strategies of the leading financial and communication centers. Developing countries in particular risk being marginalized if they do not tie into this network and accept more liberal international competition in services.

In short, a scramble is under way to rethink and reform the regulation of domestic service industries and the management of services internationally. The choices that governments make will significantly influence the future prospects for their national economies and their international competitiveness. It is hardly surprising that the United States has been pressing for freer trade in services and that this initiative has raised worries in many developing countries. Developing countries are being pulled in opposite directions and must find a new balance between protecting their domestic service markets and opening them up to the world.

The debate is particularly intense because the transitions toward service economies and toward the emergence of a world information economy, like all economic transitions, will leave some countries and companies winners and others losers. To the extent that countries and companies perceive themselves as winners or losers, they will act to speed or delay change. The winners will stress that, in aggregate, there will be economic growth, and that adjustment is necessary. The losers will try to slow down the process and to minimize their losses by exacting compensation from the winners.

## Services, Growth, and Competitiveness

The service economy gets bad press. Thus *Business Week*, for example, has lamented that "the decline of manufacturing threatens the entire U.S. economy"[7]; and in the same issue, Akio Morita, the chairman of Sony, was reported to observe that the result is a "hollowing of American industry"—a U.S. abandonment of its status as an industrial country. A recurring theme in the industrial policy literature is simply that "manufacturing matters"; without a strong domestic manufacturing industry, the United States cannot thrive and be competitive.[8] What is implied, and sometimes stated explicitly, is that services *matter less*—that they are the "empty calories" feeding economic growth.

At best, services are seen as an important input into manufacturing health. At worst, they are considered a negative force because they distract attention from the production of goods.

Others cheer on the growth of the service sector while also acknowledging the importance of manufacturing. They argue that services are critical for at least three reasons. First, the percentage of gross domestic product and employment accounted for by services such as finance, telecommunications, travel and tourism, accounting, advertising, education, health, and entertainment is increasing everywhere. In the United States, for example, the rise in services employment has dwarfed gains in the manufacturing sector. From 1948 to mid-1983, the number of U.S. workers producing manufactured goods rose by just over 50 per cent, from 15.6 million to 22.7 million, including 3.1 million employed in knowledge-intensive manufacturing. During the same period, employment in services more than tripled, expanding from 20.9 million to 74.1 million workers. Some services employment gains, however, are due to the increasing practice of manufacturers to hire outsiders to perform services they once performed themselves. Furthermore, the "McDonaldization of America" is greatly exaggerated. Much of the growth in the service sector is in productive high-technology services—not labor-intensive services. By the end of 1985, just over half (38.1 million) of these service jobs were in knowledge-based services.[9]

Second, the services component of manufactured products is rising. Although some 3.8 million new manufacturing jobs were created in the United States between 1948 and 1978, only about one-sixth of these were in production. Similarly, between 1950 and 1980, the percentage of U.S. manufacturing workers engaged in production fell from 82 per cent to 70 per cent. The integration of services into manufacturing is making manufacturing more productive. For example, when General Motors builds a car, or Boeing a new airplane, it increasingly relies on computer-aided design and computer-aided manufacturing to change designs and adjust machine tooling. Similarly, software-programming services now account for approximately 80 per cent of the development costs of new computers and new digital telecommunications switches. Fifteen years ago, these figures were reversed, with the development of the hardware for all of these products accounting for about 80 per cent of the cost.

Third, just as the transportation system made possible the long-distance exchange of goods, the telecommunications infrastructure promotes the sale of new services. In the emerging world information economy, the actual location of a worker providing many services is less important because all workers are connected through a communications network.[10] As a result, many services can now be efficiently and profitably traded. For example, American construction/engineering firms employ architectural drafters in the Philippines and India; South Koreans contribute abstracts for legal data bases; and data-entry facilities for American Airlines and other U.S. firms are located in Barbados.

Two contentious questions remain. First, how *productive* are services? The switch from goods to services usually is blamed for slowing productivity in the economy as a whole. This idea persists in many quarters, although it is now clear that the emergence of certain services improves the efficiency of firms and increases the synergy and productivity among sectors of the economy.[11] Services may, however, be significantly more productive in industrial than developing countries. Understanding the relative productivity of various services within a national economy and compared to manufacturing and agricultural activities is a key to devising sound economic policies.

Second, are manufacturing jobs "better" than services jobs? Labor leaders maintain that unionized, highly paid workers in manufacturing industries will continue to lose their jobs. If they can find work at all, it will be in non-unionized, lower-paid services jobs. Others respond that this adjustment process is inevitable, and that knowledge-based service industries hold the key to future productivity in both manufacturing and services. They argue that new production processes will generally require fewer manufacturing workers.

Over the past century, the dramatic decline in agricultural workers in industrial countries did not lead to falling agricultural production. Similarly, although the total number of manufacturing jobs in industrial countries will probably decline in coming decades, manufacturing output should increase substantially. Higher productivity should allow domestic production of manufactured goods to continue to increase even if employment declines.

At the extremes, a debate rages between those who believe that prosperity can *only* be built on a strong manufacturing sector, and those who argue not only that services are the wave of tomorrow, but also that new service industries will help bolster manufacturing production and competitiveness, if not employment. The two positions are not as far apart as they at first appear. The focus and tactics diverge, but the objectives and even the visions are similar. What is needed is a balance between efforts to promote manufacturing and services. Industrial economies cannot survive without the ability to manufacture critical products domestically. The possibility that manufacturers will favor domestic rather than foreign service inputs into the manufacturing process is real. At the same time, new services are both productive in their own right and able to increase the productivity and competitiveness of manufacturers. Politicians will have to decide what manufacturing sectors are critical, and how large a domestic production capacity is needed to maintain economic and political security. They will need to be careful, however, not to confuse the promotion of certain sectors with the protection of jobs. Modern manufacturing success will depend increasingly on new capital and information-intensive technologies. Inevitably, services will continue to provide the bulk of new jobs in industrial countries. The goal for policymakers is to ensure that policy does not tilt in favor of either manufacturers or services producers.

## Services and Development

How can developing countries use their domestic service industries to promote development and exports? What reforms are desirable? These two questions are the focus of this section.

Today, certain labor-intensive service industries thrive in developing countries. In addition, many knowledge-based service companies located in developing countries provide domestic and international services. For example, Banco do Brasil was for many years among the most profitable banks in the world. UPI news agency is now under Mexican ownership. India's software industry is well respected. Developing countries' shipping firms and airlines—such as Singapore Airlines and Cathay Pacific, are well respected. Singapore Telecom is an innovative leader, as is Palapa, Indonesia's satellite communication system. South Korean and Taiwanese construction-engineering firms are world leaders. And the Philippines are becoming a force in animation, architectural design, and drafting.

Moreover, developing-country prospects for increased services exports (and increased foreign exchange earnings) are real. Jagdish Bhagwati argues that "it would be totally wrong to infer that developing countries cannot find traded services that they can export successfully."[12] It is clear that newly industrializing countries as well as more inward-looking countries such as India have the skills to develop export advantages in an increasing range of electronic services that are now tradeable.

Nonetheless, the service sectors of most developing countries are in bad shape. Predictably, the upsurge of interest in services has caused many countries to begin to take a closer look at the role that services play in the process of development. They want to learn how to use services to better promote development.[13]

One problem is that services may play a different role in developing countries than in developed countries. The structure of domestic service industries and the structure of the global service economy may penalize service sectors in developing countries and hamper their growth and development. For example, although statistics are poor, it appears that high-technology, knowledge-based services such as finance and telecommunications ("other services" in most statistical compilations) are growing more rapidly in developed than in developing countries. In addition, most service-sector workers in developing countries are poorly paid, and their productivity is low. Without growth in knowledge-intensive services, jobs in this sector in most developing countries remain the employment of last resort—and, the relative productivity of service-sector jobs in developing countries in most cases remains lower than in the developed world.

Part of the problem appears to be that, in most developing countries, knowledge-based services usually are heavily regulated to achieve narrow objectives and often are provided by government monopolies that are not explicitly linked to the development process. (Labor-intensive services are more often provided by small, inefficient entities.) Telecommunications services, for example, are almost always provided by large, usually inefficient, government post, telegraph, and telecommunications monopolies designed to achieve three main goals. They create large numbers of jobs, they use cross-subsidies to redistribute benefits among domestic groups, and they are sources of revenue for the national treasury. None of these goals is compatible with broad-ranging development objectives. Indeed, growth, efficiency, and development are likely to lag if service monopolies in developing countries are protected from competition and isolated from new technologies available abroad. To succeed, therefore, almost every developing country needs to reform and revitalize its knowledge-based service sectors.

A continuum of interlinked strategies for promoting development is available to developing countries, as illustrated by the three models outlined below. First, developing countries can try to build up their own world-class industries and domestic monopolies by adopting infant-industry strategies. Second, developing countries can try to stimulate their domestic manufacturing and service industries by modernizing telecommunications, finance, and other service sectors; these services, in turn, can be used to promote and channel development.[14] Third, they can introduce more domestic competition in the provision of certain services and experiment with privatization. A variant of this strategy is to allow foreign service providers to compete in the market alone or in partnership with local firms.

Countries favoring an infant-industry model protect domestic service industries from foreign competition. The modernization model is built around government efforts to stimulate domestic industries to be more efficient. The competition model relies on the market to produce innovation and efficiency. Although an infant-industry or a competitive approach to the provision of services can stand alone, both can be integrated with the modernization model. Indeed, either strategy is likely to yield better results when linked to a modernization strategy. As long as foreign competition is excluded, it is conceivable for developing countries to combine elements of all three models.

### 1. The Infant-Industry Model

A first path pursued by some developing countries is based on their conviction that their future prosperity depends on building indigenous industries in key knowledge-based services. They are concerned that, without government assistance, their sovereignty will be undermined as their domestic service providers are overwhelmed by multinational firms. They fear that if the operation of the world economy is increasingly dependent on global networks, they could be at a permanent disadvantage—or be left out of the "game" entirely. This leads some countries, most visibly Brazil and India, to advocate the adoption of an infant-industry strategy for informatics and other knowledge-based service industries.

So far, however, the short-term results of these infant-industry strategies are mixed. Brazil, for example, buys only those informatics goods and services that it cannot or does not want to produce in the medium or long run. Its goal is to emulate its earlier success in domestic manufacturing, such as the aircraft industries. To this end, Brazil has diverted some of its best technological talent into the computer, telecommunications, and software industries. These sectors are expanding and learning is taking place. But so far most outputs are expensive by world standards, saddling consumers and domestic manufacturing industries with higher costs. The United States, convinced that Brazil is resorting to measures prohibited under the GATT to protect its industries, imposed over $100 million in new tariffs on Brazil in November 1987. The long-term results of the Brazilian experiment with an infant-industry strategy for services are still in doubt, but new products, services, and technologies are introduced so quickly in the emerging world information economy that any country that isolates itself and its economy from these developments risks being hopelessly outdistanced. So far it appears that, although this strategy for reforming knowledge-based service sectors retains the most domestic control, it also is the riskiest approach to guaranteeing future growth, jobs, and development. It is not clear that an infant-industry strategy can be applied successfully to services. If so, countries that go down this path could find themselves falling farther and farther behind as they become more isolated from the world economy.

In essence, services—particularly knowledge-intensive services—are expensive and inefficiently provided in most developing countries. At the same time, the central role of services for future growth makes it imperative that developing countries rationalize their service industries. A key priority for developing countries is to improve their services infrastructure, because these services are interlinked with all other activities and are thus critical to development. Efficient services beget other services. Similarly, efficient domestic service industries are an important factor in the creation of competitive domestic manufacturing sectors.

### 2. The Modernization Model

The key to this approach is for governments to begin to transform public service providers, particularly monopolies, from revenue generators into engines of development. Service providers such as telecommunications authorities need to be used to further the overall process of development. As a first step, profits need to be reinvested into the service providers. This would allow new infrastructure to be installed and make it possible to introduce service innovations more easily. In addition, service providers need to be pushed to be more sensitive to the needs of large domestic and foreign users. It is possible to combine the modernization model with the infant-industry model and exclude domestic or foreign competition. However, without competition, the ability to refocus the goals of service providers may be limited, and the absence of foreign competition could leave developing countries isolated from technological changes emerging elsewhere.

Telecommunications provides an excellent "laboratory" for the application of the modernization model to a key domestic service sector. Typically, despite changes in global technology, countries continue to treat their telecommunications monopolies as providers of jobs and as sources of cash for the national treasury. Most developing countries underinvest in telecommunications. Applicants seeking new telephone connections often outnumber lines in service. The wait to be connected is typically between two and ten years.[15] Inevitably, domestic business is retarded, and foreign investors are discouraged by such an environment. This needs to change. Even though it may hurt the treasury, undercut domestic suppliers of communications equipment, and reduce subsidies for smaller users, adopting a modernization approach could contribute to overall national development.

### 3. The Competition Model: Opportunities and Risks

Although the modernization model can be applied without resorting to privatization or increased competition, some countries may decide to follow such strategies. Competition can be introduced in a wide range of variations, many of which will not provoke domestic political opposition. One additional advantage for developing countries of exploring competition in conjunction with modernization is that this would link them more closely to the world economy. That may also be its greatest disadvantage.

The dilemma is real, as significant opportunities and risks are involved. The emerging structure of the world economy makes development difficult *without* integration and competition, yet the price of integration is greater dependence on the industrial world and less flexibility in domestic policies.[16] Developing countries walk a tightrope, balancing the acceptance of interdependence and the retention of independence in proportions that allow for future prosperity. The balance is different for each country.

When the sale of international services depended on investment and labor movement, most services in developing countries were produced and consumed domestically. The globalization of telecommunications and finance makes it possible for developing countries to be part of the world economy. Small countries such as Singapore and Barbados have carefully crafted niche strategies that welcomed foreign service firms. Eventually, foreign firms may spin off some of their operations to domestic firms. In addition, easy, affordable linkage to international services networks can, if countries so choose, be used as a way to attract foreign investors and tourists.

For example, China entered into joint ventures with Cable & Wireless Inc. because foreign oil companies operating in the South China Seas complained about the difficulties they had with voice and data communications with their headquarters. The new fiber optic cable between Hong Kong and southern China gives foreign investors access to world-class communications at competitive prices. This is an attractive selling point for would-be foreign investors. By the same token, networks that allow travellers to plan air, hotel, and car rental details in a single stop can be used to attract tourists. The globalization of credit networks already allows American Express and others to provide worldwide access to funds and other services.

*Adding Domestic Competition Only.* One way to avoid the integration-dependence trade-off and still gain some benefits is for developing countries to continue to exclude foreign competition but introduce more *domestic* competition by partial privatization of domestic monopolies, coupled with the licensing of new domestic service suppliers. National control can be maintained and efficiency promoted by adding domestic competitors. Thus in India the four competing, government-owned providers of property/casualty insurance are far more efficient than the sole government-owned provider of life insurance. China is breaking up its national airline into competing government-owned companies. Partial or total privatization of post and telecommunication authorities and of other public service providers also may contribute to the output of domestic services.

*Joint Ventures.* A variant of this strategy would be to allow foreign firms to enter into joint ventures with the state-run monopoly or other domestic providers of services. For example, giant South Korean firms such as Samsung, Daewoo, and Lucky Gold Star already collaborate with foreign firms in manufacturing, and they might extend their cooperation to services. This tactic could give service providers in developing countries access to the latest technology and at the same time leave control of most of the domestic distribution system in local hands.[17]

*Foreign Competitors in Domestic Markets.* The next step would be to permit foreign competitors. The range of possible variations of competition are illustrated by the telecommunications sector. All of these arrangements would permit developing countries to become part of a global services market, at least for knowledge-intensive services like telecommunications, data processing, and finance.

The United States provides the most ambitious model of liberalization, deregulation, and increased competition. Since 1984, the United States has permitted monopolies for the provision of local phone service, but all other services are open to competition. West Germany and Canada are now considering a second variant, under which the telecommunications monopolist would retain control over the physical transmission facilities but would be required to allow competitors access to the facilities so that they, too, could offer services. A third variant, favored by Japan and the United Kingdom, permits competition in both facilities and services but limits the number of competitors that can be licensed. In this way the number of foreign competitors can be even more stringently controlled. A fourth alternative, being experimented with in France, seeks to distinguish between basic and enhanced or "value-added" services. The monopoly maintains control over most facilities and all basic telephone services, but competition in enhanced services is permitted.

For developing countries, the danger of adopting such strategies is that some control is sacrificed. If IBM, for instance, develops a new technology or relocates some of its operations, the nascent industry can be undermined. (U.S. service firms may face the same risk if they grow too dependent on foreign manufacturing facilities.) In addition, changing technologies may first employ and then dismiss workers. For example, a thriving data-entry industry could be demolished when computers can cheaply and reliably recognize and process audio and visual inputs.

*International Services Only.* A middle ground that could allow countries to promote development and still maintain considerable control over vital domestic service industries might be to allow service monopolies to retain their control over all domestic services, but permit competition in the provision of most international services. Some models already exist. Many countries have international banking zones that allow foreign financial institutions to operate in specific places and provide international services and certain domestic services to the international community. The idea of international banking zones could be extended—perhaps to allow the creation of international data zones, granting foreign firms several special guarantees. Foreign companies could be allowed to operate in international data zones in countries that otherwise restrict their operations. Countries could still impose data restrictions outside of such special zones.

Likewise, international communications might be managed in ways similar to the regulation of international aviation. As with airlines, while there is competition on international routes, no foreign competitors are allowed to provide domestic services. This model would enable developing countries to regulate the provision of domestic services as they chose as long as they accepted new rules governing international services.

Variations of the competition model, particularly when coupled with the adoption of a modernization model, would have three main advantages for developing countries. First, countries could choose to leave the bulk of the local monopoly untouched. Reforms would provoke less domestic resentment, since international services are little used by most consumers. Second, this approach would allow countries to provide large, influential users with efficient, cheap, and innovative services. Later, developing countries could choose whether to extend competition to their domestic service markets. Third, this arrangement would allow government service monopolies to continue to provide most of their traditional subsidies to users.[18]

To summarize, the growing importance of traded services for future growth and development presents developing-country governments with choices that will significantly influence their future prospects. Continued domination of domestic services by domestic monopolies and firms will maintain government independence, but diminish opportunities for growth and diversification. If efficient, competitive services are made available, they will stimulate economic activity and may attract foreign investors. This may, however, undermine national sovereignty, create dependency, and undercut entrenched domestic firms. In the short run, a strategy that modernizes domestic service providers and allows competition at least in the provision of international services may be optimal for many large developing countries. Some developing countries, particularly smaller countries and newly industrializing countries, may also find it in their interest to extend competition and liberalization to their domestic service markets.

# Trade and Investment in Services

The debate over services and the international exchange of services is about self-interest and domestic politics. Industrial countries want to bolster their manufacturing industries. They also want to liberalize trade in those services in which they have a comparative advantage. The developed countries argue that freer trade in services will also benefit developing countries. Most developing countries remain skeptical and are reluctant to open up their service sectors to multinational firms from abroad.

### The Path to Services Negotiations

With the exception of movies, services are not mentioned in the GATT Articles. Until the passage of the Trade Act of 1974, services were not even mentioned or covered in U.S. trade legislation. But during the past few years, a handful of service companies championed the inclusion of services in U.S. trade legislation and persuaded U.S. negotiators to press for the inclusion of services in the new GATT Round. Services were given equal billing with goods in the Trade Agreements Act of 1979 and were made a high negotiating priority by the Trade and Tariff Act of 1984. Ultimately, the U.S. government saw services as a way to gain new supporters for free trade at a time when traditional backers were tempted by protectionism. They also believe that freer trade in services will promote large efficiency gains in the world economy and improve the climate of global economic relations. With more than two-thirds of all trade in services taking place among industrial countries, the United States was confident that ultimately it could push services onto the agenda.

Most developing countries opposed any treatment of services within GATT; they contended that trade in services was beyond the competence of the GATT, that services was an investment issue, rather than a trade issue, and that rules and principles appropriate to deal with border tariffs on goods could not be applied adequately to services.[19] Although services are now on the GATT negotiating agenda, developing countries still feel that industrial countries have not lived up to their obligations to lower barriers that hamper their exports of goods. They fear that services will overload the GATT and distract attention from unfinished work on important issues such as tropical products, textiles, quantitative restrictions, agriculture, and safeguards. Consequently they remain skeptical about opening their borders to industrial countries' services. They also worry, for good reason, that industrial countries will focus service negotiations on knowledge-intensive services in which they enjoy a clear comparative advantage and ignore politically sensitive, labor-intensive services, such as construction-engineering, which involve cheap labor moving across borders, with some benefits for developing countries in the form of employment-creation and foreign exchange remittances.[20]

The Reagan administration was rebuffed when it sought new multilateral trade negotiations at the GATT ministerial meeting in November 1982. The only small victory for the United States was reaching agreement to prepare national studies on services; the reports that the United States and other industrialized countries subsequently prepared formed an important empirical basis for later negotiations. Over the next four years, most *industrial* countries were persuaded of the need for including services in the negotiations. Even a number of *developing* countries (including most Asian NICs, many African states, and some smaller Latin American countries) were persuaded to agree to placing services on the negotiations agenda. Entering the September 1986 GATT ministerial meeting that launched the Uruguay Round, the staunch foes of services were reduced to a core Group of 10, led by India and Brazil and also including Argentina, Cuba, Egypt, Nicaragua, Nigeria, Peru, Tanzania, and Yugoslavia. By late 1987, Argentina had become a services supporter and Egypt had assumed a more neutral position.

Proponents and opponents of services negotiations both came away from Uruguay claiming victory. Services are on the agenda and GATT rules and procedures will apply to the negotiations. However, the negotiations on services are separated from those on goods, investment issues, and other topics. At the end of the multilateral talks—which are scheduled to last four years—the GATT contracting parties will decide whether the results of these negotiations will be integrated with the other agreements reached in the round.

### The Basic Issues of Services Negotiations

A boulder atop a peak can be dislodged and aimed in a general direction with relative ease. Once it is in motion, however, major course corrections become nearly impossible. Therefore it is imperative to start it moving in the right direction and then let momentum take over. Negotiations on trade in services are now at the top of the peak waiting for guidance.

Four broad issues must be settled if the negotiations are to succeed.[21] First, there are issues of *definition and coverage.* Defining services is controversial. Should construction-engineering, for example, be treated as part of the goods sector, or the service sector, or as something else altogether? How should services that are embedded in goods be treated? If manufacturing firms provide services in conjunction with goods (for example, maintenance or pilot training for aircraft), how should they be treated? In short, for the purposes of negotiations, what *are* services? Trade in services is hard to define because of disagreements about what constitutes trade, and what constitutes investment, in services. Although today's global telecommunications network makes services more tradeable, the boundaries separating trade and investment in services remain fuzzy. Developing countries that wish to slow the progress of negotiations argue that nothing should be done until all countries agree on definitions. Industrial countries argue that this boundary issue can *never* be fully resolved, so that an ad hoc consensus is needed that allows progress. They suggest that, as a start, negotiators might agree to define traded services simply as "services essentially produced in one country and paid for by residents of another country."[22] Ultimately, countries might agree that, as a rule of thumb, when the domestic regulatory system requires a local presence as a condition for doing business, the right of establishment (and access to the local distribution system) should become a negotiable trade issue rather than an investment issue.

*Which* services should be covered by negotiations? Developed countries claim that they want coverage to be as wide as possible, while developing countries worry that developed countries are only willing to deal with high-technology, knowledge-based services—many of which can be provided most efficiently by large multinational enterprises. They fear that labor-intensive services, in which they have a comparative advantage, will be left out of the negotiations. They therefore prefer services negotiations to focus on specific sectors, not on developing a broad general framework agreement.

Second, negotiators must resolve the conflict between *international management and national regulations.* Crafting an international agreement covering trade in services will require revising or abolishing some legitimate national or sub-national regulations that hamper or distort trade flows. Efforts to liberalize trade in services will affect, and be affected by, these national regulations. Negotiators will need to determine which regulations are "appropriate" and may continue in place, and which are "protectionist" and should be modified or eliminated. The first step will be for negotiators to try to make regulations more transparent, so that their appropriateness can be assessed more easily.

Third, negotiators are instructed by the Uruguay declaration to assure that liberalization of trade in services promotes the "economic growth of all trading partners and the development of developing countries." Developing countries fear that negotiations could leave them at a competitive disadvantage, even as industrial countries extol the advantages of freer trade in services. In contrast, industrial countries contend that the main reason developing countries received little during the Kennedy and Tokyo Rounds of trade negotiations was that they were unwilling to give very much in return.

The optimal approach would be to treat developing-country concerns within a broad services agreement and extend full rights and obligations to all signatories.[23] It is likely that domestic political constraints in industrial countries will limit progress on such key developing-country concerns of labor migration and immigration in multilateral services negotiations. Therefore, some compensation will have to be found for developing countries. Although the value of past concessions for developing countries under the Generalized System of Preferences is debatable, developing countries once again may be granted some form of special and differential treatment. Developing-country signatories to a services agreement might receive three benefits. First, services technology will be transferred to them. Second, they will be allowed a longer transition period before opening their markets to full competition from abroad. Third, their services exports might be accorded preferential access to industrial-country markets. It may even be possible to establish export platforms for telecommunications and other services. However, such preferences probably would be extended only for a limited time.[24]

Finally, negotiators will be challenged to make any agreement *evolutionary and enforceable*. If such an agreement does not evolve, it will be out of date before it comes into force. Similarly, without a working dispute-settlement mechanism, any services agreement will be too weak to be useful. A more evolutionary process is needed to make a dispute-settlement process viable, since it is harder to amend an agreement once it is in place. And, as the number of signatories increases, it is harder to achieve meaningful reform. Yet without ongoing reforms, any system of rules quickly runs aground. The challenge is to create a mechanism that learns from experience. Governments have not succeeded very well in this task in the past, but they must tackle the issue head-on this time.

# Recommendations

In many cases, developing-country service industries are not efficient or competitive. Unless at least the financial and telecommunications sectors are made more efficient, long-term development prospects across all sectors will suffer. Decisions about telecommunications (and banking) need to be thought through more broadly and thoroughly. This does not mean that developing countries must privatize or break up their monopolies or even allow foreign competitors to compete in the domestic market. However, if developing countries wish to become full partners in an increasingly interdependent world-information economy, they will need to create mutually advantageous arrangements with multinational enterprises—and probably also provide a more liberal environment for the international exchange of services. But developing countries have to be clever about how they manage their global interconnections; for many of them, substantial autonomy in their national economies remains desirable.

In contrast, the United States—the "champion" of the inclusion of trade in services in the Uruguay Round—was insensitive to developing-country fears. The United States (and Brazil and India) overly politicized negotiations on services. Now that services *are* on the negotiating agenda, the United States should take three steps. First, it should try to take services out of the limelight, so that work can proceed with less overt conflict. Second, the United States should encourage developing countries to undertake careful analyses of the role of their own service sectors in their economies and of the implications of trade liberalization. Third, the industrial countries should either broaden discussions to include labor-intensive services and cover labor movement to some extent, or acknowledge that some compensation will have to be given to developing countries as the price for excluding these issues. Having experimented with trade in services in bilateral negotiations with Israel and Canada, the United States should now focus on multilateral negotiations. Later, whether these negotiations succeed or fail, they may work to extend services agreements through further bilateral negotiations or plurilateral negotiations among small numbers of like-minded countries.

Real conceptual problems and the need for unanimity make it highly unlikely that the GATT Articles will be amended to cover services. Although a separate General Agreement on Services could emerge, it seems more likely that a services agreement will in some fashion be attached to existing GATT Articles and codes.

The first major effort will be the development of a general framework agreement (a leaky umbrella) that would cover as many services as possible. As those negotiations take form, work on several separate sectoral accords could proceed. Only countries that signed the framework agreement would be entitled to participate in sectoral codes. Signatories to the framework agreement could choose which sectoral codes they wanted to participate in. Only signatories would gain the benefits of agreements.[25] It would be far easier to make exceptions to a general agreement than to try to build an umbrella accord out of a series of disparate sectoral codes.

In addition, despite talk about separating goods and services negotiations, ultimate agreement will need to be coordinated because of the interrelationship between goods and services. (Ironically, as negotiations proceed, developing countries have started to temper their preference for separate negotiations on goods and services and for sector-by-sector services negotiations. They now suspect that linkage may work to their advantage. Simultaneously, industrial countries are wondering whether separation might not better serve their interests. If GATT negotiations on services fail, then swifter agreement among like-minded countries might prove possible.) As long as negotiations proceed in the GATT, however, the broader their coverage, the greater the opportunity to thwart domestic political pressures that could doom an agreement before it is reached.

In conclusion, knowledge-based services are a key to national development, and the international exchange of these services promotes growth and provides jobs. The economic health of nations and future global prosperity depend more and more on these service industries. If GATT negotiators reach an agreement on services, this will be an important step toward overhauling the management of the world economy to foster growth and development.

## Notes

[1] For one comprehensive classification, see Harley L. Browning and Joachim Singelmann, "The Transformation of the U.S. Labor Force: The Interaction of Industry and Occupation," *Politics and Society*, Vol. 8, No. 3–4 (1978), pp. 481–509.

[2] Dorothy L. Riddle, *Service-Led Growth: The Role of the Service Sector in World Development* (New York: Praeger Publishers, 1986).

[3] Ann Hutcheson Reid, "Trade in Telecommunications Services: The Current Institutional Framework and the Potential for Change" (Paper prepared for the Committee for Information, Computer and Communication Policy, Organization for Economic Cooperation and Development, Paris, September 9, 1985), pp. 16–25.

[4] Jagdish Bhagwati, "Trade in Services and the Multilateral Trade Negotiations," *World Bank Economic Review*, Vol. 1, No. 4 (September 1987), pp. 549–569.

[5] Joan Spero, "The Information Revolution and Financial Services: A New North-South Issue?" (Paper presented at the TIDE 2000 Conference on Telecommunications, Information and Interdependent Economies, Tokyo, November 13, 1985).

⁶ Kenichi Ohmae, in *Triad Power: The Coming Shape of Global Competition* (New York: Free Press, 1985), makes this argument, which is accepted by many newly emerging corporate alliance strategies. This poses a danger for developing countries if large firms marginalize all but the largest, most important developing countries in their strategic planning.

⁷ *Business Week*, March 3, 1986, pp. 57–85.

⁸ Stephen S. Cohen and John Zysman, *Manufacturing Matters: The Myth of the Post-Industrial Economy* (New York: Basic Books, 1987).

⁹ Eli Ginzberg and George Vojta, "The Service Sector in the U.S. Economy," *Scientific American*, Vol. 244, No. 3 (March 1981); U.S. Congress, Office of Technology Assessment, *International Competition in Services*, OTA-ITE-328 (Washington, D.C.: Government Printing Office, July 1987).

¹⁰ Debates rage over which services can be traded and which require foreign investment to be exchanged across national borders. This distinction is critical because the General Agreement on Tariffs and Trade (GATT) technically does not have authority over investment issues. See, for example, Gary P. Sampson and Richard H. Snape, "Identifying the Issues in Trade in Services," *The World Economy* Vol. 8, No. 2 (June 1985), pp. 171–181.

¹¹ The real problem may be that we cannot "productively" consume services. "We cannot simultaneously play squash, attend a lecture, visit the doctor. The consumption of goods does not necessarily take any time at all. We can buy things—and then stack them up in the corner of our rooms and not take any notice of them. The consumption of services, however, takes time." Jonathan I. Gershuny, "The Future of Service Employment," in Orio Giarini, ed., *The Emerging Service Economy* (New York: Pergamon Press, 1987), p. 121.

¹² Bhagwati, op. cit.

¹³ SELA (Latin American Economic System), *Services and the Development of Latin America*, SP/RCLA/SERV/DT No. 2/Rev. 1 (Caracas: SELA, July 31, 1984).

¹⁴ John Zysman, *Governments, Markets, and Growth: Financial Systems and the Politics of Industrial Change* (Ithaca, NY: Cornell University Press, 1983); Clark Reynolds, "Bankers as Revolutionaries in the Process of Development," in Jonathan D. Aronson, ed., *Debt and the Less Developed Countries* (Boulder: Westview Press, 1979), pp. 129–156; Bjorn Wellenius, "Telecommunications and Third World Development," in Maurice F. Estabrooks and Rodolphe H. Lamarche, eds., *Telecommunications: A Strategic Perspective on Regional, Economic and Business Development* (Ottawa: The Canadian Institute for Research on Regional Development, 1987).

¹⁵ Wellenius, op. cit., p. 154.

¹⁶ Choices about telecommunications infrastructures demonstrate this point. When developing countries choose new telecommunications equipment, they can go with older, cheaper, more reliable analog technolgies or opt for more expensive digital equipment. In general, analog technology is superior for internal communications within developing countries. State-of-the-art digital technologies are superior for linking into the global telecommunications network. In every case known to the author, developing countries have chosen the newer digital equipment. Indeed, Siemens lost a large order when it tried to persuade the Turkish government to accept an older technology. To the extent that developing countries can afford new facilities, they can leapfrog industrial countries that have large, old installed equipment bases that cannot be replaced quickly.

¹⁷ There have always been numerous joint ventures between firms from developed and developing countries. What is new is that many leading corporations in industrial countries are forming international corporate alliances among themselves. In the future, these competitive networks of firms could compete for the majority of the global market in most products and services. If these emerging alliances prove to be durable and stable, it may be imperative for firms from developing countries to ally with such groups to maintain their position.

¹⁸ To illustrate, a U.S. international carrier such as AT&T could carry a conference call from New York to Bombay. Parties in New Delhi could be added to the conference call, as well as parties in London. AT&T could run the conference call entirely on its own facilities without local partners, so long as traffic moved only between points in the United States and "ports of entry" in other signatory countries. However, to interconnect the call to a non-port—say, Madras—AT&T would need to use a local partner. The local Indian carrier would have to offer AT&T comparable terms to those afforded Indian international carriers on the connection to Madras. That would be India's only international obligation. Chapter 9 of Jonathan Aronson and Peter Cowhey, *When Countries Talk: International Trade in Telecommunications Services* (Cambridge: Ballinger Publishing Co., 1988), develops these models more fully.

[19] Ironically, Brazil and India argue that infant-industry strategies designed for goods are applicable to services. They expect to leapfrog past other countries and create industries that are competitive internationally. At the same time, they contend that goods and services are so dissimilar that they should not be dealt with in the same GATT trade negotiations.

[20] Deepak Nayyar, "International Trade in Services: Implications for Developing Countries," (Export-Import Bank of India Commencement Day Lecture, Bombay, 1986).

[21] John B. Richardson, "Negotiating on Services—the Central Issues" (Paper for the Centre for Applied Studies in International Negotiations, Geneva, February 12, 1987, mimeo.).

[22] Organization for Economic Cooperation and Development, Working Party of the Trade Committee, "The Elements of a Conceptual Framework for Trade in Services," 1C/WP(85)79 (Paris: OECD, December 1985).

[23] On April 22, 1985, the United States and Israel signed a Declaration on Trade in Services in conjunction with a Free Trade Agreement covering trade in goods, which established a set of principles for trade in services between the two countries. Subsequently, the United States and Israel entered into negotiations on three sectoral annotations covering tourism, telecommunications, and insurance. The conceptual work begun here was applied, in part, by the United States to its negotiations with Canada. On October 3, 1987, U.S. and Canadian negotiators agreed to a comprehensive trade agreement. Services are an important element of the pact, which must be approved by Parliament and Congress before taking effect. It is too soon to tell how much impact these bilateral agreements will have on GATT services negotiations.

[24] This paper presumes that any services agreement will be a stand-alone code applicable only to those who sign it. In *When Countries Talk*, Peter Cowhey and I suggest that preferences for developing countries should last for seven years from the time an agreement goes into force. If a country became a signatory two years later, it would receive preferences for only five years. Any qualifying country that became a signatory five or more years after the agreement went into force would get preferential treatment for two years.

[25] Although it possibly could undermine the GATT, sectoral service codes, like the Tokyo Round codes before them, are likely to be based on *conditional* most-favored-nation treatment. This departs from Article I of the GATT, which requires *unconditional* MFN treatment.

# Chapter 3

# U.S. Agriculture and the Developing World: Opportunities for Joint Gains

## Robert L. Paarlberg

During the first half of the 1980s, U.S. agricultural exports to the developing world declined by 30 per cent. U.S. farmers, who earlier had been encouraged to look to the developing world as a source of foreign market growth, jumped to several pessimistic conclusions. First, they concluded that a new surge in developing-country agricultural production must have been a major cause of their loss in sales. They noticed that some of their former poor-country customers, including China and India, had recorded significant internal farm production gains, and were—apparently as a consequence—emerging as occasional net *exporters* of some food staples. Second, they concluded that U.S. farms must have lost some of their earlier competitive advantage in the struggle for market shares in the Third World. The U.S. share of world wheat exports, which stood at nearly 50 per cent in 1981, fell by 1985 to less than 30 per cent, while Australian, Canadian, and European Community shares expanded. Agricultural success in the developing world, plus the faltering competitiveness of U.S. farming, were thus portrayed as key elements in the larger U.S. farm trade and farm income crisis.[1]

This chapter argues that these widespread perceptions are mistaken. While there are some good reasons to be pessimistic about the future of U.S. agricultural trade with developing countries, these are not the right reasons.

# Third World Farm Production Trends

A careful look at the evidence reveals that agricultural output in the developing world has not recently surged above historical production trends. The slowdown in developing-country imports that began in the early 1980s was caused not by any "sea change" in Third World agricultural production, but by a sudden turnaround in global macroeconomic conditions, which worked to constrain both developing-country consumption and trade.

There were some impressive individual farm production success stories in the Third World early in the 1980s, most notably China (where total agricultural output increased by an astonishing 50 per cent between 1978 and 1986). But for the rest of the Third World, agricultural production had not suddenly increased above the historical growth trend. Between 1980 and 1985, according to the U.N. Food and Agriculture Organization, the volume index of agricultural production for all the developing market-economy countries (excluding China) increased at an average annual rate of just 2.76 per cent. This represented no significant change from the annual rate of increase of 2.74 per cent that was noted for these same countries during the previous "food crisis" decade of 1970–80.[2] From the perspective of the developing countries' acute nutritional needs, and given high population growth rates, these recent farm production growth trends of course remain inadequate. Agricultural production *per capita* in the developing market economies has scarcely increased at all over the last fifteen years.

What changed world agricultural markets in the 1980s was not a sudden rise in farm production in the developing world. Production was surging above trend in some of the developed regions, including North America and Western Europe, due to a combination of good weather and technological improvements driven forward by price subsidies. But in the *developing* world, where agriculture tends to be taxed rather than subsidized, and where technological improvements are more difficult to adopt, historical production trends were only maintained.

It was a worldwide consumption slump, not a Third World production boom, that depressed world farm markets in the 1980s. Worldwide growth in per capita food consumption slowed in the 1980s to less than two-thirds the pace of the 1970s.[3] Foreign grain consumption, which had increased at an average rate of 34 million tons per year throughout the 1970s, fell to only an average yearly increase of 19 million during the first half of the 1980s. Under the constraint of growing debts and under the belated discipline of much tighter monetary policies in the United States, the inflationary growth of the 1970s had finally come to an end. Real foreign GDP growth rates, which had averaged a strong 5.5 per cent between 1970 and 1974, and which held at a respectable 3.7 per cent between 1975 and 1979, fell to a low of 1.6 per cent in 1981, and then averaged only 2.4 per cent between 1982 and 1986. In some parts of the developing world, economic growth came to a complete stop. In Latin America, for example, real GDP growth fell from a strong 6.3 per cent yearly average during the 1970s to a *negative* 0.8 per cent average between 1981 and 1983. These lower economic growth rates meant lower food and farm product consumption levels, and hence fewer imports. Further evidence that there had been no sudden explosion in poor-country farm production can be seen from changes that took place in the *net* agricultural trade balance of the developing countries. When the economic slowdown hit, the agricultural exports as well as the agricultural imports of the poor countries stopped growing. In 1981 and 1982, in fact, the poor countries actually experienced a rare *deficit* in their net agricultural trade.

### A Closer Look at Performance Variations

Agricultural production averages are of course deceiving: Some developing countries and regions have done much better than others. Between 1975 and 1985, per capita agricultural production increased by a strong 21.2 per cent in Asia, but only by 6.9 per cent in South America. Per capita production meanwhile *declined* in Africa, by a disastrous 12.2 per cent, and also in Central America. These widely diverging performances have no simple explanation. Where agro-climatic conditions, human resource development, and public policy supports have allowed "green revolution" technologies to spread—as in many parts of Asia—remarkable crop yield increases and aggregate production gains have been realized. Where these technologies have not been so easily adopted, especially in Africa, production gains have fallen behind population growth.

It must be emphasized that the use of modern farming techniques is still a physical impossibility in large parts of the Third World. About 80 per cent of all cultivated land in the Third World is still non-irrigated, and hence unable to support the much higher yields that at present can be achieved only through a careful combination of increased water and fertilizer use. Even when such physical difficulties are overcome, other technical barriers remain to the spread of modern farming. Agricultural production requirements (much more than industrial production requirements) tend to be highly location-specific. Small differences from one location to the next in soil, topography, infrastructure, farm size, or growing season can severely alter the gains from adopting a new farm production technology. Whether imported or home-grown, the technology therefore must always be adapted to fit unique local agro-climatic conditions. This can only be accomplished where the local stock of organized scientific and technical manpower is large enough to perform this sophisticated task. In the poorest countries of the tropics, adequate scientific and technical manpower often tends to be missing.

Internal policy barriers can also stand in the path of farm production breakthroughs in poor countries. In their impatience to industrialize, many poor countries have embraced policies that overtax the farm sector.[4] These countries provide extremely low levels of public investment for agriculture while holding in place low farm commodity prices, price-depressing marketing restrictions, overvalued exchange rates, commodity export taxes, industrial import restrictions, and various other measures that are either intentionally or unintentionally biased against profitable farming. Where this policy bias has remained strong, as in most of Latin America and Sub-Saharan Africa, farm production has suffered. Wherever this internal policy bias against farming has been relaxed—as in India in the 1960s, and more recently in China in the late 1970s—a gratifying production response has been observed. In some of the most advanced developing countries—such as Taiwan and South Korea—farm production has recently been favored through national pricing and exchange rate policies that are actually biased in favor of the countryside.

What would be the impact on international agricultural trade, and on U.S. agricultural trade in particular, of a decision by more developing-country governments to move away from internal policies that overtax the farm sector? If the result were a genuine breakthrough in developing-country farm production, would this be helpful or harmful to U.S. agricultural trade? Most U.S. farmers worry that each added bushel of Third World farm output under these circumstances would only mean one less bushel of potential U.S. farm exports. This is why many U.S. farm organizations now oppose bilateral and multilateral agricultural development assistance to poor countries. But once again a closer look at the evidence points toward a different conclusion.

# Agricultural Success in Poor Countries: What Impact on Agricultural Imports?

U.S. farmers know from bitter experience that agricultural growth in wealthy industrial regions—such as Western Europe—can displace their own foreign sales. Fortunately, Third World agricultural success can have just the opposite trade effect. Agricultural success in developing countries can lead to a larger demand for food as well as to a larger supply, because a much larger share of the total population in the developing world earns its income from farming, and because much of the income growth that results from farm production success is spent immediately on dietary enrichment. Much of this dietary enrichment takes the form of added protein from high-quality food grains and cereal-fed animals, the final consequence of which can be additional grain imports from countries (such as the United States) that are efficient producers of grains and animal feedstuffs.

Rapid growth in such income-driven food import demands will usually have to await the onset of successful urban industrial development. Rural agricultural development, however, is usually a precondition for successful urban industrial development.[5] The most successful industrializers—from England, to Japan, to Taiwan—all used an initial growth in agricultural productivity to create a labor and capital surplus and to generate internal consumption demand needed to get industrial growth broadly under way. In most developing countries today, the vast majority of underutilized economic resources—especially human resources—are to be found in the countryside. The most obvious way to mobilize this resource potential, so as to get the process of rapid wealth creation under way, is to expand and improve agriculture.

### Evidence of "Joint Gains"

The paradoxical tendency of agriculturally successful less developed countries to *increase* their imports of farm products is now widely recognized inside the academic and research community. It has been documented recently in at least half a dozen separate studies whose highlights deserve scrutiny.

In a 1985 study, John Lee and Mathew Shane examined two developing countries—Brazil and Malaysia—in which local agricultural success is commonly thought to have displaced U.S. agricultural trade.[6] The authors found that both countries, despite their rapid agricultural growth between 1967 and 1983, increased their farm imports along with their farm exports. On a wheat equivalent basis, Malaysia's imports of food, feedgrains, and oilseeds (primarily U.S. soybeans) increased from 1 million tons to almost 2.4 million tons during this period. Brazil showed a similar pattern. Lee and Shane concluded that "Contrary to what seems to follow from common sense reasoning, economic development in the developing countries along comparative advantage lines is not competitive with [U.S.] export interests, but generally complementary to it."

In another 1985 study, Earl Kellogg reached similar conclusions. This study examined per capita changes in agricultural imports in 18 significant developing countries (out of 92) exhibiting the most rapid growth in per capita food production over the period 1970-80, and compared these changes to those in 13 countries exhibiting the least rapid food production growth. Kellogg found that this first category of agriculturally successful developing countries increased its dollar value of per capita agricultural imports by 47 per cent, compared to only a 37-per-cent increase among the second group of agriculturally unsuccessful countries.[7]

In a subsequent study, Richard Kodl amplified Kellogg's findings. Using a regression analysis with time series and cross-sectional data on 77 developing countries, Kodl found no significant negative correlation between per capita agricultural production in developing countries and their per capita imports of agricultural products; in six of thirteen equations, he found a significant *positive* correlation.[8]

Further evidence to support this same conclusion was presented in James P. Houck's 1986 study based on a 44-nation sample and 1983 data. Houck found a relatively close association between agricultural productivity, per capita GDP, and per capita cereal imports. He concluded that "the burden of proof clearly rests with those who argue that agricultural assistance for low-income nations is usually a trade-stifling undertaking."[9]

The most recent in this remarkable series of studies is Kym Anderson's short examination of correlations across developing countries between real growth in agricultural GDP per capita (or per farm worker) and real growth in imports (or just agricultural imports) from developed countries. For 53 developing countries with populations in excess of one million, Anderson found *positive* correlations between agricultural output (or labor productivity growth) and growth in imports from the developed world over the period 1970-84; the correlations were even positive betweeen agricultural growth in developing countries and *agricultural* imports from the developed world. Anderson argues that successful agricultural development assistance projects in poor countries might actually benefit rich country agricultural exporters: ". . . by setting out to do good, they may well end up doing well."[10]

The thrust of these aggregate findings can best be illustrated through a simple comparison between the large markets that have been developed for U.S. agriculture in East Asia, where farming is a considerable success, and the more meager markets that have been developed in Africa, where farming has recently been a tragic failure. Two small and agriculturally successful East Asian developing countries, South Korea and Taiwan, import more wheat and coarse grains every year than all of the much larger and "hungrier" nations of Sub-Saharan Africa combined.

With so much evidence now circulating to support this view, why have U.S. farm groups not yet become enthusiastic supporters of more agricultural development assistance? Those groups have in fact recently stepped up their campaign against agricultural development aid. In July 1986, farm state representatives pushed through Congress the so-called "Bumpers Amendment" (Section 209 of PL 99-349), which stipulates that no U.S. foreign aid funds shall be used in poor countries to assist the production of agricultural commodities for export in competition with similar commodities grown in the United States. A parallel restriction, the so-called Foreign Agricultural Investment Reform Act (the FAIR Act), has more recently been promoted in Congress to limit the agricultural development activities of multilateral assistance institutions such as the World Bank.[11]

### Doubts About Joint Gains

In fact, there *are* some good reasons for U.S farm organizations to resist any sweeping conclusion that farm success in poor countries will *always* benefit U.S. agricultural exports. U.S. farm organizations have first looked beneath the surface of the aggregate data presented above, and have found numerous exceptions to the overall rule of "joint gains" between U.S. and developing-country farming. In some prominent cases, agricultural success appears to have been followed by a *reduction* rather than a growth in farm imports: China, India, and some of the agriculturally export-oriented countries of Latin America—including Argentina—are frequently mentioned in this regard. Also, many countries that are agriculturally unsuccessful—for example Egypt, and some of the OPEC countries—nonetheless remain large importers.

Two of these exceptional cases—China and India—do deserve special mention. Between 1978 and 1986, the value of farm production in China rose by a phenomenal 50 per cent, in large measure due to price and incentive reforms (the "family responsibility system"), and resulted in sizable per capita income gains. This did not produce the expected increase in demand for imported food and feedstuffs, however, in part because larger consumption demand was not being accommodated by the cautious and slow-moving Chinese bureaucracy. Chinese officials became particularly worried about a rapid deterioration in China's overall foreign trade balance after 1984, and so they decided to cut food imports and promote food exports. The result was a drop in U.S. wheat sales to China and a termination of all purchases of U.S. corn. China even began exporting corn in direct competition with the United States.

This initial Chinese trade response is now on its way to being adjusted. After staying out of the market for two years, China began purchasing U.S. corn again in October 1986. Chinese wheat purchases began to expand as well—to 7.5 million tons in 1986–87, with 9.5 million tons projected for 1987–88, the largest volume since 1983–84. China may yet use its agriculturally generated income gains to become (like its East Asian neighbors) an ever-better customer for U.S. agricultural exports. To meet its own projected internal feed needs in the current five-year plan, which runs through 1990, China would in fact have to import roughly 50 million tons of grain.

India has also at times responded to internal farm production gains by reducing imports. India's recent emergence as an occasional net exporter of small quantities of wheat was not, however, of major commercial trade significance.[12] India did import large quantities of U.S wheat in the 1960s, but strictly in the form of food aid, on concessional rather than commerical terms. Moreover, it began exporting some wheat in the mid-1980s not because its own internal food needs had all been met, but because low personal income within India restricted the purchasing power of the population. India's disastrous monsoon of 1987 has now in any case returned that nation to the status of a net wheat importer.

U.S. farm organizations are, however, correct to argue that farm success in poor countries does not *invariably* lead to more U.S. farm exports. There is nothing at all automatic about this paradoxical relationship. If a proper mix of policy actions is not being taken at both ends of the relationship, farm success in poor countries can actually result in lower U.S. farm exports.

## Policies to Promote Joint Gains

The accompanying figure lists some of the policy measures that must be undertaken to establish and build positive links between farm production success, income growth, dietary enrichment, and larger agricultural imports from the United States. At Step 1 in this process, where farm production success is in question, the heaviest burden of policy action rests with the developing countries themselves. In many of the developing countries that have yet to enjoy rapid farm production gains, especially those in Africa, too many powerful policy instruments—price policies, marketing policies, tax policies, exchange rate policies, and public investment policies—remain biased *against* rural farm producers. Developing-country governments may find it difficult to retain their urban political support when attempting to redress the balance between city and countryside in national food-sector planning.

In recent years, however, a number of African countries have taken significant strides to correct "urban biased" pricing-policy distortions.[13] U.S. bilateral and multilateral assistance policies can help boost poor-country farm production at this step in the process (just as some kinds of U.S. "program" food aid policies, motivated only by political or "surplus disposal" imperatives, can at times hurt), but the decisive supporting measures will be those either taken—or not taken—by the developing countries themselves.

The same holds true at Step 2 in the process, where broad-based income growth and dietary enrichment is the goal. The heaviest burden of supporting policy action again rests with the developing countries themselves. Policies must be in place to ensure that a full majority of the rural population, and not just a wealthy elite, enjoys equitable access to land, credit, education, water, technology, cattle, or whatever it is that is driving forward the agricultural development process. If this equitable access is not provided, most of the income gains from rapid agricultural development will go into the pockets of a wealthy few, and not be spent by the population at large on more food consumption, including larger food imports. If narrowly earned, these profits will be spent on the wasteful import and consumption of luxury goods, or they will simply disappear into foreign bank accounts and do nothing to boost U.S. agricultural trade.

Unfortunately, this problem of narrow income gains from farming is widespread in the developing world—in Africa, in large parts of Asia, and especially in Latin America, where unequal access to land, in particular, reduces the likelihood that income growth from agriculture will be broad-based. The introduction of modern, highly productive agricultural techniques into a setting where some have access to land but most do not can actually have the effect of *reducing* employment and income gains for the poor majority. The poor may find themselves pushed off the land by wealthy elites who move in to dominate a suddenly profitable agricultural development process.[14]

At Step 3 in the process, however, a larger share of the policy burden begins to shift to wealthy industrial countries such as the United States. At this step in the process, the goal is for developing countries to use the income they have generated (through broad-based agricultural and industrial success) to begin importing more farm products, thus capturing efficiencies through trade—in the manner of South Korea or Taiwan. To take this step, developing-country leaders must be willing to increase the specialization of their own farm production along "comparative advantage" lines—for example, exporting their high-value crops while importing products (such as animal feed) in which they may lack a comparative advantage. To pursue such a specialized and trade-oriented development strategy successfully, they

## Figure 1. Policies to Promote Additional Farm Production and Income Growth in Developing Countries Simultaneously with Additional U.S. Farm Exports to Developing Countries

|  |  | Step 1<br>Farm Production in<br>Developing Countries | Step 2<br>Broad-Based Income Growth<br>and Dietary Enrichment |
|---|---|---|---|
| Developing-Country Policies | Farm | More public investment in agriculture.<br><br>Fewer farm market restrictions biased against agricultural producers. Give producers access to market prices. | Social and institutional change to ensure more equitable access to land, water, cattle, technology, credit, etc.<br><br>Expansion of livestock and animal production. |
| Developing-Country Policies | Non-farm | Tax, credit, wage, education, and exchange-rate policies that are less biased against agriculture. | Policies that increase and diversify rural employment. Policies that stimulate balanced industrial growth. |
| U.S. Policies | Farm | Increased bilateral and multilateral farm development assistance.<br><br>Less reliance on "program" food aid for pursuit of purely surplus-disposal or foreign-policy objectives. |  |
| U.S. Policies | Non-farm | Increased bilateral and multilateral non-farm development assistance. | Foreign policies that tolerate rapid social and institutional reform in developing countries. |

| | | Step 3<br>Increased Developing-<br>Country Farm Imports | Step 4<br>Increased U.S. Farm Exports<br>to Developing Countries |
|---|---|---|---|
| **Developing-Country Policies** | Farm | | |
| | Non-farm | Development strategies founded on openness to trade. | |

| | | | |
|---|---|---|---|
| **U.S. Policies** | Farm | Relaxation of import restrictions on tropical farm products, accompanied by structural adjustments to reduce domestic production. | Market-oriented farm commodity policies to ensure competitive U.S. export prices.<br><br>Trade-liberalizing agreements with other developed countries. |
| | Non-farm | Industrial trade policies, international debt policies, and macroeconomic policies designed to produce world trade expansion, including expansion of developing-country exports. | Fiscal policy discipline and international monetary policy coordination to preserve and stabilize lower dollar exchange rates. |

will need an appropriate policy response from the outside, and especially from the United States, the dominant power in the world trading system. If political leaders in the United States decide to embrace protectionist trading policies that cut off foreign exchange earning possibilities, or if they adopt shortsighted international financial policies that prevent debt-rescheduling or if they pursue undisciplined macroeconomic policies that stand in the way of stable exchange rates and strong economic growth, then even the most trade-oriented developing countries may find Step 3 more difficult to take.

The recent protectionist drift in U.S. manufactured trade policy is a case in point. If U.S. policy makes it difficult for developing countries to earn foreign exchange by selling their manufactured products to the United States, it may inadvertently make it impossible for them to buy agricultural products from U.S. farmers. This important link between U.S. manufactured trade protection and a loss of agricultural exports was underscored in 1983–84, when China retaliated against a sequence of unilateral U.S. textile import restraints by not going ahead with anticipated wheat purchases worth some $500 million. No wonder most U.S. agricultural exporters feel threatened by trade provisions such as the "Gephardt Amendment," which would require U.S. retaliation against any country running excessive trade surpluses with the United States. This amendment implicitly targets a number of developing countries that are currently good customers for U.S. farm exports, including both Taiwan and South Korea.

U.S. international financial policies that make it difficult for poor countries to reduce and reschedule their burdensome foreign debts are another unfortunate barrier to the successful completion of Step 3 in Figure 1. The Third World debt burden was made unbearable by a sudden change in global macroeconomic conditions early in the 1980s—a deflationary recession, brought on in part by a sudden change in U.S. monetary policy that surprised international lenders and borrowers alike. Until recently, however, only the borrowers were asked to endure the pains of adjustment. Most commercial banks continue to insist—with implicit support from the U.S. government and the IMF—that the heavily indebted poor countries put themselves through a wringer of "austerity," cutting their own present and future economic growth in order to service their foreign debts. The consequences for U.S. agricultural trade, particularly with Latin America, have been severe. Pressure on Latin debtor countries to slash imports and boost exports has resulted in fewer purchases of U.S. farm products. Between 1981 and 1985, the total value of Latin American agricultural imports from the United States declined by 33 per cent.

Because of the importance of these larger international macroeconomic circumstances, we cannot today conclude with total confidence, on the basis of trade data from the 1970s, that all agriculturally successful low-income countries will be able to boost their farm imports as much today. Poor countries now have fewer opportunities to earn or to borrow foreign exchange. Until U.S. trade, financial, and macroeconomic policies begin to provide more effective support to the foreign exchange position of the developing countries at Step 3, the successful completion of Steps 1 and 2 may not be enough to trigger the hoped-for response. We may never get to Step 4.

Some critics might argue, however, that the weakest of all the links in this "joint gains" hypothesis is precisely at Step 4, where it is necessary that the developing countries decide to satisfy their growing agricultural import needs by making larger purchases *from the United States*—rather than from any number of rich-country competitors such as Canada, Australia, and the European Community, or from some new developing-country exporters such as Argentina and Brazil. Even if agricultural success in poor countries can someday help world farm trade to expand, what evidence is there that *U.S.* farmers can count on getting an adequate share of the new business?

# The Export Competitiveness of U.S. Agriculture: In Long-Term Trouble or Not?

Trade trends during the first half of the 1980s seemed to indicate that U.S. agriculture was losing its ability to capture a profitable share of world farm exports. The U.S. share of world agricultural trade, which had grown from 14.4 per cent up to 19.3 per cent between 1971 and 1981, suddenly stopped growing, and quickly fell back down to just 16.6 per cent by 1985.[15] Between 1981 and 1985, the U.S. share of world wheat exports fell even more sharply, from a high of 48 per cent all the way down to just 29 per cent. These dramatic losses in market share led some to conclude that U.S. agriculture had permanently lost its competitive edge.

Those who saw this decline in U.S. competitiveness as a durable trend searched for explanations in the global spread of new farm production technologies. The "green revolution" in plant genetics that began in the 1930s initially produced large gains almost exclusively for U.S. farming—especially with hybrid corn. The application of this new technology did not spread very far beyond the United States until the 1960s, when high-yielding varieties of wheat and rice were at last developed for Asia and Latin America. Now, however, improved varieties have been developed for grain and rapeseed in Western Europe, oil palm for Southeast Asia, sorghum and cassava for Africa, sun-flowerseed for a dozen countries, white corn and beans for Latin America, and mustardseed for Bangladesh.[16] The movement of such new production technologies from the laboratory into the field has aroused fears that U.S. farming has lost its traditional edge, and that any future growth in Third World markets therefore may benefit rival agricultural exporters—such as Canada, Australia, and the European Community, or perhaps Argentina and Brazil—much more than the United States.

A closer analysis of recent developments does not, however, uphold such fears of permanently lost advantage. U.S. agricultural exports did indeed become less competitive during the first half of the 1980s, but for reasons that had little or nothing to do with a loss of U.S. agricultural productivity. Much of the sudden loss of competitiveness experienced by U.S. farmers early in the 1980s was only a consequence of fluctuating currency exchange rates. Dollar exchange rates increased by roughly 70 per cent between 1980 and 1985, forcing foreign customers to pay that much more (in their own currency) to purchase U.S. farm products. The U.S. share of world farm exports fell accordingly. This was in part just a reversal of what had earlier happened during the first half of the 1970s, when two dollar devaluations (in 1971 and 1973) helped trigger a strong growth in U.S. farm market shares. Now the dollar has again fallen sharply—to record postwar lows in late 1987 against the deutschmark and the yen. If the dollar remains low for the remainder of the 1980s, much of the damage that was done to U.S. farm market shares during the first half of the decade can eventually be repaired.

This restoration of competitiveness through lower dollar exchange rates has so far been uneven and incomplete.[17] Still, the competitiveness effects of lower dollar exchange rates are beginning to be felt. In *unprocessed* farm-product markets, the budget cost to the European Community of subsidizing exports to third countries (mostly in the developing world) has gone up dramatically since the dollar's decline. The EC Commission estimates that every 5 per cent devaluation of the dollar since 1985 has added 400 million ECU to the Community's badly overstrained farm budget.[18] It is not clear, assuming that the dollar remains low, how much longer the Community will be able to pay these much higher export subsidy costs. In high-value *processed* farm product markets, meanwhile, a dramatic trade response to the lower dollar already has been registered. European and Japanese import markets for high-value processed farm products are not as heavily protected by variable levies and quotas, so exchange rate fluctuations have had a direct and highly positive impact. In fiscal 1986, the volume of U.S. high-value agricultural exports (such as feeds and ingredients, seeds, poultry meat, fresh fruit, processed fruit, and processed beef and vegetables) increased almost 16 per cent from the previous year, and in the first quarter of 1987 a 24-per-cent increase over the 1986 first quarter pace was recorded.

The temporary loss of international trade competitiveness suffered by U.S. farm exporters after 1981 can also be traced back, at least in part, to high and inflexible domestic farm program price guarantees. These price guarantees, which took the form of high commodity "loan rates" and high "target prices," were permitted to creep upward during the 1970s under the cover of temporarily higher market prices that had been brought on by inflation and a worldwide commodity boom.[19] When this inflationary commodity boom came to an end after 1981, and when world agricultural export markets suddenly slackened, U.S. farm exporters found themselves disadvantaged because high domestic commodity-price supports were pricing them out of world markets realities.

The error of this policy was recognized by the time Congress sat down to reauthorize U.S. farm legislation in 1985. The new farm bill written in that year contained a number of provisions intended to boost exports by allowing domestic prices to fall. These provisions included a sharp lowering of commodity loan rates (loan rates tend to set the floor under market prices), as well as several other price-cutting innovations such as "marketing loans" (for cotton and rice) and the use of "generic certificates" (especially for corn), which would permit farmers to retain their own personal income guarantees while selling their crops into the market at prices even *below* the loan rate. This long-overdue downward adjustment in U.S. domestic commodity price support levels, in combination with lower dollar exchange rates, has now gone a long way toward reestablishing the international competitiveness enjoyed by U.S. agriculture before 1981.

In the long run, lower U.S. prices will stimulate additional total foreign demand, and additional demand for U.S. products in particular, leading to a revived growth in U.S. farm export revenues. Getting to the long run will, however, take patience. Export demand in agricultural markets is price *inelastic* in the short run—meaning that for a year or so a fall in export prices produces a less than proportionate increase in sales volume. During this difficult transitional period, export volume will increase, but because of lower prices, total export revenues will actually fall. This is what happened in 1986. By mid-1987, however, U.S agriculture was finally beginning to emerge from this difficult short-run period of adjustment. The total volume of U.S. grain exports was moving up sharply (by 1 billion bushels, or about one-third), the largest annual volume increase in history. Forecasts for fiscal 1987 anticipate a strong 17-per-cent increase in the total volume of U.S. farm exports, to a level of 129 million tons—the first such increase in 7 years. Total export value is lagging behind but is nonetheless forecast to increase by 4 per cent to $28 billion.[20]

Can U.S. agricultural producers survive while competing at lower price levels? Current farm legislation ensures that they will in the short run, since it generously subsidizes farm income with direct cash "deficiency payments," which are calculated against a high price standard (the "target price") that was *not* sharply reduced by Congress in 1985. Evidence suggests, however, that the most efficient U.S. farm exporters will not need such costly cash subsidies from the taxpayer to make it in the long run. This is because production costs in large parts of the U.S. farm sector remain highly competitive. Even in an unsubsidized price competition against foreign producers, most export-oriented U.S. farmers would be able to survive.

Comparing U.S. and foreign farm production costs is made difficult by such things as fluctuating land prices and currency exchange rates. However, the U.S. Department of Agriculture has studied comparative *variable* costs of production (not including labor, land, and depreciation) using data from 1980-82 (before the strongest surge in dollar exchange rates). These studies show U.S. wheat, corn, and soybean farmers in a strong competitive position even against some of the world's lowest-cost foreign competitors in Australia, Canada, and the developing world. Average variable production costs per bushel for U.S. wheat on the Northern Plains were almost identical to Canadian costs in Saskatchewan, and U.S. national average costs were below Australian national average costs. Average U.S. variable costs for soybeans in the cornbelt were well below variable costs in both Argentina and Brazil. Argentina can produce corn more cheaply than the United States, but high internal transportation costs nullify most of this advantage.[21] Of course, not all U.S. agricultural goods can become competitive from a fall in the value of the dollar, as the roots of their problems lie elsewhere. U.S. sugar and dairy producers, for example, have lost their international competitiveness over the years while producing within a sheltered domestic market.

Farm production costs are only part of the story. Downstream from the generally low-cost U.S. farm production system is the world's largest, most flexible, and most efficient agricultural handling and marketing system. The physical capacity of this U.S. system was greatly expanded during the 1970s; the United States has individual grain export elevators large enough to handle volumes equal to the *total annual sales* of some smaller export competitors abroad. Some of these smaller competitors are currently straining against the limits of their installed handling infrastructure; the United States, in contrast, would have no trouble doubling its current export volume with the handling capacity it already has in place. Along with the huge size of this system comes an efficient set of price discovery mechanisms, based on well-developed commodity futures markets and highly competitive private sector trading operations. These private U.S. traders (unlike the slow-moving government monopoly "marketing boards" that are widely employed elsewhere) have developed the flexibility to offer each foreign buyer a customized blend of desired price, quality, and services.[22]

What danger is there that these important U.S. agricultural trading advantages will be lost at some time in the future due to an accelerating worldwide spread of new agricultural production technologies? In fact, it is precisely the United States that has the world's most impressive record for moving new farm technologies quickly from the laboratory to the field. Three important factors will usually enable U.S. farm operators to improve their competitive posture *first* whenever a new technology becomes available: (1) the high education level on U.S. commercial farms; (2) a long-functioning public sector "extension" service that has close links to land-grant university research facilities; and (3) intensive private sector product development and advertising campaigns.

Between 1970 and 1982, the average productivity of U.S. farmland increased by a phenomenal 39 per cent, compared to an overall 27-per-cent increase in the rest of the world. The average productivity of U.S. agricultural labor rose by 97 per cent, compared to a 22-per-cent increase in other countries, and compared to just a sluggish 15-per-cent increase in the productivity of the *non-agricultural* U.S. labor force. Even the average product per unit of farm machinery increased in the United States, while it was actually falling in the rest of the world.[23] There is no end in sight to this implied capacity of U.S. farmers to continue staying one step ahead of the competition. Due to recent breakthroughs in biotechnology and genetic engineering, productivity growth in the U.S. farm sector is now forecast to increase at an accelerated annual rate as high as 2.4 per cent, which is significantly above the average rate of growth experienced since 1950.[24]

Rapid productivity growth in the U.S. farm sector has increased the wealth of that sector dramatically, but it is sometimes viewed as a liability, because of the socially and politically difficult resource adjustments (such as the movement of labor out of farming) that usually follow. Farm interest groups feel threatened by productivity growth, no matter how much more wealth it promises to bring to the farm sector, because it sometimes reduces the need for farm labor, and hence the number of farmers. This was certainly true for the productivity growth that was made possible by capital-intensive chemical and machinery technologies during the postwar period, which increased farm size and reduced farm numbers. Fortunately, the next generation of highly productive agricultural technologies is likely to be less capital intensive. Some of the information-intensive and management-intensive production technologies of tomorrow will be less likely to replace labor with capital. More often, they will replace low-skill labor with high-skill labor—a more agreeable transition, one that will reward investments in "human capital," and one that political and social leaders in rural America should be eager to embrace.

U.S. agricultural productivity growth does become a threat when the more competitive prices made possible by productivity growth are blocked by farm program price-support levels and production restrictions. U.S. farm operators can choose to cash in on their productivity through market expansion abroad, by underpricing their less efficient foreign competitors. Only if they refuse to do so, or if public policy prevents them from doing so, will they find themselves heavily burdened by labor adjustment problems at home.

# Opportunities for Joint Gains

In summary, the reasons most often given for concern about the future of U.S. farm sales to the developing world are largely insubstantial. There has *not* been any dramatic upsurge in Third World farm production in the 1980s. Even if such an upsurge did take place in the future, it would stimulate demand along with supply, and therefore would *not* necessarily displace trade in developing-country agricultural imports. And if rapid market growth does take place in the developing world, U.S. agriculture, because of its recently restored competitiveness, will be well positioned to capture a large share of the benefits. This is the good news.

The bad news is that a variety of less visible factors nonetheless justify a certain amount of pessimism regarding short-run trade prospects for U.S. agricultural exports to developing countries. Prominent among these are the continuing Third World debt crisis, sluggish rates of economic growth worldwide, and the increasing closure of rich-country agricultural as well as industrial markets to Third World exports. Other negative factors include the inadequate and uneven progress that the poor countries themselves are achieving toward agricultural and trade-driven development and the recent faltering of U.S. and other rich-country assistance in support of their efforts.

With the proper policies in place, U.S. and developing-country agriculture can prosper at the same time. In the developing world, this means that "urban-biased" national policies that overtax the farm sector—such as low farm commodity price policies, lagging public investment in rural extension and infrastructure, overvalued exchange rates, marketing restrictions and monopoly marketing boards—must be replaced by policies that promote productive employment and income growth in the countryside. To ensure broadly based results, these policies must be designed to weaken rather than reinforce rural concentrations of land ownership, wealth, social status, and political power.

In developed countries such as the United States, the most important policy steps waiting to be taken are not in the narrow agricultural sector itself, but in the larger arena of international trade, financial, monetary, and development assistance policy. Protectionist trade policies must be avoided, debt policies must stress growth, discipline must be reimposed on U.S. fiscal policy (to make room for less stringent use of monetary policy), and the trend away from generous U.S. support for bilateral and multilateral development assistance must be reversed.

Those U.S. farm groups hoping to revive their exports to the developing world should be leading the fight to set such policies in place. The sooner they do, the greater the likelihood that U.S. and Third World agriculture will begin to prosper side by side.

## Notes

[1] In a widely cited 1985 *Foreign Affairs* article entitled "A World Awash in Grain," Barbara Insel observed that "[T]he world is learning how to feed itself . . . [W]e have entered an era of permanent grain surpluses, of a buyer's market for grain exports, where the United States can no longer set the rules."

[2] U.N. Food and Agriculture Organization, *FAO Production Yearbook 1980*, Volume 34, Table 5, p. 78, and *FAO Production Yearbook 1985*, Volume 39, Table 5, p. 80; U.S. Department of Agriculture, Economic Research Service, *World Indices of Agricultural Production, 1975–84*, Statistical Bulletin No. 730, Washington, D.C.

[3] "Global Trends in Agricultural Supply and Demand," (Remarks by Robert L. Thompson, Assistant Secretary for Economics, U.S. Department of Agriculture, at Outlook '87, the 63rd Annual Agricultural Outlook Conference, U.S. Department of Agriculture, December 2, 1986).

[4] World Bank, *World Development Report 1986*, Chapter 4.

[5] See John Mellor, "Agriculture on the Road to Industrialization," in *Development Strategies Reconsidered*, John P. Lewis and Valeriana Kallab, eds. (New Brunswick, N.J.: Transaction Books for the Overseas Development Council, 1986).

[6] John E. Lee, Jr. and Mathew Shane, "United States Agricultural Interests and Growth in Developing Economies: The Critical Linkage" (U.S. Department of Agriculture, Economic Research Service, June 1985), p. 16.

[7] Earl Kellogg, "University Involvement in International Agricultural Development Activities: Important Issues for Public Education" (Speech at the 1985 Annual Meeting of the Association of U.S. University Directors of International Agricultural Programs, Athens, Georgia, May 31, 1985), p. 135.

[8] Richard Kodl, "An Analysis of Agricultural Growth in Developing Countries and U.S. Agricultural Exports" (Masters thesis, Department of Agricultural Economics, University of Illinois, 1985).

[9] James P. Houck, "A Note on the Link Between Agricultural Development and Agricultural Imports" (Staff Paper 86–26, Department of Agricultural and Applied Economics, University of Minnesota, July 1986).

[10] Kym Anderson, "Does Agricultural Growth in Poor Countries Harm Agricultural-Exporting Rich Countries?" (Background paper for address given at the Australian Center for International Agricultural Research, Canberra, May 14, 1987).

[11] FAIR is currently endorsed by a powerful coalition of domestic U.S. farm interest groups—including the American Farm Bureau Federation, the American Soybean Association, the American Fertilizer Institute, the National Association of Wheat Growers, the National Cattlemen's Association, and the American Association of Meat Processors.

[12] India had also been a net exporter of wheat in 1978–80, at the peak of the U.S. export boom, and even for a brief time in 1972, following the first successful surge in "green revolution" wheat production in India. See Robert L. Paarlberg, *Food Trade and Foreign Policy* (Ithaca: Cornell University Press, 1985), p. 48.

[13] Cheryl Christensen and Lawrence Witecki, "State Policies and Food Scarcity in Subsaharan Africa," in LaMond Tullis and W. Ladd Hollist, eds., Food, State, and the International Political Economy (Lincoln: University of Nebraska Press, 1986), pp. 37–73.

[14] Robert G. Williams, *Export Agriculture and the Crisis in Central America* (Chapel Hill: University of North Carolina Press, 1986), Chapters 3 and 6.

[15] "Studies Prepared for the Use of the Republican Members of the Joint Economic Committee, Congress of the United States, by the Congressional Research Service, Library of Congress," Joint Economic Committee Print, 99th Congress, 2nd Session, October 1, 1986, Table 1, p. 50.

[16] Dennis T. Avery, "Our Huge Stake in Farm Trade Reform" (Speech delivered before the National Conference of State Legislatures, Kansas City, Missouri, November 20, 1986), p. 2.

[17] This is because not all U.S. farm trade customers and competitors have allowed their currencies to move up against the dollar, and also because not all are equally sensitive in their agricultural trade when exchange rates do fluctuate. The dollar has fallen most sharply against the European Currency Unit (ECU) and against the Japanese yen, but the European Community and Japan tend to protect their farm markets against U.S. commodity exports with such things as "variable" levies and quantitative restrictions, which screen out exchange rate effects.

[18] Commission of the European Communities, "Commission Proposals on the Prices for Agricultural Products and on Related Measures (1987/88): Financial Implications," COM(87) 1 final, Brussels, February 24, 1987, p. 6.

[19] By 1982–85, real price-support levels for U.S. wheat were 20 per cent above the levels of 1968–72. Target prices for wheat, cotton, corn, barley, and sorghum were each higher in real terms in 1985 than they had been in 1974. See D. Gale Johnson, "Commentary," in Randall B. Purcell and Elizabeth Morrison, eds., *U.S. Agriculture and Third World Development: The Critical Linkage* (Boulder: Lynne Rienner Publishers, 1987), p. 172.

[20] U.S. Department of Agriculture, *Agricultural Outlook*, November 1987, p. 53.

[21] See "U.S. Agriculture Still Has the Edge," *Farmline*, Vol. 6, No. 10 (November 1985), pp. 8–9.

[22] Robbin S. Johnson, "Implications for U.S. Agribusiness Strategies" (Remarks delivered at the 63rd Agricultural Outlook Conference, U.S. Department of Agriculture, Washington, D.C., December 1986).

[23] "U.S. Agriculture Still Has the Edge," op. cit.

[24] Economic Report of the President, 1987, p. 162.

# Chapter 4

# The Changing Demand for Industrial Raw Materials

## Raymond F. Mikesell

Since 1973–74, the trend in raw material prices (in constant dollars) has been downward, with the decline especially sharp during the 1980s. This trend has been caused in considerable measure by a decrease in the rate of growth in world demand for these materials. The lower rate of growth in world consumption in turn reflects a major change in the structure of world demand brought about by technological change and a shift in the composition of world output. Although this development has had an adverse impact on raw material producers in all countries, its effects have been especially severe for developing countries that are heavily dependent on raw materials for their earnings.

The secular decline in demand for raw materials has refuted the projections made by most resource economists during the 1960s and 1970s. A rise in the real prices of metals had been expected to result from rapid growth in the world consumption of durable goods and from the depletion of known mineral resources. Agricultural prices also had been expected to rise—due to expanding world demand and limited availability of land suitable for crops. Warnings of scarcity of natural resources and consequent limitations on world economic progress were sounded by an MIT research team in *Limits to Growth* in 1972.[1] For reasons detailed in this chapter, these predictions were not realized, and a substantial rise in the real prices of raw materials is unlikely to occur in this century.

The commodities with which this chapter is mainly concerned are metals and agricultural raw materials such as cotton and rubber that are industrial inputs. Special demand and supply conditions distinguish these raw materials from other primary commodities such as food, beverages, and fuel. Technological developments have had a greater impact on the demand for raw materials than on other primary commodities, and further such advances seem likely to depress demand for traditional metal products. This chapter (a) considers whether past trends in prices and world demand for raw materials are likely to continue; (b) examines the implications of these trends for developing countries; and (c) discusses policy options for dealing with the adverse effects on developing countries.

To put the problem confronted by developing countries in perspective, these countries as a whole are currently much less dependent on raw material exports than they were a quarter of a century ago. In 1963, agricultural raw materials, nonferrous metals, and ores constituted 23 per cent of the total value of developing-country exports; in 1984, they accounted for only 8 per cent of the total.[2] Nevertheless, nearly one-fifth of all Third World countries are dependent on one or two raw materials for over half their export earnings, and most of these countries are very poor. Therefore any agenda for alleviating world poverty and restoring global growth must address the problem of raw material exports.

# Market Developments and Outlook

Average prices of agricultural raw materials (in constant dollars) reached their post-World War II peak in the early 1950s and have been sliding downward ever since. Average prices of metals and minerals reached their highest postwar levels in the mid-1960s, and although they rose sharply in the first half of the 1970s, they declined to less than half their postwar high in 1985–86 (see Table 1). Long-run trends in commodity prices over several decades usually can be explained by changes in production costs; there has been a substantial reduction in real costs of most metals and of some agricultural raw materials as a consequence of increased productivity achieved through better technology and improved efficiency. However, the very sharp drop in raw material prices during the 1980s must be explained in large part by *imbalances between the growth of world consumption and the growth of productive capacity*. Since raw material prices continued to fall through 1986—well beyond the world recession of 1982–83—the price decline cannot be regarded as cyclical. In the cases of most raw materials relevant to this study, the rate of growth in consumption has declined while productive capacity has adjusted only sluggishly to new market conditions.

Average annual rates of growth in world consumption of raw materials declined sharply between the 1970s and the first half of the 1980s (see Table 2). The largest declines between the two periods occurred for jute, timber, copper, iron ore, nickel, bauxite, and lead. In the latter period, average annual rates of growth in consumption for jute, timber, iron ore, and tin were negative. Average annual rates of growth in consumption between the 1970s and the first half of the 1980s declined more in industrial countries than in developing countries. In industrial countries, the weighted average of annual rates of growth in consumption of both agricultural non-food materials and of metals and minerals was negative in the 1979/81–1984/86 period.[3] Rates of growth of exports of these two commodity groups also declined between the two periods, but the decline was greater for raw material exports of industrial countries.[4]

The prices of most major raw materials declined between 1979/81 and 1985 (see Table 2). The exceptions were cotton, jute, and zinc; in the cases of cotton and zinc, world consumption growth rates were sustained or actually increased. The weighted average price index of non-food agricultural materials (in constant dollars) declined by 42 per cent between 1979/81 and 1986, while the corresponding decrease for metals and minerals was 38 per cent. In the first half of 1987, however, most raw material prices experienced a recovery. Although the World Bank's Commodity Markets Division projects an increase in prices (in constant dollars) by 1995 from the low levels of 1986,[5] the projected levels for 1995 and 2000 nevertheless are well below those for 1979/81 or the average of the 1970/80 period (see Table 1). The downward trend in raw material prices from the levels of the 1950s and early 1960s appears likely to continue through the remainder of this century.

### Reasons for Declining Prices

In explaining the fall in raw material prices over the past decade, we can distinguish among three types of price movements: (a) short-term fluctuations caused by seasonal or cyclical factors or other sources of imbalance, such as crop failures, that are reversible in nature; (b) long-term price trends that reflect changes in production costs; and (c) medium- to long-term price trends that result from structural shifts in demand in relation to productive capacity (discussed in detail later in this chapter) that may require a decade or more for restoration of demand-supply balance. During any particular year, prices may be responding to all three factors, including speculative forces based on expectations.

Raw materials sold on competitive world markets are subject to a higher degree of short-term price fluctuation than are manufactures.

## Table 1. Weighted Indices of Prices of Agricultural Raw Materials and Metals and Minerals[a] (1979–81 = 100)

| | Constant dollars annual averages[b] | | Current dollars annual averages | |
| --- | --- | --- | --- | --- |
| | Agricultural (Non-food) | Metals and Minerals | Agricultural (Non-food) | Metals and Minerals |
| 1948 | 140 | 97 | 39 | 27 |
| 1949 | 129 | 105 | 34 | 28 |
| 1950 | 228 | 122 | 53 | 28 |
| 1951 | 271 | 132 | 73 | 36 |
| 1952 | 179 | 148 | 50 | 42 |
| 1953 | 142 | 137 | 39 | 38 |
| 1954 | 144 | 134 | 39 | 36 |
| 1955 | 173 | 154 | 47 | 42 |
| 1956 | 153 | 155 | 43 | 44 |
| 1957 | 145 | 136 | 42 | 39 |
| 1958 | 131 | 126 | 39 | 37 |
| 1959 | 152 | 124 | 44 | 36 |
| 1960 | 157 | 124 | 46 | 37 |
| 1961 | 131 | 120 | 39 | 36 |
| 1962 | 129 | 115 | 39 | 35 |
| 1963 | 121 | 114 | 36 | 34 |
| 1964 | 121 | 137 | 37 | 42 |
| 1965 | 117 | 155 | 36 | 48 |
| 1966 | 115 | 150 | 37 | 51 |
| 1967 | 108 | 134 | 35 | 43 |
| 1968 | 113 | 138 | 36 | 44 |
| 1969 | 115 | 144 | 39 | 49 |

Note: Commodities in the non-food group are cotton, jute, rubber, and tobacco. Commodities in metals and minerals are copper, tin, nickel, bauxite, aluminum, iron ore, lead, zinc, and phosphate rock.
[a] Weighted by 1979–81 developing countries' export values.
[b] The weighted indices of commodity prices in constant dollars are deflated by the unit value index of manufactured exports (MUV) from five industrial market economies to developing countries on a c.i.f. basis. The countries and weights in the MUV index are: France (0.091); Federal Republic of Germany (0.104); Japan (0.185); United Kingdom (0.081); and United States (0.537).
Source: World Bank, *Half-Yearly Revision of Commodity Price Forecasts*, September 17, 1987.

| | Constant dollars annual averages[b] | | Current dollars annual averages | |
|---|---|---|---|---|
| | Agricultural (Non-food) | Metals and Minerals | Agricultural (Non-food) | Metals and Minerals |
| 1970 | 101 | 142 | 36 | 51 |
| 1971 | 97 | 117 | 37 | 44 |
| 1972 | 91 | 106 | 38 | 44 |
| 1973 | 124 | 133 | 59 | 63 |
| 1974 | 114 | 144 | 66 | 84 |
| 1975 | 89 | 113 | 58 | 73 |
| 1976 | 111 | 110 | 73 | 72 |
| 1977 | 102 | 103 | 74 | 74 |
| 1978 | 97 | 92 | 80 | 76 |
| 1979 | 102 | 103 | 96 | 97 |
| 1980 | 106 | 105 | 109 | 108 |
| 1981 | 92 | 92 | 95 | 95 |
| 1982 | 82 | 83 | 84 | 85 |
| 1983 | 95 | 88 | 84 | 88 |
| 1984 | 90 | 85 | 88 | 83 |
| 1985 | 74 | 79 | 75 | 78 |
| 1986 | 58 | 62 | 68 | 72 |
| Projected: | | | | |
| 1990 | 65 | 64 | 87 | 85 |
| 1995 | 75 | 70 | 115 | 108 |
| 2000 | 76 | 72 | 165 | 157 |

# Table 2. World Consumption and Prices of Major Raw Materials[a] (percentages and constant U.S. dollars)

| Commodity | Average Annual Rates of Growth in Consumption[b] (percentages) | | | Unit | Price[c] ($ dollars) | | | |
|---|---|---|---|---|---|---|---|---|
| | 1969/71–1979/81 | 1979/81–1984/86 | Projected 1984/86–2000 | | 1969/71 | 1979/81 | 1985 | Projected 2000 |
| **Agricultural** | | | | | | | | |
| non-food[d] | 1.99 | 0.66 | 1.42 | — | — | — | — | — |
| Cotton | 1.81 | 1.78 | 1.52 | lb[e] | 1.72 | 1.51 | 1.56 | 1.38 |
| Jute | 1.06 | −0.74 | 1.43 | mt[f] | 7.76 | 3.21 | 5.83 | 3.00 |
| Natural rubber | 2.31 | 2.07 | 2.22 | lb | .61 | .64 | .42 | .50 |
| Tobacco | 2.15 | 1.96 | 1.68 | lb | 1.21 | 1.01 | .86 | .79 |
| Timber | 2.04 | −0.62 | 1.13 | n.a. | n.a. | n.a. | n.a. | n.a. |
| **Metals and** | | | | | | | | |
| Minerals[d] | 2.75 | 0.61 | 1.32 | — | — | — | — | — |
| Copper | 2.49 | 0.86 | 1.44 | lb | 1.66 | 0.88 | 0.64 | 0.73 |
| Iron ore | 2.01 | −0.43 | 0.68 | mt | 37.00 | 24.00 | 23.00 | 14.00 |
| Tin | 0.22 | −3.21 | −1.05 | lb | 4.33 | 6.75 | 5.41 | 3.34 |
| Nickel | 2.83 | 0.97 | 1.06 | lb | 3.38 | 2.75 | 2.23 | 1.69 |
| Bauxite | 4.21 | 0.14 | 1.95 | mt | 33.00 | 39.00 | 30.00 | 26.00 |
| Lead | 1.52 | 0.21 | 0.42 | lb | .35 | .43 | .18 | .17 |
| Zinc | 1.31 | 1.84 | 1.27 | lb | .37 | .35 | .36 | .36 |

[a]Excluding foods, beverages, and fuels.
[b]Evaluated in 1979/81 average prices.
[c]Average price. Current dollars deflated by manufacturing unit value (MUV) index: 1985 = 100.
[d]Weighted average.
[e]Pound.
[f]Metric ton.
n.a. = not available
Source: World Bank, *Price Prospects for Major Primary Commodities*, October 1986, Vols. I, III, and IV, Annex Tables.

Table 3 shows indices of fluctuations of annual prices for major raw materials for the 1955–81 period. Long-term price trends, with which we are mainly concerned in this chapter, may be explained to some degree by slowly declining costs of production. But the sharp decreases in prices in the 1980s were largely generated by the decline in the growth of world consumption of individual raw materials. This has given rise to overcapacity, especially in the mining industry. Mines continue to operate as long as revenues cover operating costs, indicating that output is not sensitive to a downturn in prices. Overcapacity in world mining was generated by a high level of investment during the 1970s, made with the expectation that metal consumption would continue to grow at the rates of the 1960s and early 1970s. The subsequent decline in consumption growth rates resulted in large overcapacity and low prices for most metals.

A number of bauxite, copper, iron ore, lead, and nickel mines are operating at less than capacity or have been shut down because prices do not cover operating costs. Some of these mines will be restored to full production when prices rise, but many will be permanently closed. *The important question is whether the metal prices of the 1970s will be restored once overcapacity has been eliminated by the gradual growth in demand.* This will depend on the full cost of production of new capacity, including a rate of return on capital necessary to induce new investment. The World Bank projects that metal prices will recover somewhat from the 1986 level, but will remain well below the levels of the 1970s (see Tables 1 and 2). The main reason for this outlook is that the real costs of metals, including the full cost of new capacity, are expected to decline—as they have done throughout much of this century.

Structural demand-supply imbalance arising mainly from a decline in the rates of global consumption growth has also been a factor in the decline in prices of agricultural raw materials. Adjustment to overcapacity in agriculture may be difficult—either because producers are reluctant to shift out of traditional crops or because, given soil and climate conditions, there may not be alternative uses for the land that promise better returns. In addition, the replanting cycle for commodities such as rubber spans several decades. Real costs have also been falling in agriculture, and the World Bank projects that real prices in the year 2000 will be lower than those of the 1970s and early 1980s (see Tables 1 and 2).

### Fluctuating Exchange Rates

Constant U.S. dollars tend to be used as the unit for measuring changes in raw material prices, but during the 1980s, the dollar has fluctuated widely in relation to other major currencies. This raises the

## Table 3. Indices of Fluctuations in Commodity Prices, 1955–81 (percentages)

| | Deviations from moving averages[a] | | Annual average change[b] |
| | 3-year | 5-year | |
|---|---|---|---|
| Cotton | 4.7 | 6.8 | 10.1 |
| Jute | 6.9 | 9.2 | 15.6 |
| Rubber | 7.9 | 12.1 | 16.3 |
| Tobacco | 6.1 | 5.8 | 10.8 |
| Copper | 9.1 | 15.3 | 18.5 |
| Tin | 5.3 | 8.1 | 10.4 |
| Nickel | 2.6 | 4.6 | 7.1 |
| Aluminum | 2.4 | 4.6 | 6.2 |
| Lead | 9.2 | 14.7 | 18.8 |
| Zinc | 8.4 | 14.4 | 17.8 |
| Iron ore | 4.1 | 5.7 | 8.4 |
| Bauxite | 3.7 | 5.6 | 8.0 |
| Manganese ore | 4.0 | 7.2 | 10.3 |
| Phosphate rock | 6.7 | 13.8 | 17.4 |

[a]The average percentage deviation from the moving average of prices in 1981 constant dollars.
[b]Average of annual percentage changes, devoid of sign.
   Source: World Bank, "The Outlook for Primary Commodities," *Staff Commodity Working Paper No. 9*, 1983, p. 45.

question of whether changes in the exchange value of the dollar have had a depressing effect on raw material prices. For example, between 1982 and 1984, the average price of copper in pounds sterling rose by 22 per cent while the average price in dollars fell by 7 per cent. An obvious question is, did the world price of copper rise or fall? This question cannot be answered, however, under a system of floating exchange rates for which there is no international standard of value. The more relevant question is how much of the decline in the dollar price of copper was due to a shift in the world demand-supply balance for copper, and how much was due to the appreciation of the dollar. Copper producers blame the large appreciation of the dollar between 1981 and 1985 for at least a part of the fall in copper prices during that period. Between 1983 and 1984, the average annual dollar price of a pound of copper declined from 72 to 63 cents, while the dollar appreciated against a basket of fifteen major currencies (excluding the dollar) by 7 per cent. In 1984, however, consumption of refined copper in the market economies rose as a result of the world recovery, while production decreased by about 1.5 per cent between 1983 and 1984. Commercial copper stocks also declined during 1984. Thus, in the absence of an appreciation of the dollar, it would be expected that the dollar price would rise. A statistical analysis of the various factors affecting the dollar price of copper found that, had the dollar exchange rate remained the same in 1984 as in 1983, the price of copper in 1984 would have been about 70 cents per pound, or some 11 per cent higher than the actual average of 63 cents.[6] Changes in the dollar price of copper cannot, however, always be attributed to changes in the exchange value of the dollar. Between 1984 and 1986, for example, the average dollar price of copper remained about the same, although the dollar depreciated against fifteen other major currencies.

In sum, a portion of the decline in raw material prices between 1981 and 1984 may be attributed to the appreciation of the dollar. In 1985-86, the dollar depreciated sharply. In the absence of fundamental demand and supply factors tending to push down raw material prices, a depreciation of the dollar should have resulted in a rise in the dollar prices of raw materials. Instead, there was a substantial decline in the prices of both agricultural raw materials and metals. Therefore the decline in the dollar prices of raw materials was caused in large measure by fundamental market factors. The rise in raw material prices during 1987 is likely to be simply a short-term fluctuation, not a reversal of the long-term trend.

### Major Exporters of Raw Materials

Although the 32 countries listed in Table 4 account for the bulk of the developing-country exporters of raw materials, they constitute only about one-fourth of the countries categorized as developing. Moreover, not all of these countries depend on raw materials as their major source of export earnings, and several depend on raw materials for less than 10 per cent of their export income. Individual countries differ greatly in their dependence on raw material exports, and exports of particular raw materials tend to be heavily accounted for by a few developing countries. For example, four developing countries account for 95 per cent of world natural rubber exports; three developing countries account for 90 per cent of world jute exports; and five developing countries account for 95 per cent of world tin exports.

Table 5 shows the ratio of export earnings from raw materials to total export earnings for 39 countries with ratios of 15 per cent or more. Of this group, six depend on raw materials for 80 per cent or more of their export earnings. These six countries are all located in Africa and are among the poorest in the world. Another 11 countries depend on raw materials for 50-79 per cent of their export earnings; seven of these are in Africa and four are in South America. Of the 17 countries that

## Table 4. Major Developing-Country Exporters of Selected Raw Materials (thousands metric tons)

| Commodity | 1985 Export Volume (thousands metric tons) |
|---|---|
| **Cotton** | |
| China | 347 |
| Pakistan | 345 |
| Sudan | 196 |
| Egypt | 174 |
| Brazil | 152 |
| Turkey | 120 |
| Mexico | 65 |
| Total developing-country | 2,649 |
| **Jute** | |
| Bangladesh | 266 |
| India | 4 |
| Thailand | 3 |
| Total developing-country | 310 |
| **Natural rubber** | |
| Malaysia | 1,465 |
| Indonesia | 1,050 |
| Thailand | 670 |
| Sri Lanka | 123 |
| Total developing-country | 3,598 |
| **Tobacco** | |
| Brazil | 200 |
| Turkey | 100 |
| Zimbabwe | 100 |
| Greece | 85 |
| India | 64 |
| Malawi | 53 |
| Total developing-country | 901 |
| **Copper** | |
| Chile | 1,356 |
| Zaire | 499 |
| Zambia | 475 |
| Peru | 351 |
| Philippines | 217 |
| Papua New Guinea | 169 |
| Total developing-country | 3,535 |

Source: World Bank, *Price Prospects for Major Primary Commodities, Vols. III: Agricultural Raw Materials* and *IV: Metals and Minerals*, October 1986.

| Commodity | 1985 Export Volume *(thousands metric tons)* |
|---|---|
| **Tin (metal)** | |
| Malaysia | 55 |
| Indonesia | 22 |
| Brazil | 20 |
| Thailand | 18 |
| Bolivia | 10 |
| China | 7 |
| Nigeria | 1 |
| Total developing-country | 154 |
| | |
| **Bauxite** | |
| Guinea | 12,700 |
| Jamaica | 2,325 |
| Guyana | 2,200 |
| Indonesia | 930 |
| Suriname | 500 |
| Total developing-country | 26,250 |
| | |
| **Iron ore (metal content)** | |
| Brazil | 63,687 |
| India | 16,889 |
| Liberia | 10,835 |
| Venezuela | 5,533 |
| Total developing-country | 119,300 |
| | |
| **Lead (metal)** | |
| Mexico | 104 |
| Peru | 64 |
| Morocco | 46 |
| Total developing-country | 312 |
| | |
| **Zinc (metal)** | |
| Peru | 119 |
| Mexico | 70 |
| Total developing-country | 384 |

obtained 50 per cent or more of their export earnings from raw material exports in 1985, only two had per capita incomes over $1,000, and most had per capita incomes under $500.

It should also be noted that the countries listed in Table 5 represent less than half of the developing countries for which recent trade data are available; the remainder depend on raw materials for less than 15 per cent of their export income. Some of the latter countries are very poor, and there is no significant correlation between their per capita income and the degree of their dependence on raw material exports. The three countries accounting for the vast bulk of the world's poor—China, India, and Pakistan—do not rely significantly on raw materials for their export income.

## Factors Influencing the Decline in the Growth of World Demand for Raw Materials

The annual rates of growth in the consumption of all major agricultural materials and metals declined sharply during the 1970s and the first half of the 1980s from the rates of the 1960s. In the *industrial* countries, average annual rates of growth of consumption were negative for cotton, jute, tobacco, tin, iron ore, and zinc during 1970–84. For natural rubber, refined copper, nickel, and lead, average annual rates of growth of consumption in these countries were less than 1 per cent over this period. The decline in consumption growth rates since the 1960s was especially sharp for metals. The World Bank projects a slight rise in the rate of growth in consumption for some of these raw materials during the 1985–2000 period, but projected annual growth rates for cotton, tobacco, tin, and iron ore to the year 2000 continue to be negative. Only in the case of aluminum is the projected average annual growth rate above 1 per cent (see Table 6).

In the *developing* countries, average annual rates of growth in consumption of raw materials have been substantially higher than in the industrial countries over the same period. This disparity was mainly due to differences in composition and rates of growth of GNP in the two groups of countries: The consumption of manufactured goods in most developing countries has been rising relative to the rates of growth in consumption of other goods and services, and developing countries grew somewhat faster than developed countries over the 1970–84 period. However, the World Bank has projected a decline in rates of growth of raw materials consumption in developing countries for the 1985–2000 period.

Four major factors contribute to the decline in rates of growth of world demand for agricultural raw materials and metals: (a) the de-

## Table 5. Ratio of Export Earnings from Raw Materials as a Percentage of Total Export Earnings, Selected Countries (percentages)

| Country | Per cent | Year of Data | Major Exports |
|---|---|---|---|
| Zambia | 90 | 1985 | copper, cobalt |
| Liberia | 90 | 1984 | iron ore, rubber |
| Guinea | 90 + | a | bauxite, alumina, diamonds |
| Chad | 87 | a | cotton |
| Botswana | 82 | 1986 | diamonds, copper/nickel |
| Niger | 82 | 1983 | uranium |
| Suriname | 79 | 1984 | bauxite-alumina |
| Jamaica | 66 | 1984 | bauxite-alumina |
| Zaire | 63 | a | copper, cobalt, diamonds |
| Chile | 59 | 1984 | copper and other metals, wood products |
| Mali | 57 | 1984[b] | cotton |
| Paraguay | 56 | 1985 | cotton, timber |
| Sudan | 52 | 1985 | cotton |
| Central African Republic | 51 | 1985[b] | cotton, diamonds, wood products |
| Burkina Faso | 50 | 1984 | cotton |
| Togo | 50 | 1984 | phosphates |
| Mauritania | 50 | 1983 | iron ore |
| Malawi | 45 | 1984 | tobacco, oil seeds |
| Gambia | 44 | 1985[b] | oil seeds |
| Guyana | 44 | 1985[b] | bauxite |
| Zimbabwe | 42 | 1984 | tobacco, cotton, metals |
| Bolivia | 41 | 1985 | tin and other metals |
| Peru | 39 | 1985[b] | copper |
| Ghana | 35 | 1981 | bauxite, wood |
| Papua New Guinea | 34 | 1985[b] | copper concentrates, wood products, vegetable oil |
| Nicaragua | 34 | 1984[b] | cotton |
| Jordan | 33 | 1984 | phosphates |
| Morocco | 32 | 1984 | phosphates |
| Malaysia | 31 | 1983 | rubber, tin, timber |
| Sierra Leone | 30 | 1984[b] | diamonds |
| New Caledonia | 25 | 1983 | nickel |
| Uruguay | 21 | 1984 | wool |
| Ethiopia | 20 | 1982 | hides, oil seeds, cotton |
| Philippines | 17 | 1983 | wood products, copper |
| Brazil | 17 | 1983 | iron ore |
| Egypt | 16 | 1985 | cotton |
| Bangladesh | 15 | 1985 | jute |
| Thailand | 15 | 1984 | rubber, tin |
| Tanzania | 15 | 1984[b] | cotton, sisal |

Note: This table excludes countries for which no trade data are available for recent years.
[a]Current trade data not available; author's estimate.
[b]Based on major raw material exports only.
   Sources: United Nations, *1985 International Trade Statistics Yearbook, Vol. I: Trade by Countries*, 1986; and International Monetary Fund, *International Financial Statistics*, various issues.

## Table 6. Industrial- and Developing-Country Actual and Projected Annual Rates of Growth in Consumption of Major Raw Materials (percentages)

|  | 1961–84[a] | 1970–84[a] | Projected 1985–2000[a] |
|---|---|---|---|
| **Cotton** | | | |
| Industrial countries | −1.9 | −2.2 | −1.0 |
| Developing countries | 4.0 | 3.7 | 2.3 |
| Industrial and developing countries | 1.8 | 1.8 | 1.7 |
| **Jute** | | | |
| Industrial | −4.4 | −5.6 | 0.2 |
| Developing | 2.7 | 2.8 | 1.8 |
| Industrial and developing | 0.5 | 0.6 | 1.6 |
| **Natural Rubber** | | | |
| Industrial | 2.3 | 0.9 | 1.4 |
| Developing | 7.3 | 5.3 | 3.6 |
| Industrial and developing | 3.9 | 2.5 | 2.4 |
| **Tobacco** | | | |
| Industrial | 0.3 | −0.3 | −1.9 |
| Developing | 3.2 | 3.6 | 2.9 |
| Industrial and developing | 2.0 | 2.1 | 1.7 |
| **Refined copper** | | | |
| Industrial | 2.0 | 0.9 | 0.8 |
| Developing | 7.1 | 6.9 | 3.9 |
| Industrial and developing | 2.7 | 1.8 | 1.6 |
| **Tin metal** | | | |
| Industrial | −0.7 | −2.3 | −2.4 |
| Developing | 1.4 | 0.9 | 0.6 |
| Industrial and developing | −0.3 | −1.7 | −1.5 |
| **Nickel metal** | | | |
| Industrial | 3.3 | 0.7 | 0.9 |
| Developing | 6.4 | 6.9 | 3.7 |
| Industrial and developing | 3.6 | 1.3 | 1.3 |
| **Aluminum** | | | |
| Industrial | 4.6 | 1.6 | 1.2 |
| Developing | 11.7 | 8.1 | 3.0 |
| Industrial and developing | 5.4 | 2.6 | 1.6 |
| **Iron ore** | | | |
| Industial | 1.7 | −2.2 | −0.4 |
| Developing | 6.0 | 4.0 | 2.5 |
| Industrial and developing | 2.8 | 0.2 | 0.7 |
| **Lead metal** | | | |
| Industrial | 1.6 | 0.2 | 0.1 |
| Developing | 5.8 | 4.6 | 1.9 |
| Industrial and developing | 2.3 | 1.1 | 0.6 |
| **Zinc metal** | | | |
| Industrial | 1.3 | −1.3 | 0.5 |
| Developing | 6.7 | 6.1 | 2.9 |
| Industrial and developing | 2.3 | 0.2 | 1.3 |

[a] Average annual rate.

Source: World Bank, *Price Prospects for Major Primary Commodities, Vols. III: Agricultural Raw Materials* and *IV: Metals and Minerals*, October 1986, Annex Tables.

cline in the GNP growth rate in the industrial countries; (b) changes in the composition of both output and consumption in industrial countries; (c) conservation in the use of materials in particular applications; and (d) substitution of new materials for traditional ones.

### Changes in Developed- and Developing-Country Growth Rates and Composition of Output

The industrial countries have experienced a substantial decline in the rate of growth of real GNP since the early 1970s. Their average annual growth of real GNP was 5.1 per cent during the 1960s but declined to 3.2 per cent during the 1970s and to only 2.2 per cent during the first half of the 1980s. The rate of growth of industrial production in these countries slowed even more than their rate of GNP growth. Thus the industrial production index grew at an average annual rate of 4.7 per cent during the 1961-73 period and at 2.9 per cent during the 1973-84 period. This decline is structural rather than cyclical, and the growth rates of the 1960s are unlikely to be restored in this century. Real GNP growth rates also declined in *developing* countries between the 1960s and the 1970s, with a sharp downturn during the first half of the 1980s.

The composition of output in the industrial countries has been shifting from agriculture and manufactures to services. In 1960, 46 per cent of the GNP of the industrial countries consisted of agricultural and industrial output and 54 per cent of services. By 1984, 38 per cent of the GNP of industrial countries was produced by agriculture and industry, while 62 per cent consisted of services.[7] Since raw materials constitute a much smaller proportion of the value of services than they do of agricultural and industrial production, the shift in product composition has contributed to the decline in the growth of world demand for raw materials. In the case of developing countries, there has been an increase in the proportion of GNP produced by industry; this has tended to increase their demand for raw materials and their relative share of world imports of raw materials. It seems likely that these trends in the composition of GNP in developed and developing countries will continue at least for the remainder of this century.

### Conservation and Substitution[8]

Conservation in the use of materials and substitution of materials for traditional ones have contributed heavily to the reduction in consumption of raw materials exported by developing countries.

Most substitution does not involve an increase in the demand for one raw material that offsets a decrease in demand for another raw material of equal value. Instead, it entails replacing a traditional material either with a synthetic or, if with another raw material, then one a significant portion of whose value derives from processing and energy. Thus when aluminum is substituted for copper in a range of uses, demand for bauxite rises, but the value of bauxite in aluminum is small relative to the value of copper ore in copper metal; the cost of aluminum is largely represented by processing.

Synthetic fibers have been substituted for cotton, wool, jute, and sisal for a number of decades, and synthetic rubber has replaced natural rubber in important applications since World War II. As most synthetic materials are derived from petroleum or natural gas, the several-fold increase in petroleum prices during the 1970s increased the competitive position of agricultural raw materials. However, new processes leading to substantial energy savings in the production of synthetics offset the effects of higher oil prices. With the exception of natural rubber, all agricultural raw materials were less competitive in relation to synthetics in 1982 than they were in 1972.[9] However, some agricultural raw materials—cotton, wool, and natural rubber—have characteristics that make them superior to synthetics, and an important market for these commodities is assured even though their prices are higher than those of their synthetic counterparts. Cotton has continued to represent about 31 per cent of total fiber usage in clothing in the United States and the European Economic Community over the past decade, and natural rubber as a proportion of total tire consumption increased from 31 per cent in 1972 to 37 per cent in 1982.[10] On the other hand, substantial displacement by synthetics has occurred in jute and sisal over the past 15 years. The main synthetic competitor, polypropolene, is lighter, stronger, and more supple. The only end-use in which jute is preferred on technical grounds is secondary carpet backing. Sisal twine has some advantages over polypropolene twine.[11]

Over the past fifteen years, conservation and substitution of traditional metals has occurred very rapidly due to developments in materials technology and in the materials requirements for new and improved products. The sharp rise in the cost of fuel in the 1970s stimulated demand for smaller cars and lighter materials to produce them. High-strength, low-alloy steel has replaced carbon steel and cast iron for a subsequent saving in car weight. In addition, aluminum has replaced copper and plastics, and composite materials have been substituted for metals in auto production. Metals technology has produced thinner-walled and smaller-gauged copper tubing, and the revolution in the design of electrical and electronic circuits has resulted in a reduction in the use of copper wire.

Dramatic advances in the aerospace industry have resulted in the use of composites made of carbon, silicon, and glass fibers, and of metal alloys that economize on traditional metals such as steel and aluminum. The new composite materials economize on weight and function more efficiently at the high temperatures in aerospace engines. Ceramics may eventually replace metals in jet engines and in a number of other industrial products.

A substantial amount of substitution has taken place in the communications industry with the development of microwave radios, satellite transmission, fiber optics, and other innovations. Between 1970 and 1984, the U.S. telecommunications industry consumed an average of 200,000 metric tons of copper per year, but consumption is expected to decline by half for the period 1984–90. Nearly all new long-distance cables and many new local cables are optic fibers made from glass. In addition, electronic carrier systems increase the message-carrying capacity of copper lines.[12]

Several decades ago, aluminum was substituted for copper in overhead high-voltage power cables. In the future, however, electric power will be carried by superconducting cables. The basic materials for producing the new superconductors are rare earths mixed with copper oxides and other elements. Since there are abundant supplies of "rare earths" in developed countries, they are unlikely to constitute an important export for the developing world.

# Implications for Developing-Country Exporters

The secular decline in real prices of raw materials has had a significant impact on the export earnings of about half of the developing countries. It has most severely affected the earnings of very poor countries that are heavily dependent on one or two material exports whose prices have declined significantly in real terms. The experiences of Zambia, Liberia, and Bolivia illustrate this predicament. The value of Zambia's exports (in constant dollars) declined by more than half between 1980 and 1985. Since Zambia depends on copper for over 90 per cent of its export earnings, its outlook for a substantial increase in earnings is exceedingly poor. Not only are real copper prices unlikely to return to their 1980 level, but Zambia's copper-producing capacity is projected to diminish over the next decade. Liberia's export earnings, largely accounted for by iron ore and rubber, declined by nearly 40 per cent in real terms between 1980 and 1985, and the outlook for iron ore prices is also very bleak. Bolivia, which is heavily dependent on tin exports, has experienced a similar decline in export earnings.

Not all developing countries that rely on exports of raw materials have experienced a substantial fall in export earnings. In some cases, the real prices of their major exports have not declined significantly since 1980, and in others, the volume of exports has risen to offset the drop in price. For example, countries whose principal export is cotton (including Chad, Paraguay, and Mali) fared much better than those whose principal exports are metals. Chile, whose main export is copper, has been partly able to offset the decline in prices by increasing the volume of its copper exports. Botswana has increased its export income during the 1980s by nearly doubling diamond exports.

The structure of production and of exports has changed markedly in developing countries over the past three decades. *First*, the relative importance of raw materials as a source of export income has decreased significantly. For example, the decline in cotton exports of developing countries is partly explained by increases in textile production for home consumption and export by the major cotton-producing countries—Bangladesh, India, and China. *Second*, developing countries are gainers as well as losers from a decline in real prices of raw materials. In 1984, for example, developing countries *imported* an amount of raw materials from developed countries ($13.5 billion) equal to 56 per cent of exports of raw materials by developing countries to developed countries ($24.1 billion). Most of the raw materials exported by developing countries—for example bauxite, copper, cotton, and tobacco—are also exported by developed countries. Moreover, developing countries' raw material exports to other developing countries are increasing in relative importance: In 1984, about one-third of developing-country agricultural raw materials went to other developing countries. *Third*, the impact of declining world raw material prices on individual developing countries differs enormously—with some benefiting and some losing. *Fourth*, to a substantial degree, the lower prices of raw materials reflect lower production costs rather than simply a gain for consumers at the expense of producers.

It is frequently argued that developing countries have been harmed by declining terms of trade.[13] A distinction should be made, however, between a decline in export prices that reflects a reduction in cost due to increased productivity and a decline arising from world overcapacity or competition from cheaper sources. When prices fall due to increased productivity, both exporting and importing countries may *gain*. An increase in productivity means that a country can produce more output with the same quantity of labor, land, and capital resources. If there is a decline in world prices proportional to the improvement in productivity, a country can earn the same export income by increasing its output with the same resources. Alternatively, it may export the same volume and consume more raw materials domestically, or it may shift some of the resources used to produce raw materials to other industries for export or domestic consumption.

On the other hand, a decline in export prices arising from over-capacity or competition from cheaper sources may mean a long period of reduced foreign exchange income. Unlike the case of a cyclical downturn of exports, adjustment is usually not automatic and may require a special response by the industry or a change in government policies—or both. In the event of an extended decline in the real prices of its major export or exports, a country may pursue several forms of adjustment. One course is to develop new raw material exports for which world demand is growing and price prospects are favorable. Another course is to increase the output of those raw material exports for which world markets are expanding. For example, Pakistan more than doubled its cotton exports between 1979-81 and 1986 to considerable advantage. However, it may not be possible for a country to promote an alternative raw material export with good prospects. Instead, a country may increase its exports of food products or of processed goods or manufactures; thus Brazil increased the volume of its soybean (and soybean products) exports by over 50 per cent during the first half of the 1980s, and Argentina doubled its soybean exports. Soybean prices have held up better than most primary commodities during the 1980s. Mauritania, experiencing a decline in the value of its traditional iron ore exports, increased the value of its fish exports fourfold between 1980 and 1986—making fish its principal export.

The most important form of adjustment to declining raw material prices has been the expansion of manufactured exports. Most non-oil-exporting countries that have had successful rates of growth over the past decade have reduced their dependence on primary commodity exports in favor of manufactures. Developing countries together in aggregate increased their manufactured exports at an average annual rate of 8.4 per cent during 1980–86, while their primary goods exports rose at an average annual rate of 1.3 per cent. Countries that are heavily dependent on raw material exports but that have increased their exports of manufactures several-fold over the past decade include Brazil, India, Thailand, and Turkey. For small, very poor countries, however, producing manufactures for export may not be an option.

Some countries have been able to expand manufacturing based on a raw material whose export price has declined. Countries that produce cotton and jute are increasingly exporting cotton textiles and rugs and other products made from jute. Brazil has shifted some its iron ore production to steel to become a major steel exporter in the 1980s. Another form of adjustment—also resorted to by Brazil in recent years—is for a country to reduce costs and expand its share of the world market—even though the total market may be declining or stagnating. This is how Brazil became the world's largest iron ore exporter in the 1980s in the face of world overcapacity and declining iron ore prices. It is also how Chile became the largest exporter of copper in the 1980s despite world overcapacity and declining prices. Chile's success was due in part to a dramatic decrease in production costs achieved through an increase in productivity; it now has the lowest costs of any copper-producing country.

How countries adjust to extended periods of sluggish demand and low prices for their exports is an essential part of their development strategy. In a dynamic world economy, nearly all countries, whether developed or developing, sooner or later confront this problem. The more successful developing countries, principally the newly industrializing countries (NICs), have adopted policies that have enabled them to reduce dependence for export income on primary products with stagnating or declining demand and to shift resources to those with growing demand. Some other countries, however, have continued to depend on exporting the same primary commodities during the past three or four decades despite declining real prices. The reasons for this include government price controls, credit allocation favoring high-cost products for domestic consumption, and the absence of incentives for foreign investment. Positive government policies—such as tax incentives and technical assistance, as well as the removal of restrictions—may also be required to achieve economic flexibility and export diversification. For many developing countries foreign equity investment has promoted the establishment of new industries—both primary and manufacturing. In Africa, several countries have increased their export earnings over the past decade by encouraging foreign investment in their diamond and petroleum industries.

Some very poor countries that are heavily dependent on one or two raw materials whose prices have fallen cannot adjust to the decline in export earnings simply by changing government policies. In addition to providing incentives to domestic agriculture and industry, these countries require external capital and technical assistance to develop new primary and industrial products in which they can be competitive in world markets. The nature of this adjustment depends on the physical and human resources available in the country.

In general, countries that have been able to diversify their exports have made the greatest economic progress. In the 1960s, for example, coffee exports constituted over half of Brazil's export income. Although Brazil exported about the same amount of coffee in 1985 as in the 1960s and 1970s, by 1985 coffee represented only 9 per cent of the value of its exports. Brazil had diversified into more remunerative exports, notably iron ore, steel, and a variety of manufactures as well as soybeans; between 1965 and 1983, it reduced its dependence on primary commodity exports from 92 per cent to less than 60 per cent and increased the share of manufacturing exports in total exports from 9 per cent to

40 per cent. Chile reduced its dependence on copper exports from 79 per cent in 1975 to 46 per cent in 1985, while at the same time increasing the *value* of its copper exports by 3.5 times and the *volume* by 2.5 times. Both countries have had satisfactory growth rates in recent years, and both are in the upper-middle-income group of developing countries. In contrast, Zambia has not reduced its dependence on copper exports significantly between 1965 and 1985. Zambia's GNP in constant dollars was higher in 1968 than in 1985, and real per capita income has declined sharply. Bolivia and Liberia are encountering similar problems.

# Policy Issues

Countries that export raw materials face problems that are arising from a dynamic world economy in which the demand structure is changing more rapidly than ever before. Nations cannot maintain or increase export earnings by producing the same basic materials with the same technology any more than they can compete in world markets for manufactures with the same technology and product quality. A revolution has been taking place in the raw material industries that is tending to blur the traditional distinction between industry and the production of primary commodities. A consequence of this revolution is that demand is stagnating for many traditional raw materials, and their prices are declining.

For developing countries heavily dependent on raw material exports, a central policy issue is what kind of development strategy they should adopt to enable them to achieve the rate of increase in export income necessary for a satisfactory rate of economic growth. For the industrial countries and the multilateral assistance agencies, the central policy issue is what kind of assistance and advice will enable Third World countries to grow and thereby expand world trade and income. A full discussion of these issues involves a wide range of questions regarding development strategies, international capital flow to developing countries, and the promotion of world trade—an agenda too broad to cover more than superficially in this chapter. The following discussion will examine some of the policies advanced for dealing with raw materials problems. However, none of these initiatives can substitute for a development strategy that takes into account adequate responses to the dynamic changes in world demand.

### International Commodity Agreements

The establishment of international commodity agreements has been one of the major objectives of the U.N. Conference on Trade and Development (UNCTAD) since its establishment in 1964. The Integrated Programme for Commodities adopted at the 1976 UNCTAD conference in Nairobi called for the negotiation of price stabilization agreements or other stabilization measures covering the major raw materials important to developing countries—cotton, jute, rubber, sisal, wool, copper, tin, bauxite, and iron ore—and foods and beverages such as wheat, coffee, and cocoa. International commodity agreements have been established for only two raw materials: tin (in 1956) and rubber (in 1980).[14] The International Tin Agreement collapsed in October 1985, when the tin buffer stock ran out of funds to support the price and was left with large stocks against which substantial sums had been borrowed. Trading in tin was halted on the London Metal Exchange, and the price declined by nearly 50 per cent. The International Natural Rubber Agreement expired in October 1987. A new agreement was negotiated in March 1987 and will go into effect when ratified by a sufficient number of countries. UNCTAD has made strong efforts to establish commodity agreements in copper and jute, but without success.

The usefulness of international commodity agreements is highly controversial among economists and commodity specialists.[15] There is broad agreement that a buffer stock arrangement in which a commodity would be bought and sold in the market within a range of lower and upper support prices could modify the amplitude of price fluctuations. However, a successful operation requires that the buffer stock management be given sufficient flexibility to change the range within which prices are maintained in accordance with shifts in fundamental demand and supply conditions. In practice, buffer stocks have been underfunded in terms of both money and stocks, and support prices have been unrealistic relative to long-term demand and supply. Moreover, support prices are determined by political negotiations between representatives of producing and consuming countries rather than by commodity specialists.

Disagreements between governments of producing and consuming countries have tended to arise from differences in their objectives for reaching an international commodity agreement. Consuming countries favor reducing the amplitude of price fluctuations above and below a long-term price trend as determined by fundamental factors; they have generally objected to the use of export and import quotas for supporting prices at higher than long-term competitive levels. Producing countries, on the other hand, have favored support prices at levels regarded as "fair"—which might mean some historical real price, or one that covers the full economic costs of production. But when substantial overcapacity exists, it may be impossible to maintain a negotiated support price with the resources available to the buffer stock management. Therefore producing countries favor supplementing buffer stock activities with export quotas—a practice that has proved to be unsuccessful.

Some economists have questioned the net benefit of modifying relatively short-term price fluctuations caused by cyclical or speculative forces for the welfare of the raw material producing countries. Fluctuations in export income arising from transitory market forces usually can be handled by drawing on reserves or by borrowing from the International Monetary Fund (IMF). The more serious economic consequences for producing countries arise from long-term downward price trends that reflect overcapacity in the industry, the introduction of substitute materials, or technological developments that reduce production costs for some producers who are then able to capture a larger share of the market at the expense of higher-cost producers. The economic consequences of such developments cannot be satisfactorily dealt with by international commodity agreements. The secular declines in real prices of many raw materials during the 1970s and 1980s are unlikely to be reversed. Spending billions of dollars to support these prices for temporary periods encourages additional capacity and delays adjustment.

### International Financial Assistance

To assist primary commodity-exporting countries in dealing with temporary shortfalls of export proceeds, the IMF in 1963 established a compensatory financing facility (CFF). This facility enables IMF members to obtain financing beyond their normal quota limits with the expectation that borrowings will be repaid when normal export earnings are restored, or possibly enhanced, by a cyclical upturn in demand and prices. During the 1980s, the CFF has been averaging more than 20 per cent of total IMF assistance; in 1983, it constituted 29 per cent of IMF assistance and had a value of about $7.4 billion.

Members borrowing under the CFF are normally expected to repay these credits within five years, since it is assumed that a decline in prices of primary products will be reversed within a three-year period. The facility has been especially beneficial to countries exporting commodities such as cotton, coffee, cocoa, and jute, which have been subject to *transitory* price movements. However, many metal-exporting countries whose exports have been subject to a *secular* decline in real prices have not experienced an increase in export income from which repayments to the Fund could be made. Between 1981 and 1986, outstanding obligations of the IMF arising from compensatory financing nearly tripled. This suggests that cyclical declines in the prices of some primary commodities during the 1982–83 world recession were not followed by increases in prices in the recovery period.

Perhaps the most effective financial assistance for promoting adjustment to declining raw material prices is that which helps countries diversify their exports, including the production of manufactures and processed materials. In the normal course of development, countries should reduce their dependence on raw materials for both domestic consumption and export. Success in exporting raw materials depends heavily on lowering costs through increased productivity and adapting the product to shifts in world demand. A good example of the latter is producing iron ore pellets to replace exports of iron ore. An example of shifting to processed materials is exporting alumina instead of bauxite; or, for countries with cheap power, producing aluminum for export. Such adjustments have been facilitated by external assistance or by foreign direct investment.

The more advanced developing countries have been able to adjust to declining revenues from raw material exports by adopting policies and programs that encourage import substitution and new export industries. The World Bank and the IMF have been financing this type of adjustment. This policy course may, however, present special difficulties for very poor countries that are heavily dependent on one or two export crops whose prices have fallen. Such countries might benefit by giving priority to improving production of food and essential materials for domestic consumption—thereby reducing their import requirements. But if a country is to grow, it must also find ways to increase its exports, and this is likely to require increasing the productivity and output of its traditional exports and the development of new sources of export earnings—which the very poor countries may not be able to undertake without outside assistance.

### Foreign Direct Investment

Despite the secular decline in real prices of most metals, production costs are also declining, and overcapacity in the metals industry is being eliminated. As the mineral reserves of the developed countries are depleted, the competitive advantage of developing countries with abundant mineral resources will increase. A number of developing countries with rich mineral resources need to modernize their mines and metallurgical facilities and to develop new mines to replace depleting reserves. They also must explore for additional reserves. These activities require huge amounts of capital, technology, and experience. Because of their large external indebtedness, however, most of the minerals-producing developing countries of Africa and Latin America are unable to borrow the capital required by their state mining enterprises. Foreign direct investment is especially well suited for mineral development, but a number of developing countries have adopted policies that either prevent foreign private investment or make such investment unattractive. Peru is a good example of this. On the other hand, Chile, which welcomes foreign private investment, is in a good position to greatly expand mineral output with the help of foreign capital and technology.

Although the World Bank and the Inter-American Development Bank (IADB) have made several hundred million dollars in loans to the state mining enterprises of developing countries, these sources cannot be counted on to supply the billions of dollars needed in the future. The U.S. government, with some support from Britain and Canada, has opposed such financing on grounds that it constitutes an unfair disadvantage to private mining companies competing with state mining enterprises. The U.S. government has also argued that international agency financing should not substitute for foreign private investment, and that these agencies should use their limited capital for projects and programs for which private international capital is not available. This is a debatable issue, a full discussion of which is not possible in this chapter.[16] More important is the fact that the World Bank and the regional development banks have higher-priority uses for their limited resources and are unable to provide more than a fraction of the financial requirements of Third World state mining enterprises over the next decade or so.

Foreign equity investors might be safeguarded against losses from government violation of agreements by investment insurance programs such as that provided by the U.S. Overseas Private Investment Corporation (OPIC), or by the proposed Multilateral Investment Guarantee Agency (MIGA) sponsored by the World Bank. However, it is not possible to insure against all forms of political risk that may arise when making foreign investments. Moreover, foreign investors require a favorable economic climate and attractive terms for mining contracts. Currently these conditions exist only in a few developing countries with abundant mineral resources.

### Trade Restrictions on Raw Materials

Industrial countries impose some import restrictions on raw materials exported by developing countries. These include high quotas or high tariffs on cotton, tobacco, and wool, in which some developed countries are in competition with developing countries. The United States is in competition with developing countries in copper. Despite efforts of the U.S. mining community to obtain import restrictions on raw copper, imports into the United States are subject only to a 1-per-cent *ad valorem* duty, and some copper imports from developing countries are free of duty under the tariff preferences afforded to developing countries under the Generalized System of Preferences.

Much more serious, however, are the duties and import quotas on processed materials and on manufactures such as textiles produced from raw materials. These restrictions limit the ability of developing countries to shift from export dependence on raw materials to processed and manufactured goods. These restrictions should be removed or modified during the Uruguay Round of GATT negotiations.

Members of the U.S. mining community and some government officials have advocated subsidizing U.S. production of some minerals—such as cobalt, platinum, and manganese—to reduce U.S. dependence on imports of these products. I have argued elsewhere that such a policy would be uneconomic and would provide less security against foreign supply disruptions than stockpiling strategic commodities.[17] The national security argument for import protection to promote self-sufficiency has also been made for copper and zinc, but such arguments are little more than a cloak of respectability for those seeking benefits for domestic industries.[18]

# Conclusions

The principal conclusion of this study is that the decline in most raw material prices during the 1980s has been due to secular shifts in world consumption and to technical innovations that have resulted in both substitution for traditional materials and conservation of their use. Although current overcapacity is being reduced, technological developments affecting demand and supply are likely to create further problems for raw material producers. The central policy issue is how developing countries heavily dependent on raw material exports can adjust not only to the decline in export *incomes* that has taken place in the 1980s, but also to future shifts in world *demand*. This issue is of special importance to very poor countries.

The emphasis given by UNCTAD and its developing-country members to international commodity agreements as a solution to the problem of declining earnings from primary commodities is misplaced. Not only are there formidable political and economic difficulties in formulating and managing such agreements to reduce price fluctuations, but they do not deal with the most essential problem: secular declines in raw material prices. Adjustment for dealing with this problem involves the whole range of economic policies and development strategies. Much of the need for adjustment assistance currently being provided by the World Bank and the IMF has arisen from a decline in export receipts from primary commodities. Such assistance is not designed to meet temporary reductions in export income, but to reduce import requirements and promote new sources of export earnings essential to economic growth.

Policies of developed countries should be directed to liberalizing imports of raw materials and manufactures from developing countries and promoting the flow of capital from both private and multilateral agency sources. Although foreign direct investment will depend mainly on the policies of the developing countries themselves, special encouragement should be given by industrial countries to equity investment in developing countries. Finally, industrial countries should provide increasing support to the World Bank and the regional assistance agencies to enable them to promote the adjustment process—a process that must continue in order to meet dynamic changes in the structure of the world economy.

## Notes

[1] D.H. Meadows, D.L. Meadows, J. Randers, and W.W. Behrens III, *The Limits to Growth* (New York: Universe Books, 1972).

[2] General Agreement on Tariffs and Trade, *International Trade 1985/86* and *International Trade 1969*, Geneva, 1985 and 1970, Tables A-12 and 7, respectively.

[3] Data from World Bank, *Price Prospects for Major Primary Commodities, Vol.1: Summary and Implications*, Washington, D.C., October 1986, Report No. 814/86, Tables 24, 25, 26, 27, 28, and 29.

[4] Ibid., p. 75.

[5] It should be said that these World Bank projections are controversial and, in the case of metals and minerals, are believed by many commodity specialists to be too low. The substance of this controversy does not, however, reverse the overall assessment that the long-term trend is downward.

[6] Based on Kenji Takeuchi, John E. Strongman, Shunichi Maeda, and Suan Tan, "The World Copper Industry: Its Changing Structure and Future Prospects," *Staff Commodity Working Paper No. 15* (Washington, D.C.: World Bank, 1986.)

[7] World Bank, *World Development Report 1981*, p. 137, and *World Development Report 1986*, p. 184.

[8] For a comprehensive discussion of conservation and substitution of traditional raw materials, see Walter C. Labys, "Impacts of Technology on Primary Commodity Demand with Particular Reference to Developing Country Exports" (Unpublished working paper, Department of Mineral and Energy Resources Economics, West Virginia University, Morgantown, December 1985).

[9] U.N. Food and Agriculture Organization, *Agricultural Raw Materials: Competition with Synthetic Substitutes*, Economic and Social Development Paper No. 48, Rome, 1984, p. 31.

[10] Ibid., pp. 44–45.

[11] Ibid., p. 40.

[12] See John S. Mayo, "Materials for Information and Communication," *Scientific American*, Vol. 235, No. 4 (October 1986), pp. 59–65; and Joel P. Clark and Merton C. Flemings, "Advanced Materials and the Economy," *Scientific American*, Vol. 235, No. 4, (October 1986), pp. 56–57.

[13] The argument that a decline in a country's terms of trade inevitably means a loss of economic welfare and that the terms of trade have over time moved against developing countries was popularized by Raul Prebisch in the 1970s. Raul Prebisch, *Toward A New Trade Policy for Development*, Report by the Secretary-General of UNCTAD, New York, United Nations, 1964; and *Toward a Dynamic Development Policy for Latin America*, New York, United Nations, 1986; and "Commercial Policy in the Underdeveloped Countries," *American Economic Review*, May 1959.

[14] Commodity agreements have also been established for cocoa, coffee, and sugar.

[15] For a discussion of opposing views regarding international commodity agreements, see F. Gerard Adams and Sonia A. Klein, eds., *Stabilizing World Commodity Markets* (Lexington, Mass.: Lexington Books, 1978), and "Primary Commodities in the World Economy," *World Development*, Vol. 15, No. 5 (May 1987) for the views of several commodity specialists.

[16] For a discussion of this issue, See Raymond F. Mikesell, *Nonfuel Minerals: Foreign Dependence and National Security* (Ann Arbor: University of Michigan Press for the Twentieth Century Fund, 1987).

[17] Raymond F. Mikesell, *Stockpiling Strategic Materials* (Washington, D.C.: American Enterprise Institute, 1986), Chapter 5.

[18] Ibid.

# Jobs: The Shifting Structure of Global Employment

## Ray Marshall

A number of basic trends are shifting the global structure of employment. The most fundamental of these are internationalization, demographic and labor market changes, and the spread of technological innovations—especially of the new information technologies.

Internationalization has greatly transformed the nature of global economies and the viability of traditional economic policies, institutions, and management systems. In particular, it has caused former national and international economic policies and institutions to be less effective, necessitating greater cooperation on economic policies and the modernization of international financial and trade institutions. Within countries, internationalization has subjected economic processes and management systems to the test of competitiveness. In general, competitiveness requires greater attention to productivity, quality, and flexibility. It also focuses attention on the basic determinants of the international division of labor. High-wage countries like the United States must concentrate on management systems, technology, human resource development, and the impact of their policies on the ability of their firms to operate. The United States will not be able to compete with Third World countries in terms of wages, as this would only result in a politically unacceptable decline in absolute and relative wages. Moreover, the United States has little comparative advantage in management systems. To avoid competing on the basis of wages alone, it must therefore improve its management systems and maintain its technological edge.

Global demographic forces critically influence relationships between industrial and developing countries and, unlike many other relationships, are fairly predictable. Most of the world's future population growth will be in Third World countries. Barring significant policy and institutional changes, most developing countries will not be able to generate sufficient economic growth to provide jobs for their rapidly expanding work forces—even if most countries do succeed in greatly diminishing the pace of population growth in the 21st century. The slowdown in Third World economic growth during the 1980s and these countries' consequent inability to service their external debts have important implications not only for these countries, in terms of increased poverty and joblessness, but also for the United States and other developed countries. In an interdependent world, the Third World's employment problems are also our problems—they will visit us through immigration, trade, or political and social instability.

Demographic and labor market trends in the United States also have significant implications for future U.S. relations with the Third World. Economic competition and technological change require much greater attention to education and skill development. In this competition, U.S. schools have serious deficiencies. Moreover, demographic changes will make minorities with relatively less education and training a growing proportion of the work force. The problems of many of these workers will be exacerbated by increased competition from new immigrants. Fortunately, the slowdown in U.S. work force growth and potential labor shortages could create favorable conditions to lessen these problems. Solutions also will require adequate economic growth and a worker adjustment program to facilitate the movement of people from non-competitive to competitive activities. This will not happen automatically in a very imperfect labor market.

In technology, the United States and other developed countries have substantial advantages until standardization takes place. Technology also requires fairly sophisticated education and skills that are not presently available in most developing countries. Education in fact determines the extent to which a country can assimilate technology. There also are important symbiotic relationships between human resource development and technological innovation. Aware of these relationships, many developing countries, especially the NICs, are making educational commitments that will gradually strengthen them in their competition with the United States and other developed countries.

The following sections explore a) the nature of employment trends in developing and developed countries and b) employment linkages between industrial and developing countries. The concluding section makes some policy recommendations that flow from these explorations.

# Developing Countries

Many experts believe Third World employment problems to be attributable mainly to the imbalance between rapidly expanding populations and slowly growing employment opportunities. Stagnation in the world economy during the 1980s has caused this problem to loom even larger for the developing countries than it did in the 1950s and 1960s. In general, compared to the industrialized countries, developing countries have higher rates of agricultural employment, younger work forces, lower incomes, a higher incidence of absolute poverty, greater inequalities in wealth and income, lower levels of education, and less structured labor markets.

## Work Force Trends

In 1987, there were over 5 billion people in the world—3.8 billion in the developing countries and 1.2 billion in the industrial countries. Between 1985 and 2025, about 95 per cent of the expected world population growth of 3.4 billion will be in the developing countries of Africa, Asia, and Latin America. Although Asia will experience the largest *absolute* population expansion over this period, its population growth rate will be below that of Africa and Latin America; consequently, its share of the world's population will decline from 56 to 54 per cent. Africa's population will triple (to 1.6 billion from 555 million) and Latin America's will almost double (from 374 million to 779 million).[1]

Most developing countries have 40 per cent or more of their labor force in agriculture, while industrialized countries generally have 10 per cent or less. From an economic and labor market perspective, one of the most important differences between the developed and developing countries is the number of workers in the young adult category, between the ages of 20 and 40 (see Table 1). Thus, between 1985 and 2005, all of the net increase in the world's population in the important 20–40 years age group will be in the Third World. The developed countries will actually have 14 million fewer people in this age group in 2005 than in 1985.[2]

The unstructured nature of labor markets in low-income developing countries causes unemployment figures to greatly understate their joblessness problems. Poverty is likely to be so severe that few workers can afford to be unemployed; many therefore work in the informal sector, without explicit contractual wages and fringe benefits or other legal regulations. In fact, people who are sufficiently well off to be classified as "unemployed" (i.e., active job seekers) usually need income

## Table 1. Young Adults in the Global Work Force (millions)

|                      | 1965 | 1985  | 2005  |
|----------------------|------|-------|-------|
| Industrial countries | 285  | 366   | 352   |
| Developing countries | 363  | 1,105 | 1,674 |
| World                | 921  | 1,471 | 2,026 |

Source: Paul Demeny, "The World Demographic Situation," in Jane Menken, ed., *World Population and U.S. Policy* (New York: W.W. Norton and Co., 1986), p. 60.

from the informal sector or support from the employed members of their families. In parts of Asia, the Middle East, and Sub-Saharan Africa, from 30 to 40 per cent of the urban work force is in the informal sector. In Latin America, the informal sector is generally somewhat smaller, varying from 14.4 per cent in Venezuela to 43 per cent in Peru.[3]

Women constitute a large and growing share of the work force in developing countries, especially in agriculture and in the urban informal sector. Thus in Africa, women are the main producers of food. In the Andes, "women produce a substantial part of agricultural work despite the image to the contrary given by the census data"[4]; and in Nepal, "women contribute 50 per cent of household income, compared with 43 per cent by men, and the balance by children."[5] And although women's work is concentrated in agriculture and the urban informal sector, in Latin America, women represent a growing proportion of employment in light manufacturing in the urban formal sector. Women's contributions to household income are substantially higher in *poor* households, especially in rural areas. Moreover, many women work for pitiful returns as wage laborers or traders. When all work is counted, both paid and unpaid (such as collecting water and fuel, preparing food, etc.), data in the developing world as a whole indicate that women work substantially more hours than men—especially in poor, rural households. Yet because of customs and attitudes (in developed countries as well as in the Third World), much of the work that women do continues to be "invisible"—that is, not counted at all or underestimated in official statistics—despite its importance to their families and national economies. The myth that women's work is of marginal importance thus lingers on.[6]

Underemployment and poverty levels are better indicators than unemployment levels of the severity of Third World employment problems. For example, it has been estimated that, in 1978, unemployment in the developing countries was only about 60 million, or 5 per cent of the work force; underemployment, in contrast, was 250 million, or 35 per cent.[7] The International Labour Office estimated in 1976 that about 300 million people were "unemployed or inadequately employed" in the developing world, and that about one billion workers would enter those labor markets between 1975 and 2000.

Perhaps because of the unstructured nature of Third World labor markets, the favorable rates of economic growth between 1960 and 1980 seem to have made it possible for many developing countries to absorb their rapidly growing working-age populations in more productive employment.[8] The slowdown in development during the 1980s will, however, make it much more difficult to do so.

The predicament of the developing countries with respect to employment and unemployment must of course be viewed in relation to these countries' low national GNP and per capita income levels. In 1980, two-thirds of the developing world's 3.3 billion people were living in countries with per capita incomes of $400 a year or less, while only 425 million lived in countries with per capita incomes of over $1,500 a year. Moreover, incomes in developing countries are very unequally distributed; in low- and middle-income countries, the poorest fifth receives only 3–5 per cent of income and the richest fifth, 30–45 per cent.[9]

Third World rural poverty has been intensified by social and political as well as policy constraints on agricultural development, including unequal access to land, policies that favor urban populations at the expense of the rural, and practices and policies that often place women, even when they are de facto heads of households, at a disadvantage relative to men. It has been pointed out that "the rapid expansion of employment in the developing countries, necessarily and most graphically through increases in the number of jobs for women, has proved to be the single most telling factor in the reduction of poverty."[10]

Education and human resource development—because of their importance for the growth of productivity and total output—are particularly important determinants of the extent to which the developing countries are likely to be able to improve their employment structures. This is so because, as Theodore Schultz has emphasized, human capital is at least as important to the growth of productivity and output as physical capital:

> Increases in the acquired abilities of people . . . and advances in useful knowledge hold the key to future economic productivity and to its contribution to human well being. . . . A decidedly favorable achievement of many low-income countries during recent decades is their investment in population quality. Investment in research, especially in agricultural research, has also fared well.[11]

## Figure 1. Education of the Global Labor Force
### (average years of schooling)

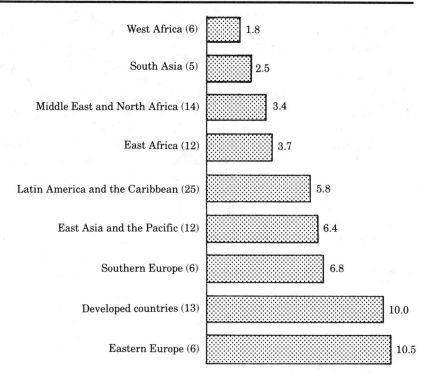

Note: Number of countries included in regional average shown in parenthesis after
region or country group.
  Source: *International Labour Review,* September-October 1987, p. 563.

Basic educational competencies will determine how well and how
fast modern technology can be adapted to Third World needs and how
effectively people in these countries can make the decisions and develop the institutions needed for personal and national development.
The education levels of various regions are shown in Figure 1 and
Table 2.

### Latin American Labor Force Trends

Due to growing economic interdependence and the proximity of Latin
America to the United States, the U.S. economy is likely to be particularly influenced, directly and indirectly, by the mismatch between
labor force growth and economic development in Latin America. While
overall real GDP in Latin America expanded by 8 per cent between

## Table 2. Education Levels, by Gender, 1985 (percentages)

| | Men's Literacy Rate | Women's Literacy Rate | Women in School 1st and 2nd Levels[a] | 3rd Level[b] |
|---|---|---|---|---|
| | *(percentage)* | | *(percentage)* | |
| World | 78 | 68 | 48 | 11 |
| Developed | 99 | 99 | 76 | 32 |
| Developing | 68 | 50 | 43 | 5 |
| Latin America | 85 | 81 | 65 | 17 |
| Europe | 95 | 87 | 74 | 18 |
| Asia | 65 | 44 | 39 | 4 |
| Oceania | 61 | 44 | 38 | 2 |
| Africa | 57 | 36 | 43 | 2 |

[a]Enrollment, first level: elementary or primary school; age range varies between 5 and 13. Enrollment, second level: middle, secondary, or high school; age range varies between 11 and 20.
[b]Enrollment, third level: higher education; generally ages 20-24.
  Source: Ruth Leger Sivard, *Women . . . a World Survey* (Washington, D.C.: World Priorities, 1985).

1980 and 1986, the labor force increased by at least 18 million, or more than 15 per cent. The employment situation in Latin America was made even worse by the 1982–83 recession, when Latin America became a net capital exporter because of rising external debts; as a consequence, the decline in labor growth during the 1980s was not translated into less joblessness.

Latin America's experience illustrates the major labor force trends taking place—to a greater or lesser extent—throughout the Third World. The region's labor force grew from less than 55 million in 1950 to just over 118 million in 1980—a net increase of 63 million.[12] Although the rate of increase is likely to slow down in the future, the region's absolute increase is expected to amount to 93 million between 1980 and 2000, compared with an estimated increase of about 34 million in the United States (whose labor force was roughly equal to all of Latin America's in 1980).

The sectoral structure of the region's work force has changed greatly; there have been massive shifts from rural to urban areas and out of agriculture into manufacturing and services. As a consequence of these shifts, the proportion of the work force in agriculture declined from over a half to less than a third over a 30-year period. The proportion of the Latin American labor force in agriculture during the 1980s was about the same as in the developed countries in the 1950s. The industrial-sector share increased in eight countries—and especially so in Mexico. The labor force participation of women in Mexico's industrial employment grew very significantly between 1950 and 1980, rising from 11.9 per cent to 27.9 per cent, while women's share of agricultural employment fell from 37.1 per cent to 19.3 per cent.[13] Women had a larger share of manufacturing employment in Mexico than in any other Latin American country, mainly because they accounted for an overwhelming majority of employees in the "maquila" plants that assemble products for U.S. (and some foreign) companies, for sale in the United States.

It is doubtful that Latin America can provide adequate employment for all who seek work; many of those unable to find adequate employment at home will emigrate to North America. Mexico's experience will be particularly important for the United States. Between 1980 and 2000, Mexico's total population is expected to increase by 61 per cent—from 70 million to 113 million—before Mexico's strong family planning program results in a significant slowdown in population growth. Between now and the year 2000, the Mexican working-age population is likely to grow at over 3 per cent a year, which means that it will more than double between 1980 and 2000 (from 20 million to 42 million). Between 1995 and 2000, Mexico—whose work force is presently half the size of that of the United States—is expected to add about as many workers to its work force each year as the United States (1.2 million in Mexico compared to 1.3 million in the United States). Without a substantial improvement in economic growth, there will be very strong pressures for Mexicans to seek work in the United States. Indeed, this conclusion can be extended to the entire Caribbean basin, where the Center for Immigration Studies estimates that, just to keep the lid on already unacceptably high levels of unemployment, 35 million additional jobs will have to be created between 1986 and 2000. Even more jobs than this will be required if the labor force participation rates of women continue to increase, as they probably will. In the Caribbean basin countries, job creation at this level will require investments of one trillion 1986 dollars; over half of this amount would be required in Mexico alone.[14]

# Developed Countries

During the 1970s and 1980s, all of the principal developed countries experienced rising unemployment, although Japan consistently has had the lowest unemployment rate of any of the industrial countries and until 1984 had relatively rapid employment growth. Canada and the United States had the fastest employment growth among the developed countries during this period, but both countries had higher average unemployment rates than Japan. West Germany had relatively low unemployment in the 1970s, but since 1984 its unemployment rates have been higher than those of the United States, and even higher than those of Italy, which historically has had relatively high unemployment rates. Over the entire 1965–1985 period, U.S. employment expanded by almost 50 per cent, compared with only 2.5 per cent in Europe and 25 per cent in Japan. No new jobs were added in OECD Europe between 1979 and 1985, while employment in the United States was growing at over 2 per cent a year, adding over nine million jobs to the American economy between 1979 and 1985.[15]

One reason for the secular rise in unemployment in both the United States and Europe has been an increase in structural problems on both the demand and supply sides of the labor market. In Europe, it is assumed that labor market rigidities account for rising long-term unemployment, but this is probably only a marginal factor. Indeed, although European labor markets are not as flexible as those of the United States and Japan, there is no evidence that labor market rigidities have increased since the 1960s. Global economic stagnation and dramatically divergent industrial-country macroeconomic policies suggest that demand conditions probably are more important determinants of rising unemployment than are market rigidities. There have, however, been important changes in labor supply—mainly increased labor force participation of women, young people, and immigrants, all of whom have higher than average rates of unemployment. There also have been significant changes in competitive conditions and in technology.

All industrial countries have had youth employment problems, but their experiences have differed. West Germany has had a relatively favorable youth employment rate, largely due to a very effective school-to-work transition system that provides training for young people and helps place them with employers. Japan also has very well-organized apprenticeship and school-to-work programs. Another factor influencing youth unemployment differences between the United States and Europe is the timing of the postwar baby boom; these people entered the work force during the 1960s and 1970s in the United States but not until about 1975 in Europe. In this case, too, Japan was the exception; youth unemployment increased slightly during the 1960s but dropped by over one-third during the 1970s. In Japan, as in most of Europe—and in marked contrast to the United States—youth labor force participation rates dropped sharply after 1960 because of rising school attendance. Youth unemployment has also worsened due to the decline in the number of unskilled and farm jobs, through which young people often entered the work force, as well as to the increased labor force participation of women and immigrants, who generally compete with young people for jobs in secondary labor markets. All of the OECD countries have experienced steady increases in the labor force participation rates for women and steady declines in these rates for men. Young black men have had particularly serious unemployment and labor force participation problems in the United States, partly because of the decline of many of the kinds of jobs they formerly held, but also because of the deterioration of conditions and the unavailability of jobs in the central parts of large metropolitan areas, in many of which blacks account for a significant share of the population.

Employment in all of the industrial countries has shifted out of agriculture—first to industry and then to services (see Table 3). This is in keeping with well-established economic theory, which predicts that as economies develop, employment will shift in this direction; this is because, as income rises, the propensity to buy services rather than goods also rises. Employment tends to shift faster from goods to services than output because of higher productivity in goods-producing activities. The United States has a relatively high proportion of total employment in services—63 per cent in 1984, compared with 54 per cent in the United Kingdom, 49 per cent in Japan, and 44.5 per cent in Germany. Moreover, it is expected that by the year 2000, over 90 per cent of U.S. employment *growth* will be in services, and services will account for 75 per cent of the American work force. Manufacturing probably will continue to decline as a source of employment, despite a continued rise in U.S. manufacturing output. The shift to services has been a factor in the slowdown[16] in productivity and real wage growth in the United States because productivity in services is lower than in manufacturing. Although the services category is so amorphous that generalization about it is difficult, many high-value-added services are tightly linked to manufacturing; thus, for example, banking, advertising, insurance, and transportation services are closely linked to the automobile industry. Hence, the soundness of the U.S. economy still depends heavily on a competitive and innovative manufacturing sector.

### Labor Force Trends in the United States

The U.S. population and work force will increase more slowly in the future than in the 1960s and 1970s. During the 1970s, the U.S. labor force grew by 24.1 million, but growth is expected to slow to 18 million during the 1980s and to 15.6 million during the 1990s.[17] Depending on what happens to immigration, technological change, education, and training of existing workers—and, most important, to economic growth—labor markets are likely to be tighter. There probably will be greater shortages of skilled and educated workers than during the 1970s, while unskilled, uneducated workers will have more difficulty finding employment. Thus the overall level of unemployment in the

# Table 3. Civilian Employment by Sector and Gender: Rapid Shift Toward Services

| | | Total Employment in: | | | Female Employment in: | | |
|---|---|---|---|---|---|---|---|
| | | Agriculture | Manufacturing *(percentages)* | Services | Agriculture | Manufacturing *(percentages)* | Services |
| World | 1960 | 60.5 | 17.6 | 22.0 | 65.0 | 13.3 | 21.8 |
| | 1980 | 50.8 | 21.0 | 28.3 | 52.9 | 16.6 | 30.6 |
| Industrial Countries | 1960 | 28.2 | 34.7 | 37.1 | 34.4 | 24.4 | 41.2 |
| | 1980 | 12.7 | 36.7 | 50.7 | 13.6 | 27.0 | 59.6 |
| Europe | 1960 | 28.5 | 38.5 | 33.1 | 31.9 | 27.3 | 40.9 |
| | 1980 | 13.7 | 39.3 | 47.0 | 14.8 | 27.6 | 57.7 |
| Developing Countries | 1960 | 75.7 | 9.6 | 14.8 | 81.3 | 7.3 | 11.5 |
| | 1980 | 65.4 | 15.0 | 19.7 | 70.9 | 11.8 | 17.4 |
| Africa | 1960 | 78.5 | 8.1 | 13.5 | 85.5 | 3.2 | 11.3 |
| | 1980 | 68.7 | 11.9 | 19.5 | 77.8 | 5.5 | 16.7 |
| Latin America | 1960 | 47.6 | 21.0 | 31.4 | 23.8 | 21.1 | 55.3 |
| | 1980 | 31.8 | 25.9 | 42.4 | 14.6 | 19.9 | 65.7 |
| East Asia | 1960 | 76.8 | 9.3 | 14.0 | 81.3 | 7.8 | 10.9 |
| | 1980 | 66.9 | 16.5 | 16.6 | 72.1 | 13.7 | 14.4 |
| South Asia | 1960 | 73.8 | 10.6 | 15.7 | 80.8 | 8.5 | 10.8 |
| | 1980 | 64.3 | 13.8 | 22.0 | 69.8 | 11.6 | 18.6 |
| United States | 1960 | 6.7 | 36.6 | 56.8 | 2.1 | 24.0 | 74.0 |
| | 1980 | 3.5 | 31.0 | 65.5 | 1.7 | 19.2 | 79.2 |
| Japan | 1960 | 33.1 | 29.5 | 37.5 | 43.7 | 20.1 | 36.3 |
| | 1980 | 11.2 | 34.3 | 54.6 | 14.1 | 26.4 | 59.6 |
| China | 1960 | 83.3 | 6.3 | 10.5 | 86.5 | 6.0 | 7.5 |
| | 1980 | 74.3 | 14.0 | 11.8 | 78.5 | 12.0 | 9.5 |
| Mexico | 1960 | 55.1 | 19.5 | 25.4 | 32.8 | 14.0 | 53.3 |
| | 1980 | 36.6 | 29.0 | 34.5 | 19.3 | 27.9 | 52.8 |

Source: International Labour Office, *Economically Active Population* (Geneva, 1985).

United States will rise, despite a continuation of the current high demand for skilled workers.

The work force will continue to age, and there will be a much smaller pool of young workers. Between 1986 and 2000, the number of people in the 35-47 age group will grow by 38 per cent, and the number in the 48–53 age group will rise by 67 per cent, while the overall population will grow by only 15 per cent. The number of those who are 65 and older will rise at a slower rate but will increase by 9.7 million between 1980 and 2000, while the number of those in their twenties will decline from 41 to 34 million, or from 18 to 13 per cent of the population. Moreover, the economic dependency rate should continue to drop. The median age of the work force will rise from 35 years in 1984 to 39 years in 2000.[18] The consequence of these developments should be to improve the quality of the work force in terms of age, experience, and education.

There will be growing participation of women in the U.S. work force (see Table 4). Women have constituted two-thirds of labor force growth for the last two decades, and this trend is expected to continue, mainly because more women with children will continue to work. The labor force participation rate of women is expected to increase from 51.5 per cent in 1980 to 57.5 per cent in 1990 and to 61.1 per cent in 2000; women's share of the work force will increase from about 45 per cent now to 47.5 per cent in 2000. However, the labor force participation rates of women will probably peak and stabilize by the year 2000, when the number of women entering the work force will no longer surpass those retiring.[19]

The share of minorities in the U.S. work force will also increase. Non-whites, who constituted 13 per cent of the work force in 1985, will account for 29 per cent of work force growth between 1985 and 2000, when their proportion of the labor force will reach 15.5 per cent. By 2000, women and minorities will constitute 63 per cent of the work force. And between now and 2000, women, minorities, and immigrants will account for over 80 per cent of the *net additions* to the labor force.[20] The structural employment problems of minorities, reflecting lower levels of educational attainment, will cause them (especially young black and Hispanic males) to continue to suffer income disadvantages. Because of the growing proportion of young working-age people among minorities, addressing the problems of these groups will be increasingly important to national economic and social welfare.

Immigrants also will be a growing proportion of the work force; they accounted for about a third of U.S. population growth between 1970 and 1980 and for a larger proportion of the growth in the work force. The share of immigrants in work force growth probably will increase in the 1990s.[21] How immigrants will do in the labor market

# Table 4. U.S. Labor Force Participation[a]
## (percentages)

| | Total | 1960 Male (*percentage*) | Female | Total | 1980 Male (*percentage*) | Female |
|---|---|---|---|---|---|---|
| OECD[b] Countries | 68.7 | 93.7 | 44.7 | 69.7 | 85.5 | 52.1 |
| Seven Major Industrial Nations: | | | | | | |
| **United States** | **68.6** | **91.7** | **42.6** | **72.4** | **85.4** | **59.7** |
| United Kingdom | 73.4 | 99.1 | 48.6 | 73.5 | 89.3 | 57.6 |
| Canada | 62.3 | 91.9 | 32.0 | 71.8 | 86.4 | 57.3 |
| Japan | 75.8 | 92.2 | 60.1 | 71.8 | 89.1 | 54.9 |
| France | 69.9 | 87.4 | 46.1 | 67.6 | 82.5 | 52.5 |
| West Germany | 70.5 | 94.9 | 49.3 | 65.4 | 81.7 | 49.3 |
| Italy | 64.1 | 93.3 | 36.7 | 60.9 | 82.9 | 39.8 |

[a]Labor force participation is the percentage of the total, male, or female population that is employed.
[b]Excluding Turkey.
Source: International Labour Office, *World Labour Report I,* 1984, p. 53.

will depend on how U.S. public and employer policies assimilate them and on their education and skills. Very little is known about the educational level of illegal immigrants, but relatively large numbers of legal immigrants are concentrated at the two extremes of the education spectrum. Of the adults who entered the work force during the 1970s, 25 per cent had fewer than five years of schooling (compared with 3 per cent of U.S. residents), while 22 per cent (and 16 per cent of residents) were college graduates. Because of the serious employment problems and low wages of the developing countries relative to the United States, and the fact that immigration networks are well established, it is likely that at least 600,000 immigrants will continue to enter the United States each year for the rest of this century. Immigration at this level would add at least 6 million people to the U.S. work force by 2000.[22]

The economic impact of this shift in the ethnic composition of the U.S. work force will depend both on the educational and skill characteristics of the immigrants and on labor force conditions in the United States. The evidence suggests that trained, educated immigrants will promote economic growth, but that untrained, uneducated immigrants will depress wages and working conditions for low-wage residents and displace them from jobs, although not on a one-to-one basis. Some analysts argue that unskilled immigrants actually benefit areas to which they migrate because they are likely to have higher earnings and lower unemployment than unskilled residents. This is true in part because immigrants from the Third World generally are more willing than more established residents to work more hours at marginal, low-

wage jobs. Moreover, the availability of immigrants at low wages dis-
courages employers from automating jobs. It would be hard to argue
that immigrants do not depress wages and working conditions or cause
any employment displacement. The United States probably can absorb
somewhat more legal immigrants during the 1990s than it has in the
1970s and 1980s, but this will require careful attention to their labor
market impact. Absorption will be easier, of course, if higher rates of
economic growth are achieved.

Finally, the skills mix of the U.S. work force will continue to
change. About 90 per cent of all new jobs will be in services and less
than 10 per cent in manufacturing. Lower-skill jobs are likely to
disappear while professional and technical jobs increase in work force
share. William Johnston has observed that:

> Ranking of all jobs according to the skills required . . . indicates
> that the fastest growing jobs require much higher math, language,
> and reasoning capabilities than current jobs, while slowly growing
> jobs require less. . . . When skill requirements in language, rea-
> soning, and mathematics are averaged, only four percent of the
> new jobs can be filled by individuals with the lowest levels of skills,
> compared to nine percent . . . today. At the other end of the scale,
> 41 percent of the new jobs will require skills ranked in one of the
> top three categories, compared with only 24 percent . . . at
> present.[23]

As a consequence of these rising education and skill requirements, job
market access will be particularly difficult for black men and
Hispanics.

## North-South Linkages

In a highly interdependent global economy, the policy challenge of
course is to make the relationships between the developed and developing countries mutually beneficial rather than destructive. The threat
in the 1980s is that the negatives of interdependence are becoming
stronger than they were in the 1970s. Due to heavy debt burdens,
many of the developing countries, particularly those in the Western
Hemisphere, have become net capital exporters and therefore are unable to resume the high levels of mutually beneficial growth that they
experienced during the 1960s and 1970s. This is a problem for the
United States not only because American banks hold significant
amounts of Third World debt, but also because in the late 1970s about
40 per cent of U.S. exports went to the developing countries. The
decline in U.S. exports to these countries during the 1980s therefore

has been costly for Americans in terms of jobs and incomes. Moreover, the inability of Third World countries to provide jobs for their rapidly growing work forces has caused employment and income conditions to deteriorate in most of these countries. Economic stagnation in the developing countries will result in domestic economic hardship as well as political instability, which will also have negative effects on the United States and other countries in the form of intensified trade problems, U.S.-Third World political tensions, and immigration. The United States therefore has a heavy stake in encouraging the kind of economic growth in these areas that could provide the basis for improved living conditions and higher productivity—which could in turn generate greater investment opportunities and markets for products and technology from the developed countries. In short, while internationalization has weakened the effectiveness of demand management in individual countries, demand management policies on a global basis could be very effective.

### The Trade-Jobs Linkage

The employment effects of international trade have become important political issues because of the secular rise in unemployment in the United States and other developed countries during the 1970s and 1980s. This issue has been underscored by the increased share of Third World exports coming to the United States and the decline of U.S. exports to the Third World—prompted in large measure by the fact that after 1982 the United States was the world's main expanding market, and Third World countries needed to increase exports and reduce imports in order to service their mounting external debts. This is illustrated by U.S. trade with Latin America: U.S. exports fell by 26 per cent between 1981 and 1986 while the U.S. share of Latin America's exports increased from one-third to 60 per cent of the total. When this issue is examined carefully, however, it is clear that, on balance, North-South trade has resulted in *net job gains* for the North. In a 1984 study for the World Bank, Bela Balassa (using a technique that in fact underestimated job gains, since it did not include the indirect effects of trade) found the net gains to the North from manufacturing trade with developing countries to be 701,000 jobs in 1973, 1,439,000 in 1978, and 1,474,000 in 1981. The largest gains were in the European Economic Community (710,000), followed by Japan (523,000) and the United States (142,000).[24] Using a similar technique, Renshaw examined the net employment effects of trade between the developed (OECD) and developing countries under a "protectionist" scenario, which showed a positive balance of 364,000 jobs, and a "liberalization" scenario, which yielded a positive balance of 387,000 jobs.[25]

A very thorough input-output study of the employment effects of North-South manufacturing trade by the U.N. Industrial Development Organization (UNIDO) confirmed these findings.[26] UNIDO studied the domestic employment impact of the trade of six principal industrial countries (West Germany, Japan, France, the United Kingdom, Italy, and the United States) with two categories of developing countries: (1) all developing countries; and (2) nine export-oriented developing countries (Argentina, Brazil, Hong Kong, Malaysia, Mexico, South Korea, Singapore, the Philippines, and Thailand).

The study concluded that, despite the fact that these were difficult economic times for the whole world, all six of the developed countries experienced substantial *net job gains* in their manufacturing trade with the South in 1975, 1980, and 1983 (see Table 5). Without this trade, all of these countries would have experienced a deeper recession and higher unemployment. However, in 1983, with the exception of Japan, all of these countries *lost* jobs as a result of trade in industrial goods with nine export-oriented developing countries. It is important to note, however, that these losses, which were largest for the United Kingdom, were more than offset by trade with other developing countries.

In 1983, manufacturing job *losses* as a percentage of the manufacturing employment from trade with the nine export-oriented developing countries mentioned earlier were: the United Kingdom, 1.8 per cent; Germany, 1.1 per cent; the United States, 0.4 per cent; France, 0.13 per cent; and Italy, 0.13 per cent. Japan's manufacturing employment *increased* 3.7 per cent as a result of its trade with these export-oriented countries. As might be expected, the employment changes by the United States as a result of trade with the South show large gains in some high-value-added sectors and major losses in low-value-added industries like apparel, leather, wood, food and paper products, and textiles and basic metals (see Figure 2). It should be noted, however, that *manufacturing* employment growth is heavily concentrated in a few developing countries. Indeed, in 22 of 28 industry branches, over half of the total output of all Third World countries is concentrated in the top five countries and areas. Although developing countries achieved greater growth relative to the developed countries in low-value-added consumer products industries between 1970 and 1980, they also had faster growth during these years in such high-value-added areas as non-electrical machinery, electrical machinery, transport equipment, and professional and scientific equipment. Despite the slowdown after 1980, the developing world's share of value-added increased in 22 of the 28 categories between 1980 and 1987.

The main reason for the competitive disadvantage of American-based companies relative to the developing countries is the fact that

# Table 5. Anatomy of Employment Change in Six Major Industrial Countries (thousands of persons)

| | Germany (Fed. Rep.) 1975-1980 | France 1975-1980 | Italy 1975-1978 | Japan 1975-1980 | United Kingdom 1975-1979 | United States 1973-1980 |
|---|---|---|---|---|---|---|
| | | | *(thousands of persons)* | | | |
| **Total Change in Employment** | **505** | **386** | **423** | **2,656** | **85** | **13,635** |
| Agriculture | −337 | −259 | −128 | −981 | −15 | −43 |
| Construction | 118 | −75 | −25 | 733 | −7 | 249 |
| Services | 1,011 | 1,079 | 590 | 3,192 | 432 | 12,752 |
| Industry[a] | −287 | −593 | −14 | −288 | −325 | 677 |
| **Change in Employment in Industry[a] due to changes in:** | | | | | | |
| Level of product demand | 932 | 817 | 202 | 3,812 | 142 | 3,593 |
| Domestic | 988 | 1,051 | −216 | 3,330 | 880 | 3,621 |
| External | −56 | −234 | 418 | 482 | −738 | −28 |
| North | −23 | −305 | 297 | 256 | −655 | −73 |
| South | −47 | 59 | 112 | 251 | −97 | −107 |
| Nine selected developing economies[b] | −43 | −31 | −15 | 116 | −84 | −149 |
| Technology | −659 | 30 | 206 | 240 | 251 | 97 |
| Productivity | −560 | −1,206 | −422 | −4,340 | −718 | −3,013 |

Note: A minus sign before a figure indicates a loss, all other figures represent gains. The discrepancy between the sum of North and South and the total external effect is due to service trade.
[a]Industry consists of manufacturing, mining, and utilities.
[b]Argentina, Brazil, Hong Kong, Malaysia, Mexico, the Republic of Korea, the Philippines, Singapore, and Thailand.
Source: United Nations Industrial Development Organization, *Industry and Development: Global Report 1986*, p.100.

# Figure 2. U.S. Net Employment Gains and Losses in Trade with the South, 1983 (thousands of man years)

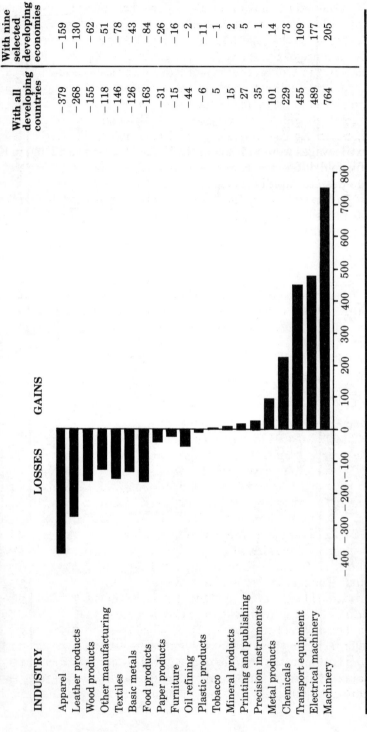

| INDUSTRY | With all developing countries | With nine selected developing economies |
|---|---|---|
| Apparel | −379 | −159 |
| Leather products | −268 | −130 |
| Wood products | −155 | −62 |
| Other manufacturing | −118 | −51 |
| Textiles | −146 | −78 |
| Basic metals | −126 | −43 |
| Food products | −163 | −84 |
| Paper products | −31 | −26 |
| Furniture | −15 | −16 |
| Oil refining | −44 | −2 |
| Plastic products | −6 | −11 |
| Tobacco | 5 | −1 |
| Mineral products | 15 | 2 |
| Printing and publishing | 27 | 5 |
| Precision instruments | 35 | 1 |
| Metal products | 101 | 14 |
| Chemicals | 229 | 73 |
| Transport equipment | 455 | 109 |
| Electrical machinery | 489 | 177 |
| Machinery | 764 | 205 |

Source: U.N. Industrial Development Organization, *Industry and Development: Global Report 1986*, p. 109.

U.S. productivity advantages are more than offset by lower labor costs, especially wages, in the developing countries. This relationship can be illustrated by the case of textiles, in which Korea is widely perceived to have a large comparative advantage. In this industry, it took 64 man-years in the United States and 245 in Korea to produce $1 million in output. Productivity in the United States was therefore almost four times greater than in Korea. However, in 1980 the average annual wage of an industrial worker was $16,406 in the United States and $2,890 in Korea—or nearly six times higher in the United States. Textile wages were $11,268 in the United States and $2,490 in Korea— a fivefold difference. Korea retains a substantial unit labor cost advantage despite rapidly increasing wages and unit labor cost increases.[27]

In general, some developing countries prospered during the 1960s and 1970s from a development strategy to finance imported technology and production growth with credit available on favorable terms from the international financial institutions. Most of these developing countries gained competitive advantage by combining standardized technology with very low-wage labor and exporting products to service their debts and sustain their growth. The average relationships for the South relative to the North in 1980 were roughly: productivity, 45 per cent of that of the North's; wages, 25 per cent; and unit cost, 63 per cent.[28]

Most of the U.S. job losses linked to trade with Third World countries have been due to a loss of exports, *not* to an inordinate surge in imports. The main reason for the growing U.S. share of world imports has been the greater growth of U.S. GNP during the 1980s. The U.S. share of world imports increased from 13.3 per cent in 1980 to 19.2 per cent in 1985, but remained about the same relative to GNP. The growing trade deficit was due to a decline in exports relative to GNP—merchandise exports fell from 8.4 per cent of GNP in 1980 to 5.3 per cent in 1985, and all exports fell from 12.9 per cent of GNP to 9.3 per cent during these years. U.S. merchandise exports to the developing countries declined more than total exports during these years, and by 24.4 per cent in real terms compared with the 11.7 per cent drop in total exports. Significantly, real U.S. exports to heavily indebted Latin America fell 30.9 per cent during these years. As John Sewell and Stuart Tucker have pointed out, the direct decline of U.S. exports to the Third World cost the United States 650,000 jobs during these years. An *additional* 1.1 million jobs were lost because of the failure of trade with the Third World to grow in the 1980s. The debt crisis was clearly a major factor in these trade problems. The decline of exports to Mexico, the most important developing-country trading partner of the United States (and third most important overall), cost the United States nearly 300,000 jobs between 1980 and 1985. And the drop in U.S.

exports to the Big Four—Argentina, Brazil, Mexico, and Venezuela—resulted in a loss of nearly 600,000 U.S. jobs, or more than one-third of all U.S. job losses attributable to the fall in U.S. exports to the Third World as a whole.[29]

## The Technology Linkage

Monumental technological innovations have interacted with internationalization to transform traditional economic relationships. Technology greatly strengthens multinational corporations and facilitates the internationalization of financial, product, and physical equipment markets. It also makes it possible to coordinate production in different parts of the world, to produce in much smaller units, to interrupt product cycles and introduce new ones, and to greatly alter the amount of labor and physical resources needed to produce a given output. This process has been particularly visible in agriculture and commodity markets—where most output improvements are due to the substitution of knowledge and information for labor as well as for capital and physical resources. Technological change has therefore weakened the Keynesian assumption that increased output would lead to increased employment.

These technological developments will have very important implications for employment relations between industrial and developing countries. Advances in agricultural techniques and the development of synthetic materials enable greatly increased output at the very time that changes in manufacturing technologies are increasing output-to-commodity ratios. Since Third World countries are mainly commodity exporters, the weakening of the connections between manufacturing output and commodity inputs tends to reduce the demand for their exports. Similarly, many Third World economies could be hurt by the decline in the labor intensiveness of production and increased skill requirements. This has led some analysts to predict that work "outsourced" to the developing countries will be repatriated as it becomes less labor-intensive.

Several studies have attempted to assess the impact of technology on the international division of labor. According to one perspective reflected in these studies, the production of standardized manufacturing products will gradually be shifted to the developing countries, leaving the production of more technologically advanced, customized, high-fashion, design-intensive, and high-value-added production in the industrialized countries.[30] Those who hold this view believe that the standardization of product designs and productive technologies make these processes readily transferable to low-wage Third World countries. Although there is some evidence to support this argument, which also seems to conform with past trends, other analysts believe the technology will, at least in some cases, reverse this process and cause the repatriation of production to the developed countries as production technology becomes more sophisticated and capital-intensive.[31] According to this view, other factors, especially the need for better trained and educated workers, the costs of materials, and proximity to customers and supplies, will outweigh labor costs in concentrating production in the developed countries.[32] The proximity of suppliers and customers could also become especially critical as the new information technology permits rapid responses to changes in demand and greater customization to meet consumer needs. There also is a trend among American companies to establish closer symbiotic relationships with suppliers who are able to customize, gain economies of scale, and undertake research and development to improve components, equipment, and processes. In addition, changes in production technology give an advantage to the close integration of design, production, and marketing.

In the 1980s, economic stagnation, debt problems, and political instability in many Third World countries make them less attractive as places for multinationals to locate manufacturing facilities. At the same time, developments in materials and chemicals production apparently have reduced the demand for primary products, which, in addition to low wages, was the chief advantage of locating in Third World countries. In this connection, however, the great diversity among developing countries must be noted. Some of the NICs, especially those in Asia, will continue to challenge the industrial countries because of the heavy emphasis they place on national human resource development. But poorer developing countries face some serious dilemmas in their policy choices concerning technological development. If they introduce technology to improve productivity and profits, they displace labor into labor markets that already have high levels of underemployment. If they do not introduce the technology, their products are not likely to be competitive in international markets, even at very low wages.

### The Labor Markets Linkage

Labor markets have not been as internationalized as financial, commodity, and manufactures markets, but they, too, have become more integrated by improvements in transportation and communication. Although economists traditionally have assumed labor to be an immobile factor of production, workers have always migrated in response to income and employment opportunities. Some consider the postwar economic "miracle" in Europe, especially in Germany, to be due in some significant measure to the labor market flexibility made possible by the importation of "guest workers" from Eastern and Southern Europe.

Migrant workers' remittances to their home countries have been an important source of foreign exchange for some countries. Between 1970 and 1980, these remittances increased at an annual rate of about 26.5 per cent. Worker remittances to the developing countries were only $3 billion in 1970 but had reached $24 billion by 1980. By 1982, it was estimated that such remittances to the middle-income oil-importing countries amounted to 34 per cent of these countries' current account deficits.[33] Worldwide, in the late 1970s, there were an estimated 20 million migrant workers, some 12 million of whom were from the developing countries. These migrants were heavily concentrated in certain regions: North America, 6 million; the Middle East, 3 million; and Western Europe, 5 million.

In the case of the United States, some estimates show that immigrants accounted for one-third of U.S. labor force growth during 1965-1985, and immigration is expected to play a larger role in the 1990s.[34] Leon Bouvier has observed that "immigration now appears to be almost as important as fertility insofar as U.S. population growth is concerned."[35]

For the United States, the most important labor market linkage is with Mexico, although immigration from other countries, especially from Asia, also has increased. As noted earlier, there are indications that immigration pressures from Mexico are likely to increase despite the U.S. Immigration Reform Act of 1986. It has been estimated that Mexico's 1980 population of over 70 million will double by the year 2000, and that a total of 31 to 33 million jobs will have to be created in Mexico over that period in order to (a) accommodate all new entrants into the labor force; (b) absorb the recent arrears of unemployed and underemployed into productive full-time employment, and (c) retain those who would otherwise migrate to the United States.[36] Even if Mexico were to regain its 1970s growth rate of 6.6 per cent a year (which it is unlikely to attain again in the 1980s), only some 20 million new jobs would be created by the end of the century, leaving a sizable deficit. It must also be recognized that no matter how many new jobs are created in Mexico by the year 2000, the real-wage differential between Mexico and the United States will draw workers across the border.

The flow of immigrants from Mexico and other developing countries into the United States is likely to continue despite efforts to control it. In a more competitive world with large (though diminishing) wage differentials, stagnating job growth, and high levels of Third World joblessness, the push and pull forces of labor supply and demand will be very strong. The demand for unskilled workers in the developed countries probably will diminish because of increasing skill requirements and the displacement of workers with limited skills and education. The rate of immigration will depend on overall economic developments in the developed and developing countries.

# Recommendations

The current high levels of global underemployment, joblessness, and poverty are very serious problems—particularly in the Third World. In most developing countries, barring dramatic improvements in the world economy, joblessness and poverty will get worse over the next 20 years. Third World joblessness is now 40–50 per cent, and many of those who do have jobs have very low incomes. Moreover, at least 600 million jobs—more than presently exist in all industrial market economies combined—will have to be created in the developing countries over the next 20 years just to keep joblessness from rising.

Although employment conditions in the developed countries are much better than in the Third World, they are not good relative to the 1960s and 1970s. Even in the United States, where job growth has been faster than in any other developed country, real wages have been stagnant since 1973, and between 1980 and 1986, unemployment averaged 7.5 per cent compared with 6.1 per cent during the 1970s. There are, moreover, deep pockets of structural unemployment in all of the developed countries. Unemployment in the developed countries not only creates serious human and economic problems but also makes those countries less willing either to promote an open and expanding trading system or to provide the kinds of financial resources needed to stimulate mutually beneficial economic development in the Third World. There is therefore a danger of a negative, degenerating world economy unless proper actions are taken to reverse the trends.

But there is also a positive side to these trends. The slowdown in work force growth in the United States and other industrialized countries will require lower rates of job growth to keep unemployment down. Indeed, growth rates like those of the 1960s could produce labor shortages in the developed countries.

### U.S.-Third World Policies

The United States must develop a comprehensive strategy for addressing the interrelated issues of immigration, technology transfer, trade, and development issues.

*Facilitate immigration.* It will be in the economic and political interest of the developed countries to permit higher levels of immigration from the developing countries, but these flows should be legal and carefully regulated to prevent adverse impact on low-wage American workers, who are the principal losers from immigration—and for whom employment and income prospects are not very bright even without higher levels of immigration. However, immigration must be considered in an international context. Job shortages in Third World countries during the 1980s and 1990s will create enormous pressures for both economic development and emigration to the more developed countries. In a world where most other industrial countries have greatly restricted immigration, most of those migration pressures are likely to be concentrated on relatively open countries like the United States. If competitive industries in developed countries require workers with higher skills, these countries will face serious problems if they have large numbers of unskilled, uneducated workers. Careful attention should, however, also be given to avoiding the adverse impact of immigration on the developing countries. Many of these countries already have serious shortages of highly skilled technical and professional workers. The best policy would be to try to help these countries make the human capital investments to produce the people needed for growing economies—assuming, of course, that international economic policies make it possible to promote an open and growing international economy. If, however, growth in developing countries is not sufficient to keep highly skilled workers or educated professionals employed—as is apparently the present situation in China and India—unemployed or underemployed workers should be encouraged to migrate to areas where these skills are in short supply.

*Strengthen international labor rights.* One way to see to it that Third World workers benefit from economic development and from foreign investment is to include internationally accepted labor standards in trade rules. Such rules include: freedom of association and collective bargaining; the prohibition of forced labor; a minimum age for employment; and acceptable standards for wages, hours, and occupational safety and health. These standards would not equalize wages or other conditions of employment, but they could make it possible for Third World workers to improve their situation. Moreover, with rising real wages, Third World countries could become a larger source of rising aggregate demand to stimulate the global economy. In addition, minimum labor standards reduce worker opposition to trade, strengthen management, and promote human resource development. In the absence of rules, companies could gain competitive advantages through substandard labor conditions. The logic of the market thus dictates a kind of Gresham's law of labor standards—bad standards tend to drive out the good. And while critics object to these measures as "protectionist," standards actually do what free-traders claim for free markets—they make it possible for everyone to benefit from exchange. In the absence of acceptable rules, in contrast, some people are able to gain at the expense of others. Critics also argue that we should not impose our labor standards on the rest of the world, but these standard worker protections have all been accepted overwhelmingly by the International Labour Organization.

## Need for a U.S. Consensus in Support of a Global Strategy

High priority should be given to building a *national* consensus for an employment-oriented global development strategy. Such a process could increase attention to international issues on the U.S. agenda and provide more and better information about the global economy and the altered role of the United States in that economy. Too many of our policies are now based on ideas rooted in earlier times, when our economic problems were very different and the United States was both more powerful relative to other nations and less dependent on international transactions. Before policies can change, both policymakers and the public must be provided with more and better information on the profound changes that are taking place in the world economy.

The consensus-building process for an employment-oriented global strategy might be guided by the following objectives:

*Avoid unilateralism.* If the United States wants to establish the institutions, policies, and mechanisms required to improve its own economic performance and to help create a widely beneficial global system, it must seek greater international economic cooperation, at least with the major industrialized and developing countries. In the present international economic climate, unilateralism on major economic policies is not only inappropriate, but often counterproductive.

*Adjust macroeconomic policy.* Before the United States can participate more effectively in international economic affairs, it must put its own economic house in better order. This will necessarily entail a number of measures, especially the development of a long-range strategy to reduce the federal budget deficit and bring down real interest rates. There also is a great need to give less attention to consumption—and more attention to strengthening both productivity and our production base.

*Develop human resources.* In a world where capital and technology are very mobile, the surest ways for any country to promote its national economic welfare are to develop its people and assure low levels of joblessness. Besides greater attention to health care, education, and job training, a human resource development strategy requires an adjustment program to shift resources from non-competitive to competitive activities. Current U.S. adjustment programs are not adequate in terms of either resources or processes, but experience in many countries suggests that effective adjustment requires adequate advance notice of major layoffs and plant closings; a feasible and comprehensive array of services to displaced workers, communities, and companies regardless of the causes of displacement; and mechanisms to permit labor, management, community, and government representatives to participate in the development and implementation of such programs. Of course the best approach to adjustment would be to have a well-educated work force adequately prepared to deal with change. The lack of basic skills has been an important obstacle to the adjustment of displaced workers in the United States.

## U.S. Competitiveness

Competitiveness is achieved by producing quality products at low prices. This, in turn, requires attention to quality, productivity, and flexibility to adjust to change. To avoid a painful compression of U.S. wages, U.S. competitiveness must be improved through management systems, technology, and public policy.

*Management systems.* Quality and productivity are mainly the consequence of management systems, technological innovation, and the quality of human resources (i.e., workers, enterpreneurs, and managers). Because the United States is an older industrial society, it has many obsolete management systems rooted in earlier, mainly national, mass-production systems. These older systems emphasized sophisticated equipment and processes and unsophisticated workers—precisely the kinds of activities most transferable to the Third World. The Japanese and some newer high-tech U.S. companies have established systems that depend on high-quality human resources and advanced technology. These more sophisticated systems require, in addition, a high degree of employee involvement in production decisions. The development of these highly competitive production systems in Japan and other countries has forced U.S. companies either to transform their own systems or to become non-competitive.

*Technology.* As noted earlier, the key to competitiveness in the U.S. system for the foreseeable future is the development and use of advanced technology. The more sophisticated technology is required for capital goods that, in turn, require large global markets for optimal economies of scale. This is an additional reason why the United States has a major stake in an open and expanding trading system.

*Public policy.* Public policies also are major determinants of competitiveness. Unfortunately, this is an area where the United States has serious disadvantages. Our policy processes, like many U.S. management systems, are obsolete. They are geared to goods-producing economies and are therefore incompatible with the requirements of an internationalized information economy. In particular, our processes are too adversarial, uncoordinated, and ideologically based. The consequences are excessive waste on litigation, uncertainty, and economic instability, all of which detract from the profitability of American enterprises that must compete against foreign enterprises whose operations rely upon consensus-based management. We also have no coherent global economic strategy and therefore tend to adopt unilateral policies based on short-run domestic political concerns, with little, if any, consideration for the impact of those policies on the competitiveness of American companies, the interests of people in other countries, or our our own long-run self-interest.[37]

Interdependencies between developed and developing countries present all countries with serious challenges as well as important opportunities. If the dangers are not averted, the international economic system could experience degenerating crises that could not be successfully managed by present institutions and policies. Such crises would undoubtedly force U.S. and other world political leaders to assign higher priority to both North-South economic relations and the need to develop consensus for new institutions, rules, and policies.

On the positive side, the competitiveness of the developed countries has been considerably strengthened since 1973. Inflation has been brought under control. There is a substantial backlog of technology that could form the basis for new industries, jobs, and economic growth. And there are considerable commonalities between the economic interests of the developed and developing countries. The leadership challenge is to avoid the crises and take advantage of the opportunities.

## Notes

[1] Population Reference Bureau, unpublished data.

[2] Paul Demeny, "The World Demographic Situation," in Jane Menken, ed., *World Population and U.S. Policy* (New York: W.W. Norton and Company, 1986), pp. 42–43.

[3] Omatunde E.G. Johnson, "Labor Markets, External Developments, and Unemployment in Developing Countries," in *Staff Studies for the World Economic Outlook*, Research Department, International Monetary Fund, July 1986, pp. 52–53.

[4] International Labour Office, *World Labor Report* (1984), p. 2.

[5] Ibid.

[6] Ibid.

[7] Yves Sabalo, "Industrialization, Exports, and Unemployment," *International Labour Review* (July-August 1980), pp. 481–495.

[8] See David E. Bloom and Richard B. Freeman, "The Effects of Rapid Population Growth on Labor Supply and Employment in Developing Countries," *Population and Development Review* (September 1986), pp. 381–414.

[9] Jacques Lesourne and Robert L. McNamara, *Facilitating Development in a Changing Third World* (New York: The Trilateral Commission, 1983).

[10] Susan P. Joekes, *Industrialization, Trade and Female Employment in Developing Countries: Experiences of the 1970s and After* (New York: U.N. International Research and Training Institute for the Advancement of Women, mimeo.), p. 3.

[11] Theodore Schultz, *Investing in People: The Economics of Population Quality* (Berkeley: University of California Press, 1981), pp. xi. and 160.

[12] Inter-American Development Bank, "Labor Force and Employment," in *Economic and Social Progress in Latin America* (1987 Report).

[13] Ibid.

[14] Leon F. Bouvier and Robert Gardner, *Immigration to the U.S. The Unfinished Story* (Washington, D.C.: Population Reference Bureau, Inc., 1986), p. 45.

[15] OECD (unpublished data).

[16] Stephen S. Cohen and John Zysman, *Manufacturing Matters: The Myth of the Post-Industrial Economy* (New York: Basic Books, 1987).

[17] Bureau of Labor Statistics, unpublished data; and William B. Johnston, *Workforce 2000* (Indianapolis: Hudson Institute, 1987).

[18] Johnston, *Workforce 2000*, op cit, p. 80.

[19] Bureau of Labor Statistics, op. cit., and Johnston, *Workforce 2000*, op. cit.

[20] Ibid.

[21] Vernon M. Briggs, Jr., "The Growth and Composition of the Work Force," *Science* (August 1987), p. 186.

[22] Bouvier and Gardner, *Immigration to the U.S.*, op. cit., p. 45.

[23] William B. Johnston, *Workforce 2000*, op. cit.

[24] Bela Balassa, "Trends in International Trade in Manufactured Goods and Structural Changes in the Industrial Countries," *World Bank Staff Paper*, 611, 1984.

[25] G. Renshaw, *Employment, Trade, and North-South Cooperation* (Geneva: International Labour Office, 1981).

[26] UNIDO, *Industry and Development: Global Report 1986* (Vienna: UNIDO, 1986). The "North" is defined as Canada, the United States, Western Europe, Eastern Europe, the U.S.S.R., and Japan. The "South" is Latin America, Tropical Africa, North Africa, West Asia, the Indian subcontinent, Southeast Asia, and China.

[27] Ibid., pp. 110–111.

[28] Ibid., p. 63.

[29] John W. Sewell and Stuart K. Tucker, "Swamped by Debt: U.S. Trade with the NICs," in Thornton F. Bradshaw et al., eds., *America's New Competitors* (Cambridge: Ballinger Publishing Co., 1987), pp. 188–192.

[30] See C.F. Sabel, *Work and Politics: The Division of Labor in Industry* (New York: Cambridge University Press, 1982).

[31] See *Fortune*, June 11, 1984, p. 152; *Electronic Business* (February 1984), p. 178.

[32] See S. Jacobbson and J. Sigurdson, eds., *Technological Trends and Challenges in Electronics: Dominance of the Industrialized World and Response of the Third World* (Lund, Sweden: University of Lund, Research Policy Institute, 1983).

[33] *The Economist*, December 8, 1984.

[34] Briggs, "The Growth and Composition of the Work Force," op. cit., p. 147.

[35] Leon Bouvier, *The Impact of Immigration on the Size of the U.S. Population* (Washington, D.C.: Population Reference Bureau, 1981), p. 23.

[36] Wayne A. Cornelius, "Immigration, Development Policy and Future U.S.-Mexican Relations," in Robert H. McBride, ed., *Mexico and the United States* (Englewood Cliffs, N.J.: Prentice-Hall, 1981), p. 108.

[37] See Peter G. Peterson, "The Morning After," in *Atlantic Monthly* (October 1987) for an analysis of the failings of recent policies.

# Statistical Annexes U.S.-Third World Interdependence

Stuart K. Tucker with
Carey Durkin Treado

# Statistical Annexes

# Statistical Note

In these *Agenda 1988* Statistical Annexes, countries are classified as "developed" or "developing" on the basis of both their per capita GNP and their Physical Quality of Life Index (PQLI). The PQLI was developed by the Overseas Development Council in the late 1970s in response to the need for a non-income measurement that summarizes many aspects of well-being. It is a composite index of three indicators—infant mortality, life expectancy at age one, and literacy. Each of the components is indexed on a scale of 0 (the worst performance in 1950) to 100 (the best performance expected by the end of the century—as estimated in 1978). For life expectancy at age one, the best figure expected to be achieved by any country by the year 2000 (77 years) is equivalent to 100, and the worst performance in 1950 (38 years in Guinea-Bissau) is 0. Similarly, for infant mortality, the best performance expected by the year 2000 (7 per thousand) is rated 100, and the poorest performance in 1950 (229 per thousand in Gabon) is set at 0. Literacy figures (as percentages) are automatically on a 0 to 100 scale. The composite index, the PQLI, is calculated by averaging the three indices (life expectancy, infant mortality, and literacy), giving equal weight to each component.[1]

The "developed" countries are those having both a 1985 per capita income of $4,130 or more *and* a PQLI of 90 or above. On the basis of these criteria, not all "high-income" countries qualify as "developed"; the thirty-two that do are so specified in Table D-1.

The term "developing" countries refers to the 144 countries in Table D-1 with 1985 per capita incomes of less than $4,130 and/or PQLIs of less than 90. Although Barbados, Brunei, Hong Kong, Netherlands Antilles, Singapore, and Trinidad and Tobago all have per capita GNPs in excess of $4,150 and PQLIs of at least 90, they have been included in the developing category; these six countries are considered by the ODC to be in transition from developing to developed status and are classified as "advanced developing countries."

The various agencies that are the sources of the data provided in these Statistical Annexes differ in their classifications of countries. The World Bank, the U.N. Conference on Trade and Development (UNCTAD), the U.S. Agency for International Development, and the Development Assistance Committee (DAC) of the Organisation for Economic Co-operation and Development do not in all instances agree as to whether a particular country should be classified as developed or developing. Inclusion of a country in one category or the other often depends on the purposes of the compiling organization. For example, the DAC list of developing countries includes all countries, territories, or other geopolitical entities that receive official development assistance or other resource flows from DAC members; thus Portugal was classified as developed while it was a member of DAC, but has been classified as developing since leaving DAC and becoming a recipient of aid from DAC members. U.N. trade data, to cite another example, are compiled according to the statistically convenient breakdown of developed market economies, developing market economies, and centrally planned economies—categories for the most part retained in those Annex A charts that are based on U.N. sources. The various agencies also differ in their definitions of Greece, Portugal, Spain, Turkey, Yugoslavia, and Israel as developed or developing. Thus UNCTAD considers all of these countries except Turkey to be developed while the World Bank and DAC designate all of them except Spain as developing. The various agencies also differ as to the placement of individual countries in regional and other classifications. Such discrepancies in agency practice are reflected in tables and figures throughout these Statistical Annexes that draw on these agencies as data sources. Thus the World Bank includes Cyprus and Turkey in Europe, while the Population Reference Bureau considers them part of Asia. And while both DAC and the IMF classify some nations as "non-oil developing countries" they differ as to the country composition of this group; DAC includes all non-OPEC developing nations in this category. The IMF, in contrast, determines whether or not a country is in the "non-oil" grouping on the basis of certain oil-export criteria—one of which is whether or not a country's oil exports accounted for at least two-thirds of its total exports during 1978-80. Countries that do not meet these criteria are included in the IMF's non-oil group—even if they are net oil exporters; thus Mexico is a "non-oil" country, as are some members of OPEC. These Statistical Annexes adhere to the IMF classification of non-oil developing countries.

In addition, these Annexes classify "centrally planned economies" in Asia as developing countries and centrally planned economies in Europe as industrial countries. It should be noted that in these Annexes, aggregate data for South America, Central America, the Caribbean, and Mexico is labeled "Latin America."

Small statistical discrepancies in the tables, unless otherwise explained, are due to the rounding of data. An entry of "n.a." signifies that information was not available. Dashes (—) indicate that amounts are negligible or less than the smallest unit. Average annual growth rates are compounded growth rates. Figures identified with the dollar sign ($) are in U.S. dollars.

---

[1]For a more extensive discussion of the PQLI, See Morris D. Morris, *Measuring the Condition of the World's Poor: The Physical Quality of Life Index* (New York: Pergamon Press, for the Overseas Development Council, 1979).

# Glossary

**Agency for International Development (AID).** The U.S. government agency that administers the U.S. bilateral economic assistance program.

**Balance of payments.** A summary of all international transactions (the sum total of the current account, capital account, and errors and omissions) undertaken by a country during a given period of time.

**Bank of International Settlements (BIS).** Established in Basel, Switzerland, in 1930 to aid in the handling of German reparations and loan payments and in fostering cooperation among the major central banks.

**Bilateral assistance.** Economic or military assistance provided directly by one country to another. The U.S. bilateral economic aid program, for instance, consists primarily of development assistance, Economic Support Fund aid, and P.L. 480 food aid.

**Capital account.** A component of the balance of payments that expresses net flows of international assets, primarily loans, purchases and sales of foreign stocks and bonds, and foreign direct investment.

**Centrally planned economies.** In these Statistical Annexes, the "centrally planned economies" are the Eastern European economies whose dominant characteristic is government ownership and control of the factors of production: Albania, Bulgaria, Czechoslovakia, the German Democratic Republic, Hungary, Poland, Romania, and the U.S.S.R. The Asian centrally planned economies—the People's Republic of China, Mongolia, the Democratic Republic of Korea, and Vietnam—are here classified as developing countries.

**Current account.** A component of the balance of payments that expresses net exports and imports of merchandise goods, services, investment income, and unilateral transfers.

**Current and constant dollars.** Values expressed in current dollars reflect prices current in the period indicated. Current dollar values thus may rise or fall in a particular year simply because of price changes. Values expressed in constant dollars reflect prices prevailing in a single base year and are called "real values", because price changes are offset.

**Customs, insurance, and freight (c.i.f.) import value.** The value of imports plus freight, insurance, and other charges (excluding import duties) incurred in bringing the merchandise from the country of exportation to the first port of arrival at the country of importation.

**Debt-service ratio.** Ratio of interest and principal payments due in a year to exports for the year.

**Deflator.** An index of relative price change that is divided into current values to yield real values.

**Development assistance.** Economic aid extended bilaterally or multi-laterally for the purpose of promoting development.

**Development Assistance Committee (DAC).** A specialized committee of the Organisation for Economic Co-operation and Development (OECD) that monitors development assistance levels and policies, as well as relations between developed and developing countries. Eighteen of the 24 members of the OECD serve on the DAC (Greece, Iceland, Luxembourg, Portugal, Spain, and Turkey are not members).

**Direct investment abroad.** Equity ownership in a foreign firm or enterprise, implying significant managerial control. According to the U.S. government, a private U.S. investment abroad is considered direct if a single U.S. resident, or an affiliated group of U.S. residents, owns "at least 10 per cent of the voting securities (or the equivalent) of a foreign business enterprise." If not, the investment is deemed "portfolio" investment.

**Economic Support Fund (ESF).** U.S. economic assistance extended to countries on the basis of special U.S. economic, political, or security needs and interests. The ESF used to be called Security Support Assistance.

**Free-alongside-ship (f.a.s.) export value.** Value of goods at the port of exportation, based on the transaction price, including inland freight, insurance, and other charges incurred in placing the merchandise alongside the carrier at the port of exportation.

**Free-on-board (f.o.b.) export value.** Value of goods on the carrier at the port of exportation, based on the transaction price, including inland freight, insurance, and other charges incurred in placing the merchandise on the carrier at the port of exportation.

**Foreign exchange.** Financial assets used in carrying out international economic transactions. The sources of foreign exchange that a country can draw upon to make international payments—foreign currency, gold, Special Drawing Rights (SDRs), or other assets that can be converted readily into foreign exchange—are collectively known as that nation's international reserves.

**General Agreement on Tariffs and Trade (GATT).** The multilateral treaty, subscribed to by 96 governments, that lays down rules for international trade. As an institution, GATT functions as the principal body concerned with negotiating the reduction of trade barriers and with international trade relations.

**Gross domestic product (GDP).** The total market value of all final goods and services produced during a given period by all factors of production that earn income within a country. GDP includes income earned by foreigners within a country but excludes income earned abroad by that country's citizens and corporations.

**Gross national product (GNP).** The total market value of all final goods and services produced in a particular country during a given period. GNP includes income earned abroad by that country's citizens and corporations but excludes income earned by foreigners in the country concerned.

**International Monetary Fund (IMF).** The multilateral financial institution that oversees the management of international financial exchange and liquidity, facilitates agreement on changes in the international monetary system, allocates additional international reserves in the form of Special Drawing Rights (SDRs), and provides loans to member countries for several purposes, but primarily to ameliorate the effects of temporary balance-of-payments deficits.

**Labor force.** Includes both a) the civilian labor force, comprised of all non-institutional population who are sixteen years old and seeking employment, and b) the armed forces.

**Long-term debt.** Debt that matures (is due) in over one year's time.

**Multilateral assistance.** Economic assistance provided to developing countries through multilateral development banks and other international organizations.

**Official development assistance (ODA).** ODA is defined by DAC as "those flows to developing countries and multilateral institutions provided by official agencies . . . which meet the following test: a) it is administered with the promotion of economic development and welfare of developing countries as its main objective, and b) it is concessional in character and contains a grant element of at least 25 per cent." ODA consists of soft (low-interest) bilateral loans, bilateral grants, and multilateral flows in the form of grants, capital subscriptions, and concessional loans to multilateral agencies.

**ODA commitments.** Obligations to provide assistance to recipient countries under specified terms. Funds may be committed in one year but not disbursed until future years.

**ODA disbursements.** The actual international transfer of financial resources associated with development assistance. Gross disbursements minus repayments on prior loans equal "net disbursements" or "net flows".

**ODA grants.** Resource flows to developing countries, in money or in kind requiring no repayment.

**Organisation for Economic Co-operation and Development (OECD).** The organization of Western industrialized nations designed to promote economic growth and stability in member countries and to contribute to the development of the world economy. Member countries of the OECD are Australia, Austria, Belgium, Canada, Denmark, Finland, France, the Federal Republic of Germany, Greece, Iceland, Ireland, Italy, Japan, Luxembourg, the Netherlands, New Zealand, Norway, Portugal, Spain, Sweden, Switzerland, Turkey, the United Kingdom, and the United States.

**Organization of Petroleum Exporting Countries (OPEC).** An organization devoted to seeking agreement among producers regarding selling prices and other matters relating to oil exports. Includes Algeria, Ecuador, Gabon, Indonesia, Iran, Iraq, Kuwait, Libya, Nigeria, Qatar, Saudi Arabia, the United Arab Emirates, and Venezuela.

**Newly industrializing countries (NICs).** Those relatively advanced developing countries that have fast-growing income and industrial diversification. There is no widely accepted definition of this category of countries. However, six countries are almost always considered to be among the NICs: Brazil, Hong Kong, Mexico, Republic of Korea, Singapore, and Taiwan. Some other sources variously consider the NICs to include some of the following: Argentina, India, People's Republic of China, Portugal, South Africa, Turkey, and Yugoslavia.

**P.L. 480 (Food for Peace Program).** The objectives of the P.L. 480 program established in 1954 as the U.S. government's program of food assistance and administered jointly by AID and the U.S. Department of Agriculture—are the provision of humanitarian food aid, the furtherance of international economic development, the expansion of U.S. agricultural and commercial export markets, and the promotion of U.S. political interests.

**Security assistance.** Economic or military aid extended to countries on the basis of U.S. strategic and political interests.

**Short-term debt.** Debt that reaches maturity (is fully due) within one year's time.

**Special drawing rights (SDRs).** International liquidity and reserves created and managed by the IMF, valued on the basis of a basket of currencies, and designed to replace gold and the U.S. dollar as the principal international reserve assets. Constituting claims on the IMF, SDRs may be exchanged for convertible currencies to settle international official transactions.

**Terms-of-trade.** The ratio of export prices to import prices. If, for instance, a country's export prices rise relative to its import prices—a terms-of-trade improvement—this means that it can buy a greater quantity of imports for any given quantity of exports. Similarly, if export prices fall relative to import prices—a terms-of-trade deterioration—this means that a country can buy a lesser quantity of imports for any given quantity of exports.

**World Bank Group.** International financial institutions providing intermediate- and long-term loans for economic development purposes. The World Bank Group consists of the International Bank for Reconstruction and Development (IBRD—or commonly, World Bank), which extends nonconcessional loans; the International Development Association (IDA), which extends concessional loans; and the International Finance Corporation (IFC), which extends loans for projects involving the private sector.

ANNEX A

# The Changing Structure of Global Trade

*In the early 1980s, global recession, rising protectionism, and the debt crisis combined to compress trade. Since 1984, the world recovery has given some impetus for renewed trade growth, but, compared to the robust 1970s, trade has not grown significantly either in value or in volume in recent years. During the 1980s, global trade imbalances became accentuated, ushering in an era of trade conflict. The United States ran trade deficits with 17 of its top 20 trading partners in 1986.*

*The collapse of commodity prices in the 1980s, coupled with the pressures of the debt crisis, forced many developing countries to resort to manufactured exports to industrial countries for their foreign exchange revenues. In the 1980s, developing countries continued to increase their share of industrial-country manufactured imports, including high-technology goods. Much of this success, however, has been concentrated in a few newly industrializing countries (NICs). Meanwhile, with merchandise trade in trouble, services trade as a percentage of total trade increased.*

## A-1. World Exports: A Decline in Real Value in the 1980s ($ billions, constant 1980 and current)

*In current dollars, world exports surpassed the $2 trillion level and reached an historic high in 1986. But in real value (corrected for inflation), world exports have not returned to the level reached in 1980. The global recession of 1980-83 and the ongoing debt crisis have greatly slowed world trade.*

*($ billions, constant 1980)*

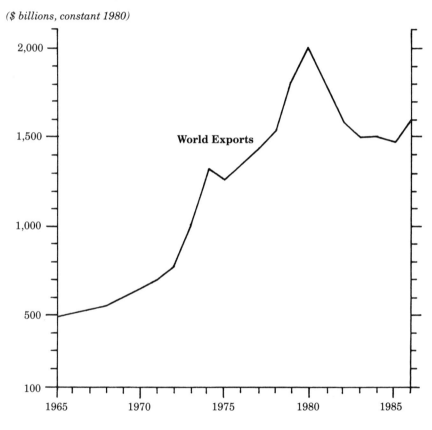

|  | 1965 | 1970 | 1975 | 1980 | 1983 | 1986 |
|---|---|---|---|---|---|---|
|  |  |  | *($ billions, current)* | | | |
| **World exports** | 186.5 | 312.0 | 872.7 | 2,002.0 | 1,813.5 | 2,133.0 |
| Share of world exports |  |  | *(percentages)* | | | |
|   Industrial countries | 68.9 | 71.9 | 66.1 | 66.3 | 64.1 | 69.0 |
|   Non-OPEC developing countries | 13.3 | 11.8 | 11.2 | 12.6 | 15.0 | 15.2 |
|   OPEC countries | 6.0 | 5.8 | 13.0 | 15.3 | 9.9 | 5.6 |
|   Centrally planned economies[a] | 11.7 | 10.5 | 9.7 | 8.8 | 11.0 | 10.2 |

[a]Includes Asian centrally planned developing economies as well as Eastern Europe.
    Sources: United Nations, *Monthly Bulletin of Statistics* (July 1981 and June 1986), Special Table B, and GATT, *International Trade 85-86*, Table A1.

# A-2. Volume of World Trade: Faltering in the 1980s (percentages)

*World trade volumes fell during the global recession of 1980-83 and rebounded only moderately. Projections for trade in 1987 and 1988 show growth considerably slower than during the 1970s.*

| | 1969–78[a] | 1979 | 1980 | 1981 | 1982 | 1983 | 1984 | 1985 | 1986 | 1987[b] | 1988[b] |
|---|---|---|---|---|---|---|---|---|---|---|---|
| | | | | | | | *(percentages)* | | | | |
| **World Trade Volume** | **6.7** | **6.4** | **1.2** | **0.7** | **-2.2** | **2.9** | **8.6** | **3.2** | **4.9** | **3.3** | **4.4** |
| **EXPORTS BY:** | | | | | | | | | | | |
| **Industrial Countries** | **7.3** | **7.2** | **3.9** | **3.7** | **-2.0** | **2.8** | **9.7** | **4.4** | **2.9** | **3.4** | **4.6** |
| United States | 6.8 | 14.1 | 9.8 | -1.6 | -10.9 | -3.8 | 7.5 | 1.6 | 7.8 | 12.7 | 13.4 |
| **Developing Countries** | **4.6** | **4.4** | **-4.2** | **-6.0** | **-7.6** | **3.2** | **7.1** | **1.0** | **8.2** | **2.8** | **5.8** |
| Fuel exporters | 3.2 | 1.9 | -13.5 | -15.1 | -16.2 | -3.2 | 0.5 | -5.7 | 9.8 | -0.4 | 4.6 |
| Non-fuel exporters | 6.1 | 6.9 | 8.5 | 5.2 | 1.1 | 8.2 | 11.6 | 5.2 | 7.7 | 3.9 | 6.2 |
| Africa | 3.1 | 8.4 | -1.2 | -14.9 | -5.1 | 3.4 | 5.6 | 7.1 | 2.2 | 1.6 | 3.9 |
| Asia | 10.8 | 9.0 | 8.8 | 8.5 | 1.1 | 10.7 | 13.6 | 5.0 | 17.1 | 6.1 | 6.3 |
| Europe | 3.3 | -1.7 | 3.9 | 3.1 | 1.7 | 8.3 | 13.4 | 4.2 | 2.4 | 3.2 | 4.9 |
| Middle East | 4.8 | 0.4 | -15.2 | -17.6 | -19.7 | -9.3 | -4.4 | -8.8 | 16.6 | -3.2 | 5.4 |
| Western Hemisphere | 1.7 | 7.6 | 1.2 | 6.0 | -2.4 | 8.2 | 8.5 | 0.0 | -8.8 | 0.1 | 7.2 |
| **IMPORTS BY:** | | | | | | | | | | | |
| **Industrial Countries** | **6.9** | **8.9** | **-1.6** | **-2.3** | **-0.3** | **4.8** | **12.4** | **5.0** | **8.9** | **4.3** | **4.6** |
| United States | 7.5 | 1.6 | -7.9 | 0.6 | -3.7 | 13.0 | 24.3 | 5.1 | 14.6 | 1.8 | 4.0 |

| Developing Countries | 7.2 | 3.5 | 7.3 | 7.8 | -4.0 | -2.4 | 1.8 | -0.2 | -3.1 | -0.2 | 2.9 |
|---|---|---|---|---|---|---|---|---|---|---|---|
| Fuel exporters | 15.0 | -4.6 | 13.4 | 18.7 | -1.5 | -10.2 | -6.1 | -11.7 | -21.5 | -12.2 | -1.1 |
| Non-fuel exporters | 4.8 | 7.4 | 4.9 | 3.2 | -5.2 | 1.7 | 5.3 | 4.5 | 3.9 | 3.3 | 4.0 |
| Africa | 7.2 | -3.5 | 8.7 | 11.3 | -8.1 | -10.1 | -0.4 | -7.3 | -11.0 | -4.0 | 1.6 |
| Asia | 8.6 | 12.3 | 9.5 | 7.2 | 0.9 | 8.3 | 5.3 | 7.4 | 4.3 | 4.9 | 4.3 |
| Europe | 1.3 | 0.0 | -2.5 | -1.4 | -8.3 | 2.6 | 6.7 | 6.1 | 5.6 | 2.8 | 4.4 |
| Middle East | 15.1 | -4.1 | 8.8 | 16.7 | 5.6 | -2.4 | -6.1 | -14.9 | -18.3 | -12.5 | -1.0 |
| Western Hemisphere | 6.4 | 8.3 | 9.7 | 3.5 | -17.8 | -22.5 | 2.8 | 2.2 | -4.8 | -0.8 | 2.4 |

[a] Annual average.
[b] IMF projection.
Source: IMF, *World Economic Outlook*, April 1987, Tables A20, A24, and A25.

## A-3. U.S. Exports: In Trouble in the 1980s ($ billions, constant 1980[a])

*U.S. exports fell dramatically during 1980-1983 after a decade of strong growth—particularly in U.S.-Third World exports. The limited growth regained since 1983 has been with industrial countries, not with the developing countries, whose demand for U.S. exports has stagnated under the burden of low growth and high debt.*

*($ billions, constant 1980)*

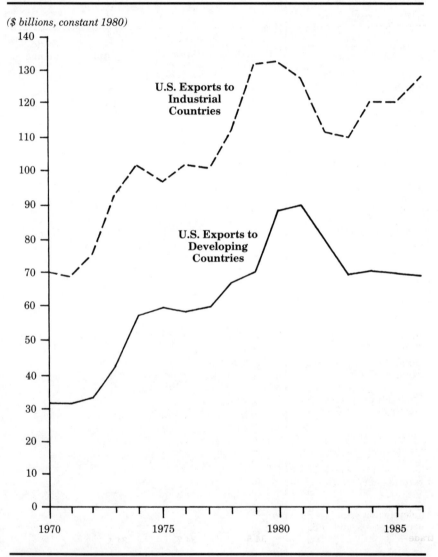

[a]Deflated by the U.S. export deflator.

Source: U.S. Department of Commerce, *Highlights of U.S. Export and Import Trade*, December issues, 1970-1986.

# A-4. Developing Countries Prominent Among Twenty Largest U.S. Trading Partners, 1986 ($ billions)

*The U.S. trade deficit is widely spread among its trade partners. In 1986, the United States ran trade deficits with 17 of its top 20 trade partners, nine of which are developing countries. The debt crisis has taken its toll on U.S.-Mexican trade, which dropped from third to fourth most important to the United States.*

| | Total Transactions | U.S. Exports | U.S. Imports | Trade Balance |
|---|---|---|---|---|
| | | *($ billions)* | | |
| Canada | 114.0 | 45.3 | 68.7 | −23.3 |
| Japan | 112.3 | 26.9 | 85.5 | −58.6 |
| Germany, Fed. Rep. | 36.7 | 10.6 | 26.1 | −15.6 |
| **Mexico** | **29.9** | **12.4** | **17.6** | **−5.2** |
| United Kingdom | 27.5 | 11.4 | 16.0 | −4.6 |
| **Taiwan** | **26.8** | **5.5** | **21.3** | **−15.7** |
| **Republic of Korea** | **19.9** | **6.4** | **13.5** | **−7.1** |
| France | 17.8 | 7.2 | 10.6 | −3.4 |
| Italy | 16.1 | 4.8 | 11.3 | −6.5 |
| **Hong Kong** | **12.5** | **3.0** | **9.5** | **−6.4** |
| Netherlands | 12.2 | 7.8 | 4.4 | 3.5 |
| **Brazil** | **11.2** | **3.9** | **7.3** | **−3.5** |
| Belgium and Luxembourg | 9.6 | 5.4 | 4.2 | 1.2 |
| **Venezuela** | **8.6** | **3.1** | **5.4** | **−2.3** |
| Australia | 8.4 | 5.6 | 2.9 | 2.7 |
| **China** | **8.3** | **3.1** | **5.2** | **−2.1** |
| Switzerland | 8.3 | 3.0 | 5.4 | −2.4 |
| **Singapore** | **8.3** | **3.4** | **4.9** | **−1.5** |
| **Saudi Arabia** | **7.5** | **3.4** | **4.1** | **−0.6** |
| Sweden | 6.5 | 1.9 | 4.6 | −2.8 |
| Total, twenty countries | 502.5 | 174.2 | 328.4 | −154.2 |
| **Total, nine developing countries** | **133.0** | **44.3** | **88.7** | **−44.5** |
| Total, all developing countries | 208.5 | 75.3 | 133.1 | −57.8 |
| Total U.S. Trade | 604.4 | 217.3 | 387.1 | −169.8 |
| | *(percentages)* | | | |
| Nine developing countries as a percentage of total U.S. trade | 22.0 | 20.4 | 22.9 | |
| All developing countries as a percentage of total U.S. trade | 34.5 | 34.7 | 34.4 | |

Note: Developing countries in bold type. Export figures are f.a.s.; import figures are c.i.f.
Source: U.S. Department of Commerce, *Highlights of U.S. Export and Import Trade*, December 1986, Tables B-22 and C-26.

## A-5. U.S. Trade with Developing Countries[a], by Region ($ millions)

*U.S. trade with Asian developing countries increased rapidly in the late 1970s. During the 1980s, however, U.S. export opportunities to all developing countries have been seriously blocked by slow growth.*

| | 1975 | | | 1981 | | | 1986 | | | Growth Rates[b] | | | |
| | | | | | | | | | | 1975–1981 | | 1981–1986 | |
| | U.S. Imports | U.S. Exports | Trade Balance | U.S. Imports | U.S. Exports | Trade Balance | U.S. Imports | U.S. Exports | Trade Balance | U.S. Imports | U.S. Exports | U.S. Imports | U.S. Exports |
| | ($ millions) | | | ($ millions) | | | ($ millions) | | | (percentages) | | (percentages) | |
|---|---|---|---|---|---|---|---|---|---|---|---|---|---|
| Asia | 11,462 | 10,400 | -1,063 | 38,315 | 27,061 | -11,254 | 68,617 | 29,235 | -39,382 | 22.3 | 17.3 | 12.4 | 1.6 |
| Latin America | 17,065 | 17,114 | 49 | 40,805 | 42,102 | 1,297 | 44,112 | 31,078 | -13,034 | 15.6 | 16.2 | 1.6 | -5.9 |
| Africa | 8,925 | 4,949 | -3,976 | 28,127 | 11,097 | -17,030 | 11,057 | 5,978 | -5,079 | 21.1 | 14.4 | -17.0 | -11.6 |
| Near East[c] | 5,779 | 6,743 | 964 | 18,300 | 12,443 | -5,857 | 8,594 | 8,415 | -179 | 21.2 | 10.8 | -14.0 | -7.5 |
| Europe[d] | 613 | 1,405 | 792 | 1,026 | 2,692 | 1,666 | 2,056 | 2,436 | 381 | 9.0 | 11.4 | 14.9 | -2.0 |
| Oceania | 135 | 112 | -23 | 191 | 272 | 81 | 110 | 227 | 116 | 6.0 | 15.9 | -10.4 | -3.6 |
| TOTAL | 43,979 | 40,723 | -3,257 | 126,764 | 95,667 | -31,097 | 134,546 | 77,370 | -57,176 | 19.3 | 15.3 | 1.2 | -4.2 |

Note: Export figures are f.a.s. transaction values; import figures are c.i.f.
[a] Excludes European centrally planned economies.
[b] Average annual growth rates.
[c] Excludes Israel.
[d] Includes Portugal and Turkey.

Sources: U.S. Department of Commerce, *Highlights of U.S. Export and Import Trade*, December 1975, Tables E-3 and I-4B; December 1981, Tables E-3 and I-6; December 1986, Tables B-22 and C-26.

## A-6. U.S. Services and Merchandise Trade Balances with Developing Countries: Both Down in the 1980s ($ billions)

*The positive effect of U.S. services trade with developing countries on the U.S. current account balance[a] began to wane in the 1980s, and the services balance surplus fell at the same time that the U.S. merchandise balance worsened.*

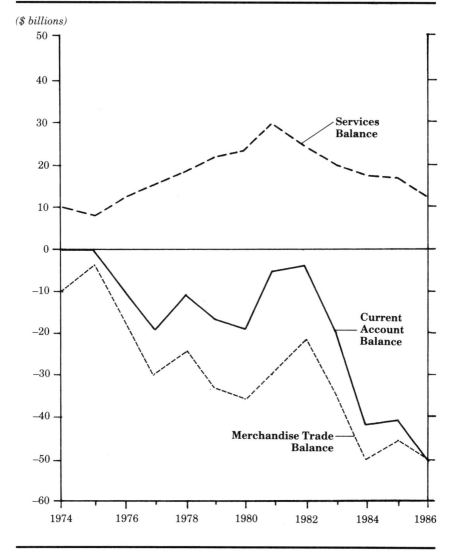

($ billions)

[a]Sum of balances on trade, services, and asset income, and unilateral transfers.

Source: U.S. Department of Commerce, *Survey of Current Business*, March editions, 1975-1987.

# A-7. Expansion in South-South Trade, 1970-1986 (percentages)

*Although it is still a small portion of world trade (6.9 per cent), developing-country trade with other developing countries has grown rapidly during the 1980s to compensate for weak demand and protectionism in industrial countries.*

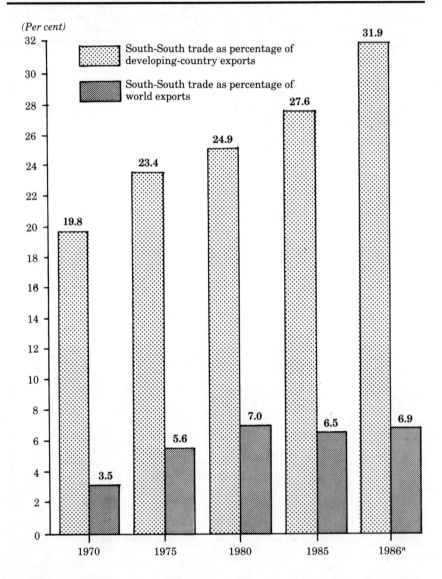

(Per cent)

South-South trade as percentage of developing-country exports

South-South trade as percentage of world exports

ᵃBased on first half of 1986.
Source: United Nations, *Monthly Bulletin of Statistics* (June and December 1986), Table B.

# A-8.  U.S. Imports of Manufactures: A Dramatic Rise
## ($ billions and percentages)

*The share of manufactures in U.S. imports rose from 59 per cent in 1983 to 71.8 per cent in 1986. During the same period, imports from the industrial countries have captured a larger share of the U.S. market.*

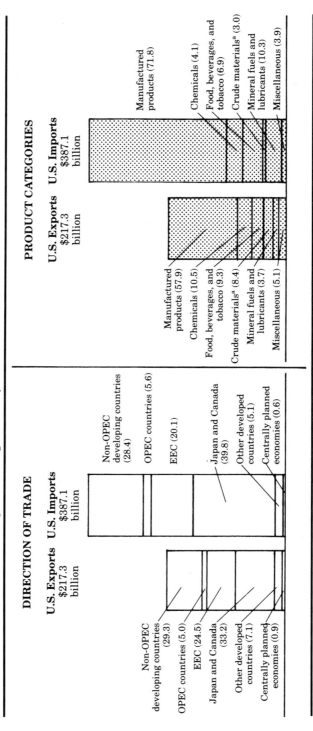

Note: Export figues are f.a.s. and import figures are c.i.f. Figures do not add up to 100 per cent due to statistical discrepancies in source data.
[a]Includes animal and vegetable oils and fats and inedible crude materials (except fuels).
Source: U.S. Department of Commerce, *Highlights of U.S. Export and Import Trade* (December 1986), Tables B-3, B-5, C-6, C-8.

# A-9. U.S. Trade with Developing Countries ($ billions and percentages)

*U.S. export and import trade with developing countries—which in recent years accounted for over 40 per cent of total U.S. trade—was down to 34 per cent of U.S. trade by 1986. The decline has been particularly evident in U.S. exports of autos and consumer goods.*

| | Total U.S. Trade ($ billions) | | | U.S. Trade with Developing Countries, as Share of Total U.S. Trade[a] (percentages) | | |
|---|---|---|---|---|---|---|
| | 1975 | 1981 | 1986 | 1975 | 1981 | 1986 |
| **EXPORTS[b]** | | | | | | |
| **Total** | **107.7** | **233.7** | **212.9** | **38.2** | **41.1** | **34.2** |
| Food, feeds, and beverages | 19.1 | 37.9 | 22.2 | 35.0 | 41.2 | 40.1 |
| Fuels | 4.8 | 10.7 | 8.2 | 15.3 | 19.5 | 30.5 |
| Other industrial supplies | 25.4 | 57.0 | 49.3 | 39.3 | 40.4 | 37.8 |
| Capital goods | 35.4 | 80.2 | 76.6 | 43.0 | 45.1 | 38.2 |
| Automotive goods | 10.1 | 18.0 | 22.1 | 27.4 | 33.7 | 17.7 |
| Consumer goods | 6.5 | 15.8 | 14.1 | 35.6 | 44.3 | 35.6 |
| Other | 6.4 | 14.1 | 20.5 | 53.3 | 42.9 | 22.9 |
| **IMPORTS[c]** | | | | | | |
| **Total** | **103.4** | **273.4** | **370.0** | **42.4** | **45.8** | **33.8** |
| Food, feeds, and beverages | 10.5 | 19.7 | 24.2 | 59.0 | 56.5 | 55.5 |
| Fuels | 28.4 | 85.1 | 38.5 | 79.5 | 79.7 | 67.5 |
| Other industrial supplies | 24.1 | 55.6 | 63.4 | 24.6 | 25.4 | 24.5 |
| Capital goods | 10.1 | 35.5 | 76.3 | 18.6 | 24.7 | 25.3 |
| Automotive goods | 12.8 | 31.0 | 78.6 | 2.1 | 3.3 | 7.8 |
| Consumer goods | 14.7 | 40.6 | 78.4 | 43.1 | 51.4 | 54.1 |
| Other | 2.8 | 5.8 | 10.6 | 23.7 | 24.4 | 20.8 |

[a] Israel is included; Oceania, Turkey, Portugal, and developing centrally planned economies in Europe are omitted from developing countries' share.
[b] Exports are f.a.s. values.
[c] Imports are c.i.f. values except for 1986 imports, which are customs values.

Sources: U.S. Department of Commerce, *Highlights of U.S. Export and Import Trade* (December 1975), Tables E-7 and I-8C; (December 1981), Tables E-7 and I-13; and (December 1986), Tables B-18 and C-20.

## A-10. Commodity Prices: A Continuing Decline (index: 1980 = 100)

*Due to the commodity price collapse in recent years, many developing countries—still dependent on commodities for a large portion of their income—have suffered severe revenue declines.*

*(index: 1980 = 100)*

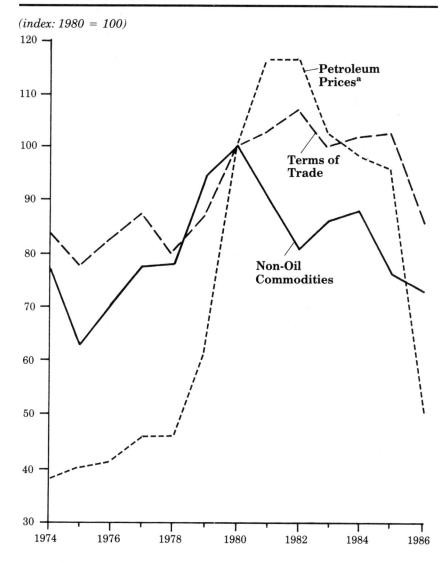

Note: Figures for 1986 are estimates.
[a]Based on the dollar price of Venezuelan petroleum.
   Source: IMF, *International Financial Statistics, 1986 Yearbook; International Financial Statistics,* March 1987 monthly edition.

# A-11. U.S. Reserves and Imports of Key Raw Materials (percentages)

*Developing countries supply the major share of U.S. imports of strategic raw metals and minerals.*

| Metal/Mineral | U.S. Reserve Base[a] (percentage of world reserve base) | U.S. Reliance on Imports in 1986[b] | Developing-Country Share of U.S. Imports in 1985[c] (percentages) | Principal Suppliers, 1982–1985 (share of total U.S. imports) |
|---|---|---|---|---|
| Columbium | * | 100 | 83 | Brazil (73%), Canada (13%), Thailand (5%) |
| Natural graphite | n.a. | 100 | 88 | Mexico (50%), China (24%), Brazil (8%), Madagascar (6%) |
| Manganese ore | * | 100 | 80 | Gabon (36%), Brazil (22%), South Africa (15%) |
| Strontium | 11 | 100 | 100 | Mexico (97%), Spain (3%) |
| Platinum[d] | 1 | 98 | 37 | South Africa (43%), United Kingdom (17%), U.S.S.R. (12%) |
| Bauxite and alumina | * | 97 | 89 | Bauxite—Guinea (45%), Jamaica (32%), Brazil (6%) Alumina—Australia (76%), Jamaica (10%), Suriname (7%) |
| Cobalt | 10 | 92 | 92 | Zaire (40%), Zambia (16%), Canada (13%), Norway (6%) |
| Diamond[e] | n.a. | 92 | 62[f] | South Africa (41%), United Kingdom (26%), Ireland (18%), Belgium-Luxembourg (10%) |
| Tantalum | * | 91 | 0 | Thailand (34%), Brazil (10%), Australia (8%), Malaysia (6%) |
| Flourspar | 3 | 88 | 70 | Mexico (47%), South Africa (30%), China (9%), Italy (7%) |
| Chromium[g] | * | 82 | n.a. | South Africa (59%), Zimbabwe (11%), Turkey (7%), Yugoslavia (5%) |
| Nickel | 3 | 78 | 10[h] | Canada (40%), Australia (14%), Norway (11%), Botswana (10%) |
| Potash | 21 | 78 | 0 | Canada (90%), Israel (6%), E. Germany (1%), U.S.S.R. (1%) |
| Tin | 1 | 77 | 96 | Thailand (22%), Brazil (20%), Indonesia (15%), Bolivia (12%) |
| Zinc | 18 | 74 | 40 | Ore, concentrates—Canada (38%), Mexico (23%), Honduras (14%) Metals—Canada (55%), Mexico (8%), Peru (7%), Australia (5%) |
| Cadmium | 22 | 69 | 8 | Canada (39%), Australia (24%), Mexico (8%), W. Germany (7%) |
| Silver | 17 | 69 | 39 | Canada (28%), Mexico (25%), United Kingdom (17%), Peru (14%) |
| Barite | 12 | 66 | 88 | China (46%), Morocco (16%), India (10%), Chile (7%) |

| Commodity | | | | Sources |
|---|---|---|---|---|
| Tungsten | 8 | 62 | 62 | Canada (17%), China (17%), Bolivia (12%), Portugal (7%) |
| Mercury | 2 | 51ⁱ | 41 | Spain (27%), Algeria (18%), Japan (12%), Turkey (11%) |
| Iron ore | 6 | 37 | 28 | Canada (62%), Liberia (13%), Brazil (12%), Venezuela (11%) |
| Gypsum | n.a. | 36 | 16 | Canada (69%), Mexico (20%), Spain (10%) |
| Silicon | n.a. | 35 | 42 | Brazil (23%), Canada (19%), Norway (16%), Venezuela (13%) |
| Copper | 16 | 27 | 60 | Chile (40%), Canada (29%), Peru (8%), Mexico (6%) |
| Gold | 8 | 21 | 13 | Canada (56%), Uruguay (12%), Switzerland (5%) |
| Lead | 18 | 20 | 100 | Ore, concentrates—Peru (67%), Honduras (22%), Mexico (4%), Canada (3%) |
| | | | 29 | Metals—Canada (54%), Mexico (23%), Australia (6%), Peru (6%), Honduras (2%) |
| Fixed nitrogen | n.a. | 17 | 29 | Canada (32%), U.S.S.R. (28%), Trinidad and Tobago (20%), Mexico (15%) |
| Beryllium | n.a. | 16 | 96 | Brazil (51%), China (27%), South Africa (6%), Switzerland (6%) |

ᵃ Reserve base refers to resources demonstrated to exist.
ᵇ Net import reliance = imports − exports + adjustments for government and industry stock changes.
ᶜ Imports for consumption by value, where available.
ᵈ Platinum group metals (platinum, palladium, iridium, osmium, rhodium, ruthenium).
ᵉ Natural stone used in industry.
ᶠ Includes uncut gem stones.
ᵍ Chromite and ferrochromium.
ʰ Primary products only.
ⁱ 1985 figure.
* Negligible or less than 0.5 per cent.
n.a. Not available.
  Sources: U.S. Department of the Interior, Bureau of Mines, *Mineral Commodity Summaries, 1987* and U.S. Department of the Interior, Bureau of Mines, *Minerals Yearbook* (1985).

# A-12. Major Primary-Commodity Exports of Developing Countries, 1981–1983 ($ billions and percentages)

*Petroleum remains the Third World's biggest foreign exchange earner, but the developing countries also account for a large proportion of world exports of other primary commodities.*

| | Developing-Country Exports | | Major Developing-Country Suppliers 1981–83 | | | |
|---|---|---|---|---|---|---|
| | ($ billions) | (percentage of world exports of commodity) | (percentage of world exports of commodity) | | | |
| Petroleum | $216.5 | 81.0 | Saudi Arabia 26.8 | Mexico 5.8 | U.A.E. 5.7 | Iran 5.6 |
| Sugar | 8.5 | 69.1 | Cuba 36.6 | Brazil 5.9 | Philippines 3.5 | Thailand 3.5 |
| Coffee | 8.3 | 91.6 | Brazil 20.0 | Colombia 16.4 | Ivory Coast 4.8 | El Salvador 4.6 |
| Copper | 5.1 | 63.8 | Chile 22.1 | Zambia 12.2 | Zaire 7.3 | Peru 4.8 |
| Timber | 4.6 | 27.8 | Malaysia 11.0 | Indonesia 3.8 | Ivory Coast 1.9 | Philippines 1.7 |
| Iron ore | 3.2 | 46.8 | Brazil 24.9 | India 5.2 | Liberia 4.4 | Venezuela 3.3 |
| Rubber | 3.0 | 98.3 | Malaysia 47.0 | Indonesia 24.8 | Thailand 15.4 | Sri Lanka 4.2 |
| Cotton | 2.9 | 43.4 | Egypt 6.5 | Pakistan 5.5 | Turkey 4.2 | Mexico 3.0 |
| Rice | 2.5 | 55.0 | Thailand 22.5 | Pakistan 9.2 | China 5.5 | India 5.2 |
| Tobacco | 2.3 | 51.3 | Brazil 9.8 | Turkey 7.4 | China 6.0 | India 4.6 |
| Maize | 2.0 | 19.2 | Argentina 8.7 | Thailand 3.5 | Yugoslavia 1.2 | Zimbabwe 0.5 |
| Tin | 1.9 | 74.7 | Malaysia 28.6 | Indonesia 13.4 | Thailand 12.7 | Bolivia 10.0 |
| Cocoa | 1.9 | 92.1 | Ivory Coast 26.4 | Ghana 16.3 | Nigeria 12.2 | Brazil 11.8 |
| Tea | 1.5 | 84.6 | India 26.6 | Sri Lanka 18.2 | China 12.8 | Kenya 8.9 |
| Palm oil | 1.4 | 81.6 | Malaysia 70.1 | Indonesia 7.0 | Ivory Coast 1.7 | Papua New Guinea 0.5 |
| Beef | 1.3 | 16.7 | Argentina 5.4 | Uruguay 2.5 | Brazil 2.2 | Colombia 1.3 |
| Bananas | 1.2 | 86.7 | Costa Rica 16.7 | Honduras 14.2 | Ecuador 13.8 | Colombia 10.2 |
| Wheat and meslin | 1.2 | 6.9 | Argentina 5.7 | Turkey 0.4 | Uruguay 0.1 | Yugoslavia 0.1 |
| Phosphate rock | 1.1 | 62.9 | Morocco 34.1 | Jordan 8.5 | Togo 4.8 | Senegal 3.0 |

Source: World Bank, *Commodity Trade and Price Trends* (1986 Edition), Tables 7 and 8.

# A-13. Industrial-Country Imports from Developing Countries: Changes in Composition (percentages)

*In the 1980s, developing countries' share of industrial-country manufactured imports has continued to grow despite the decline in their overall trade share of industrial-country imports.*

| | Industrial Countries | | | United States | | | European Economic Community *(percentages)* | | | Japan | | |
|---|---|---|---|---|---|---|---|---|---|---|---|---|
| | 1975 | 1981 | 1985 | 1975 | 1981 | 1985 | 1975 | 1981 | 1985 | 1975 | 1981 | 1985 |
| **Total Imports** | **23.8** | **26.8** | **21.2** | **40.5** | **43.4** | **30.2** | **21.5** | **21.0** | **15.8** | **56.2** | **61.7** | **52.7** |
| **Primary Products** | **49.1** | **50.1** | **40.4** | **68.2** | **72.6** | **55.9** | **43.8** | **40.7** | **30.8** | **63.8** | **71.7** | **64.3** |
| Foods, beverages, and tobacco | 28.6 | 28.1 | 31.5 | 57.1 | 55.1 | 52.1 | 18.9 | 19.8 | 22.2 | 36.9 | 29.5 | 32.1 |
| Crude materials (excluding fuels, oils, and fats) | 27.2 | 26.0 | 26.5 | 38.6 | 33.4 | 28.5 | 23.1 | 20.8 | 22.5 | 34.3 | 39.4 | 35.4 |
| Mineral fuels and materials | 70.6 | 65.2 | 49.6 | 78.9 | 81.6 | 63.4 | 71.2 | 55.7 | 39.0 | 82.9 | 88.2 | 81.5 |
| **Manufactured Products** | **6.1** | **9.3** | **11.4** | **16.2** | **22.0** | **21.5** | **5.1** | **6.3** | **7.1** | **27.8** | **29.5** | **25.6** |
| Chemicals | 4.2 | 4.4 | 5.2 | 13.1 | 14.1 | 12.4 | 2.4 | 2.5 | 2.8 | 16.1 | 16.7 | 10.4 |
| Machinery and transport equipment | 2.1 | 4.8 | 7.2 | 7.2 | 13.0 | 13.2 | 1.5 | 3.0 | 4.3 | 16.5 | 15.2 | 16.0 |
| Other manufactured goods | 10.8 | 15.6 | 18.6 | 26.2 | 33.4 | 35.9 | 8.7 | 10.4 | 11.4 | 39.2 | 42.7 | 39.1 |
| **Miscellaneous** | **23.4** | **8.8** | **9.8** | **75.9** | **21.3** | **24.6** | **8.5** | **8.2** | **9.5** | **NA** | **21.9** | **16.2** |

Sources: United Nations, *Monthly Bulletin of Statistics*, May 1981 and 1986, Special Table D; and May 1987, Special Table C.

# A-14. Industrial-Country Manufactured Imports from Developing Countries (percentages)

*Although slowed by the weak growth of the 1980s, developing-country manufactured exports to industrial countries have grown, particularly in high-technology industries.*

| R & D Intensity of Product[a] (selected items) | Developing-Country Share of Industrial-Country Imports | | | | Annual Average Growth Rate of Imports | |
|---|---|---|---|---|---|---|
| | 1970 | 1975 | 1980 | 1985 | 1970–80 | 1980–85 |
| | | *(percentages)* | | | | |
| Total Manufactures | 9.5 | 11.6 | 13.4 | 15.7 | 4.2 | 1.1 |
| High Intensity | 2.6 | 6.3 | 9.2 | 12.4 | 6.4 | 2.3 |
| Electronic components | 11.2 | 21.6 | 29.0 | 29.1 | 6.3 | 1.7 |
| Scientific instruments | 1.3 | 5.5 | 9.9 | 8.9 | 7.9 | 0.2 |
| Drugs and medicine | 6.9 | 8.3 | 7.0 | 4.7 | 3.2 | – 1.1 |
| Medium Intensity | 4.4 | 4.6 | 6.4 | 8.4 | 4.3 | 1.8 |
| Motor vehicles | 0.2 | 0.6 | 0.9 | 2.1 | 4.4 | 2.4 |
| Rubber and plastics | 6.1 | 6.0 | 8.2 | 13.2 | 6.6 | 3.8 |
| Low Intensity | 15.7 | 18.6 | 21.0 | 24.8 | 4.0 | 0.7 |
| Fabricated metal products | 2.5 | 4.1 | 7.7 | 13.4 | 5.8 | 2.2 |
| Textiles, clothing, footwear, leather | 19.0 | 25.9 | 30.5 | 38.2 | 4.4 | 1.3 |

[a] Products classified according to the intensity of research and development required in production. Categories based upon methodology described in *Selected Science and Technology Indicators: Recent Results, 1979–1986* (Paris: OECD, 1986).
Source: UNCTAD, *Trade and Development Report 1987*, p. 122.

# A-15. Major Developing-Country Exporters of Manufactures (percentages)

*The newly industrializing countries (NICs) have increased their manufactured exports—as a percentage of their own trade and production, and as a percentage of total Third World manufactured exports.*

| | Manufactured Exports as a Percentage of Total Exports | | | | | Total Exports as a Percentage of GNP | | | | Percentage of Total Developing-Country Manufactured Exports | | | | |
|---|---|---|---|---|---|---|---|---|---|---|---|---|---|---|
| | 1965 | 1970 | 1975 | 1980 | 1983 | 1970 | 1975 | 1980 | 1983 | 1965 | 1970 | 1975 | 1980 | 1983 |
| Taiwan | 46.0 | 78.6 | 83.6 | 90.8 | 93.1 | 26.3 | 34.5 | 49.4 | 50.7[a] | 4.6 | 13.8 | 17.1 | 23.4 | 26.6 |
| Korea | 52.0 | 74.9 | 76.8 | 80.1 | 83.4 | 9.4 | 24.3 | 28.5 | 32.4 | 2.0 | 7.4 | 15.0 | 18.2 | 23.2 |
| Hong Kong | 92.4 | 95.3 | 96.7 | 95.6 | 95.3 | 56.4 | 49.0 | 49.6 | 49.8 | 17.9 | 23.1 | 17.2 | 17.0 | 15.4 |
| Singapore | 28.9 | 26.7 | 39.9 | 45.6 | 48.2 | 81.1 | 94.5 | 178.0 | 132.0 | 6.3 | 4.9 | 8.3 | 11.5 | 12.0 |
| Brazil | 5.0 | 9.7 | 23.3 | 32.8 | 31.9 | 6.5 | 7.1 | 8.3 | 11.1 | 1.8 | 3.1 | 7.8 | 8.6 | 7.9 |
| Mexico | 14.1 | 30.0 | 29.5 | 11.0 | 12.8 | 3.4 | 3.5 | 8.5 | 16.8 | 3.1 | 4.3 | 3.4 | 2.2 | 3.2 |
| Argentina | 5.2 | 12.3 | 23.6 | 21.4 | 13.9 | 8.3 | 8.4 | 14.3 | 11.8 | 1.7 | 2.6 | 2.7 | 2.2 | 1.2 |

[a] 1983 GNP figure for Taiwan is an estimate.
Sources: United Nations, *Handbook of International Trade and Development Statistics*, 1976, 1983, 1984, 1985, and 1986; World Bank, *World Debt Tables* (1985–86 Edition); and Council for Economic Planning and Development, Republic of China, *Taiwan Statistical Data Book, 1984.*

## A-16. World Services Exports: Continued Growth in 1980s
   ($ billions)

|                          | 1970  | 1975  | 1980    | 1985    |
|--------------------------|-------|-------|---------|---------|
| **World Services Exports** | **63.1** | **154.2** | **264.5** | **371.5** |
| Developed-country        | 52.5  | 125.5 | 202.1   | 273.6   |
| United States            | 9.6   | 18.9  | 35.0    | 41.5    |
| Developing-country       | 9.9   | 31.1  | 62.4    | 97.8    |
| Africa                   | 1.8   | 4.5   | 8.7     | 8.4     |
| Asia                     | 1.6   | 6.9   | 16.0    | 35.3    |
| Europe                   | 1.8   | 6.4   | 10.5    | 13.8    |
| Middle East              | 1.1   | 4.4   | 9.9     | 20.2    |
| Western Hemisphere       | 3.6   | 8.9   | 17.2    | 20.1    |
| World Merchandise Exports | 267.6 | 729.6 | 1,827.0 | 1,758.6 |

Sources: IMF, *Balance of Payments Statistics, Supplement to Volume 28, 1970–76*; *Supplement to Volume 30, 1972–79*; *1985 Yearbook* (Vol. 36); and *1986 Yearbook* (Vol. 37).

# The Impact of the Debt Crisis

*Since the most serious phase of the debt crisis erupted in 1982, Third World debt has grown more quickly than export earnings. To achieve the trade surplus necessary for debt servicing, many developing countries have had to reduce their imports. Between 1981 and 1985, imports by the most heavily indebted developing countries fell by more than 30 per cent.*

*The inability of debtor countries to import has had a direct and severe impact on U.S. exports and trade-related employment. The recent evaporation of commercial and official lending to developing countries threatens to throw the crisis into yet another painful phase. Without new lending, developing countries will not be able to "roll over" (borrow to cover) their current obligations and therefore will reduce their imports further.*

# B-1. Developing-Country Debt Outrunning Export Income ($ billions)

*The debt crisis became most visible in 1982, when world trade slumped and debt-service payments consumed a high portion of developing-country export earnings. In many developing countries, the debt has grown faster than exports, forcing many of them to devote larger portions of their export earnings to debt servicing.*

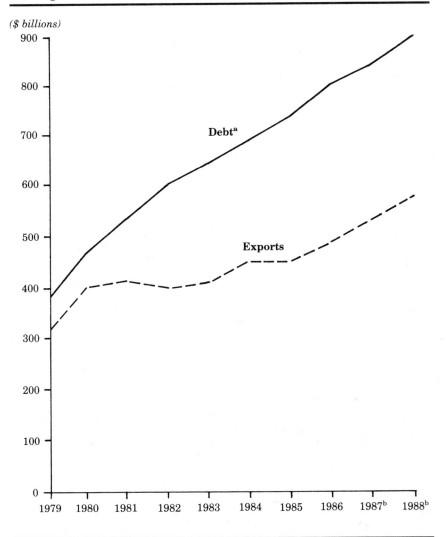

aLong- and short-term debt outstanding.
bIMF projection.
Source: IMF, *World Economic Outlook*, April 1987, Tables A46 and A51.

# B-2. Industrial-Country Net Transfers to Developing Countries[a]: Sudden Decline and Change in Composition
## ($ billions, constant 1980[b]; and percentages)

*The contraction of commercial lending and private export credits in the first half of the 1980s was largely responsible for the sharp drop in industrial-country resource transfers to developing countries.*

*($ billions, constant 1980)*

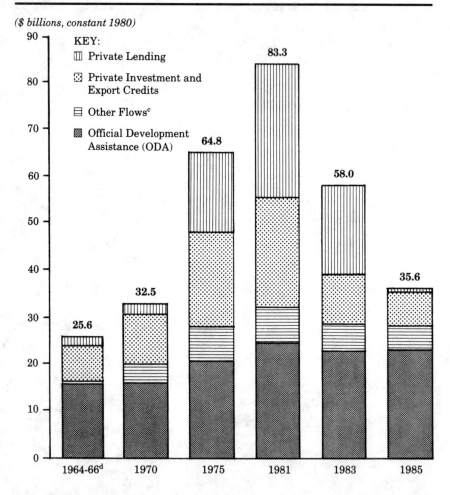

Note: Data on private voluntary grants are not available for 1964-66 average.
[a]Financial flows from DAC countries to developing countries and multilateral agencies.
[b]Deflated by the U.S. GNP deflator.
[c]Non-concessional official flows and private voluntary agency grants.
[d]Annual average.
  Source: OECD (DAC), *Development Co-operation, 1986 Report* (Paris: 1987), Table 4; *1984 Review*, Table II.A.1; and *1975 Review*, Table 17.

## B-3. IMF Lending to Developing Countries (billions SDRs)

*Since 1984, IMF lending has been negligible, and by 1986, the IMF was receiving more in repayments from developing countries than it was lending to them. This shift has been widespread, but particularly painful for the small debtor countries of Africa, which are heavily dependent upon official loans.*

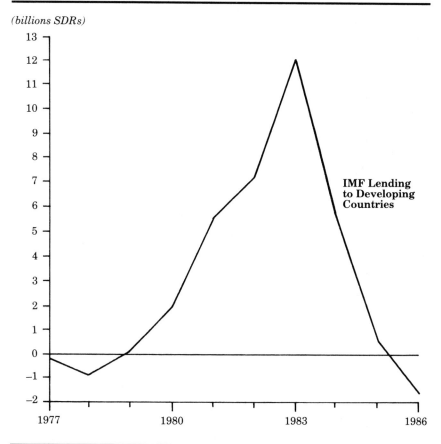

*(billions SDRs)*

IMF Lending to Developing Countries

| Net IMF Lending[a] to: | 1977 | 1980 | 1983 | 1986 |
|---|---|---|---|---|
| | | *(billions SDRs)* | | |
| **All Developing Countries[b]** | **–0.3** | **1.9** | **12.1** | **–1.7** |
| Africa | 0.1 | 0.4 | 1.5 | –0.7 |
| Asia | –0.3 | 1.2 | 2.6 | –0.4 |
| Europe | –0.1 | 0.5 | 1.4 | –0.6 |
| Middle East | 0.1 | –0.1 | 0.1 | 0.0 |
| Western Hemisphere | –0.1 | –0.1 | 6.4 | 0.1 |

[a]Purchases minus repurchases.
[b]Countries receiving IMF funds are almost entirely non-oil developing countries.
Sources: IMF, *International Financial Statistics, 1986 Yearbook* and *International Statistics,* June 1987 monthly edition.

# B-4. International Commercial Banks[a]: Withdrawal from Developing Countries ($ billions)

*The developing countries are now paying back $11.3 billion more to the commercial banks than they are receiving in new loans. Fearing that debtors are no longer good credit risks, commercial banks everywhere have declined to make new loans to most developing countries.*

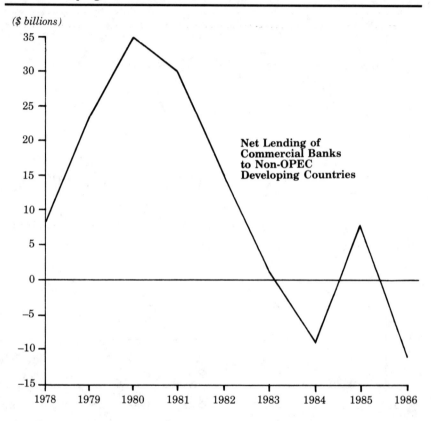

Net Lending of Commercial Banks to Non-OPEC Developing Countries

| | 1980 | 1981 | 1982 | 1983 | 1984 | 1985 | 1986 |
|---|---|---|---|---|---|---|---|
| | | | ($ billions) | | | | |
| World | 160.0 | 165.0 | 95.0 | 85.0 | 90.0 | 105.0 | 160.0 |
| **Non-OPEC developing countries** | **34.9** | **30.4** | **15.2** | **2.2** | **−9.5** | **5.4** | **−11.3** |
| Latin America | 28.3 | 25.8 | 14.0 | 2.5 | −4.8 | 1.3 | −2.0 |
| Asia | 5.9 | 2.3 | −1.2 | −1.9 | −5.0 | 5.9 | −9.0 |
| Africa | 1.3 | 1.5 | 2.5 | 0.4 | −0.9 | −0.5 | −0.2 |
| Middle East | −0.6 | 0.8 | −0.1 | 1.2 | 1.2 | −1.3 | −0.1 |

[a]Encompasses all banks reporting to the Bank for International Settlements.
Sources: Bank for International Settlements (Basel, Switzerland), *Fifty-Second Annual Report*, 1982, p. 122; *Fifty-Third Annual Report*, 1983, p. 116; and *Fifty-Seventh Annual Report*, 1987, pp. 94, 100, and 101.

# B-5. U.S. Banks[a]: Reduced Lending to Developing Countries ($ billions)

*Under the pressure of slow growth and the shrinkage of petrodollars available for recycling, U.S. banks have reduced the level of their lending worldwide. Although involuntary lending has kept some of their capital in the Third World, U.S. banks have reduced their outstanding loans to developing countries by 17 per cent since 1982.*

*($ billions, constant 1980)*

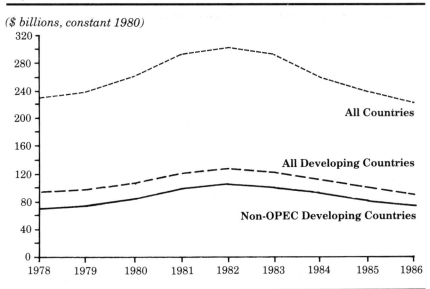

|  | 1980[b] | 1982[b] | 1984[b] | 1986[b] |
|---|---|---|---|---|
|  |  | *($ billions, current)* |  |  |
| **All Countries** | 262.8 | 351.6 | 332.2 | 296.8 |
| **Non-OPEC Developing Countries** | 88.4 | 120.6 | 117.6 | 100.2 |
| Latin America | 56.1 | 75.0 | 76.9 | 70.5 |
| Mexico | 15.7 | 24.3 | 25.8 | 23.5 |
| Brazil | 16.3 | 22.0 | 24.8 | 23.6 |
| Argentina | 7.2 | 8.6 | 8.4 | 9.0 |
| Asia | 27.7 | 41.1 | 36.9 | 27.5 |
| Korea, Republic of | 7.6 | 12.4 | 10.9 | 7.1 |
| Philippines | 4.4 | 5.5 | 5.1 | 4.9 |
| Africa | 4.6 | 4.4 | 3.8 | 2.2 |
| Egypt | 0.8 | 1.2 | 1.0 | 0.3 |
| Morocco | 0.7 | 0.7 | 0.8 | 0.8 |
| **OPEC Countries** | 20.3 | 24.4 | 22.9 | 17.4 |
| Venezuela | 9.3 | 11.2 | 10.6 | 8.7 |
| Indonesia | 1.8 | 2.7 | 3.1 | 1.9 |

[a] Includes adjustments for guarantees and indirect borrowings.
[b] End of year data.

Source: Federal Financial Institutions Examination Council, "Country Lending Exposure Survey," December issues, 1978-1986 (Washington, D.C.).

# B-6. U.S. Direct Foreign Investment
## ($ billions and percentages)

*Once thought a possible substitute for commercial lending, direct foreign investment by U.S. companies has moved away from the austere economic climate of many debtor countries for the same reasons as commercial lending.*

|  | 1975 | 1980 | 1982 | 1983 | 1984 | 1985 | 1986 |
|---|---|---|---|---|---|---|---|
|  |  |  | *($ billions)* |  |  |  |  |
| World | 133.2 | 215.6 | 207.8 | 207.2 | 213.0 | 232.7 | 259.9 |
| Developed | 89.6 | 155.9 | 152.2 | 154.0 | 156.2 | 171.8 | 193.8 |
| Developing | 36.5 | 55.7 | 50.2 | 47.5 | 51.4 | 55.4 | 61.6 |
| Share by Developing Region |  |  | *(percentages)* |  |  |  |  |
| Latin America | 61.0 | 69.8 | 56.1 | 50.8 | 49.1 | 53.2 | 56.8 |
| Asia | 15.8 | 15.3 | 24.2 | 27.5 | 29.4 | 26.8 | 26.0 |
| Africa | 10.9 | 11.0 | 12.9 | 12.9 | 12.9 | 11.4 | 8.8 |
| Middle East | 12.4 | 3.1 | 5.9 | 8.1 | 8.4 | 7.7 | 7.5 |
| Europe | 0.0 | 0.8 | 0.9 | 0.8 | 0.9 | 0.8 | 0.9 |

### Largest Developing-Country Recipients, 1986

| | All Industries<br>*($ billions)* | Key Sectors<br>*(percentage of country total)* |
|---|---|---|
| Bermuda | 14.6 | Finance, insurance, and real estate, 95% |
| Brazil | 9.1 | Manufacturing, 78% |
| Mexico | 4.8 | Manufacturing, 81% |
| Panama | 4.4 | Banking and finance, 62% |
| Indonesia | 4.3 | Petroleum, 85% |
| West Indies (U.K.) | 4.0 | Banking and finance, 96% |
| Hong Kong | 3.6 | Trade, 40%; banking and finance, 34% |
| Bahamas | 3.2 | Banking and finance, 71%; petroleum, 26% |
| Argentina | 3.0 | Manufacturing, 59% |
| Saudi Arabia | 2.5 | Petroleum, 37%; services, 22% |
| Singapore | 2.3 | Manufacturing, 62% |
| Colombia | 2.0 | Petroleum, 47%; manufacturing, 33% |
| Venezuela | 1.8 | Manufacturing, 50% |
| Egypt | 1.8 | Petroleum, 82% |
| South Africa | 1.1 | Manufacturing, 52% |
| Peru | 1.1 | Petroleum, 38% |
| Philippines | 1.1 | Manufacturing, 39%; banking and finance, 32% |
| Malaysia | 1.1 | Petroleum, 63%; manufacturing, 27% |
| Thailand | 1.0 | Petroleum, 65% |
| Total[a] | 66.9 | |

[a] Total exceeds developing-country total due to the negative investment position in the Netherlands Antilles (about −$16 billion).

Source: U.S. Department of Commerce, *Survey of Current Business*, various August issues, 1976–1987.

# B-7. Effect of Debt on Third World Imports ($ billions and percentages)

The increased debt repayment burden of the 1980s has forced the major debtor countries to run large trade surpluses in order to pay interest on their debt. For the largest debtors, this has primarily meant reducing their imports from other countries, thereby spreading economic malaise.

| | Total Debt ($ billions) | | | Debt Service/Exports (percentages) | | | Trade Balance ($ billions) | | Imports ($ billions) | |
|---|---|---|---|---|---|---|---|---|---|---|
| | 1980 | 1982 | 1985 | 1980 | 1982 | 1985 | 1981 | 1985 | 1981 | 1985 |
| **Total, ten countries** | **292.1** | **391.3** | **452.6** | **19.2** | **25.0** | **27.3** | **-5.0** | **42.7** | **160.4** | **111.0** |
| Brazil | 70.2 | 91.3 | 106.7 | 39.9 | 50.1 | 30.4 | -0.7 | 10.9 | 24.1 | 14.7 |
| Mexico | 57.5 | 86.1 | 97.4 | 50.8 | 44.7 | 45.7 | -3.6 | 7.0 | 23.0 | 17.0 |
| Argentina | 27.2 | 43.6 | 48.4 | 24.8 | 30.5 | 50.3 | -0.3 | 4.4 | 9.4 | 4.2 |
| Korea | 29.8 | 37.8 | 48.0 | 15.8 | 17.6 | 17.4 | -4.9 | -1.2 | 26.2 | 30.1 |
| Indonesia | 20.9 | 26.5 | 35.8 | 8.0 | 10.1 | 21.9 | 10.5 | 9.0 | 13.3 | 9.3 |
| Venezuela | 29.6 | 31.8 | 32.1 | 15.4 | 19.2 | 14.3 | 6.6 | 7.5 | 13.4 | 7.6 |
| Philippines | 17.5 | 24.3 | 26.2 | 10.2 | 21.7 | 27.2 | -2.8 | -0.7 | 8.5 | 5.4 |
| Chile | 12.1 | 17.3 | 20.2 | 29.3 | 27.8 | 32.5 | -2.4 | 0.7 | 6.4 | 3.1 |
| Yugoslavia | 18.5 | 20.0 | 19.4 | 6.9 | 8.9 | 11.0 | -4.9 | -1.5 | 15.8 | 12.2 |
| Nigeria | 8.9 | 12.4 | 18.3 | 1.9 | 10.2 | 28.4 | -2.5 | 6.6 | 20.4 | 7.5 |

Sources: The World Bank, *World Debt Tables* (1986–87 edition) and IMF, *Direction of Trade Statistics Yearbook, 1986.*

## B-8. Costs of Third World Debt: U.S. Export and Job Losses
## ($ billions and thousands of jobs)

*The contraction of Third World imports accompanying the debt crisis has damaged U.S. export opportunities and destroyed both existing jobs and jobs that might have been created in a more healthy economic climate. These U.S. job losses amounted to about 1.7 million jobs by the end of 1986. In contrast, several debt relief proposals that have been advanced would, in varying degrees, increase U.S. employment.*

### U.S. JOB LOSSES, 1980–1986

| Market | U.S. exports 1980 | U.S. exports 1986 | Direct job decline | Lost potential job increase | Total lost jobs[a] |
|---|---|---|---|---|---|
| | *($ billions)* | | *(thousands of jobs)* | | |
| Developing Countries | 88.0 | 75.3 | 537 | 1,198 | 1,735 |
| Latin America | 38.7 | 31.1 | 342 | 587 | 929 |
| Mexico | 15.1 | 12.4 | 127 | 230 | 357 |
| Venezuela | 4.6 | 3.1 | 55 | 69 | 124 |
| Brazil | 4.3 | 3.9 | 28 | 66 | 94 |
| Argentina | 2.6 | 0.9 | 54 | 40 | 94 |

### IMPACT OF DEBT RELIEF FOR LATIN AMERICA ON U.S. EXPORTS AND JOBS[b]

| Proposal | Third year of relief | | Tenth year of relief | |
|---|---|---|---|---|
| | New exports *($ billions)* | New jobs *(thousands)* | New exports *($ billions)* | New jobs *(thousands)* |
| 1. Reduce Interest | 2.6 | 54 | 9.2 | 190 |
| 2. "Market Value" | 5.3 | 110 | 25.1 | 520 |
| 3. Bradley Plan | 7.7 | 160 | 32.9 | 682 |
| 4. Full Capitalization | 20.5 | 424 | 59.2 | 1,226 |

Note: Proposal 1 involves reducing the interest rate charged developing countries by 1.5 percentage points. Plan 2 does this plus writes off 3 per cent of the principal each year. Plan 3 writes off 3 per cent of the principal each year and reduces interest rates by 3 per cent. Plan 4 provides for new lending at market terms to cover all principal and interest payments due. Each plan is assumed to be carried out for all ten years.
[a] Total number of jobs lost is the summation of jobs that were lost due to the decline of real exports and the jobs that would have been created if the trend of the 1970s had continued.
[b] Applies to commercial bank debt only.
Source: ODC calculations.

# Development Assistance

*The parallel collapses of private lending and investment by industrial countries to developing countries make official development aid the most important source of the external financial resources available to developing countries—especially the poorest among them. The tables in this annex provide data on the quantities and sources of aid as well as the sectoral uses of the aid.*

*In terms of official development assistance as a percentage of GNP, the United States has dropped to rank last among the eighteen OECD donor countries. Furthermore, less than one-quarter of U.S. development aid goes to the poorest nations of the world—which contain half of the world's population. More than two-thirds of the total U.S. foreign aid budget is security-related aid; in recent years, such U.S. aid to Central America and the Middle East has grown rapidly.*

# C-1. World Bank Lending: Emphasis on Agriculture, Energy, and Transportation (percentages and $ millions)

*Throughout the last decade, World Bank lending has concentrated on agriculture, energy, and transportation. In response to the debt crisis, however, the Bank has allocated more non-project funds for heavily indebted Africa and Latin America to assist with structural adjustment to the crisis.*

| | Sub-Saharan Africa | | East Asia and the Pacific | | South Asia | | Middle East and North Africa | | Latin America and the Caribbean | | Developing Countries ($ millions) | |
|---|---|---|---|---|---|---|---|---|---|---|---|---|
| | 1977–81 | 1984–86 | 1977–81 | 1984–86 | 1977–81 | 1984–86 | 1977–81 | 1984–86 | 1977–81 | 1984–86 | 1977–81 | 1984–86 |
| | (percentages) | | | | | | | | | | | |
| Agriculture and rural development | 34.5 | 24.7 | 33.0 | 20.8 | 39.7 | 31.1 | 27.4 | 23.3 | 23.9 | 28.4 | 3,064 | 4,010 |
| Energy | 8.3 | 10.4 | 18.2 | 16.3 | 22.3 | 32.9 | 12.8 | 17.2 | 21.5 | 25.6 | 1,709 | 3,371 |
| Transportation | 22.6 | 17.7 | 12.3 | 21.9 | 4.9 | 7.5 | 15.4 | 10.9 | 14.2 | 11.0 | 1,314 | 2,065 |
| Non-project | 7.8 | 17.5 | 2.2 | 3.0 | 4.2 | 3.7 | 7.9 | 4.8 | 2.6 | 10.5 | 463 | 1,109 |
| Development finance companies | 4.5 | 3.2 | 11.9 | 5.1 | 3.4 | 5.4 | 10.6 | 15.0 | 9.2 | 4.1 | 813 | 978 |
| Education | 6.9 | 4.3 | 7.8 | 12.6 | 1.2 | 2.2 | 6.4 | 5.3 | 2.1 | 2.4 | 462 | 817 |
| Industry | 3.0 | 4.9 | 1.3 | 1.5 | 8.5 | 10.0 | 9.8 | 6.5 | 7.1 | 0.1 | 612 | 685 |
| Water supply and sewerage | 4.7 | 3.4 | 4.1 | 4.7 | 4.9 | 1.4 | 5.8 | 10.7 | 8.6 | 3.2 | 572 | 675 |
| Urban development | 2.9 | 4.6 | 4.6 | 6.6 | 2.4 | 2.6 | 1.0 | 1.7 | 5.7 | 5.7 | 337 | 667 |
| Small-scale enterprises | 1.1 | 1.2 | 1.7 | 4.3 | 1.1 | 0.8 | 1.1 | 1.9 | 2.2 | 6.7 | 150 | 503 |
| Population, health, and nutrition | 0.0 | 2.9 | 1.9 | 2.8 | 1.1 | 1.8 | 0.4 | 0.5 | 0.2 | 1.3 | 75 | 285 |
| Technical assistance | 2.2 | 3.6 | 0.1 | 0.3 | 0.3 | 0.3 | 0.1 | 0.2 | 0.1 | 0.8 | 42 | 128 |
| Telecommunications | 0.5 | 2.0 | 0.9 | 0.2 | 6.0 | 0.2 | 0.7 | 1.9 | 1.1 | 0.3 | 186 | 113 |
| Tourism | 0.9 | 0.0 | 0.0 | 0.0 | 0.0 | 0.0 | 0.5 | 0.0 | 1.2 | 0.0 | 52 | 0 |
| | ($ millions) | | | | | | | | | | | |
| Annual Average Total | 1,319 | 2,004 | 2,012 | 3,323 | 1,972 | 3,630 | 2,129 | 2,620 | 2,421 | 3,818 | 9,852 | 15,395 |

Source: World Bank, *World Bank Annual Report, 1986*, pp. 80, 86, 94, 100, 106, and 112.

# C-2. Industrial-Country Concessional Aid: Emphasis on Utilities, Education, and Agriculture (percentages and $ millions)

*The sectoral aid priorities of the major donor nations differ considerably; in aggregate, however, their official development assistance (concessional loans and grants) during 1982-84 has gone primarily to public utilities, education, and agriculture.*

|  | United States | Japan | Germany | France | Total DAC[a] Donor Countries |
|---|---|---|---|---|---|
|  |  |  | *(percentages)* |  |  |
| Public utilities | 9.8 | 53.4 | 41.4 | 21.9 | 29.1 |
| Education | 8.0 | 5.6 | 20.3 | 33.3 | 15.5 |
| Agriculture | 20.8 | 13.4 | 10.9 | 9.5 | 15.1 |
| Industry, mining, construction | 0.5 | 13.9 | 5.6 | 5.5 | 7.1 |
| Health | 10.3 | 4.4 | 2.7 | 10.7 | 7.0 |
| Multi-sector | 17.6 | 2.1 | 3.7 | 2.2 | 6.6 |
| Social infrastructure and welfare | 8.0 | 3.5 | 2.1 | 6.4 | 5.2 |
| Trade, banking, tourism, services | 6.6 | 1.3 | 6.6 | 0.5 | 3.2 |
| Planning and public administration | 2.1 | 0.5 | 4.1 | 5.8 | 2.7 |
| Unspecified | 16.4 | 2.1 | 2.6 | 4.2 | 8.4 |
|  |  |  | *($ millions)* |  |  |
| **Total** | **4,138** | **3,081** | **2,220** | **3,850** | **18,260** |

[a]Member countries of the Development Assistance Committee of the Organization of Economic Cooperation and Development.

Sources: OECD (DAC), *Development Co-operation, 1984 Review*, Table II.E.3.; and *1985 Review*, Table 7.

## C-3. Net Flow of Resources from Developed[a] Countries to Developing Countries and Multilateral Institutions: Rapid Decline ($ millions)

*Official Development Assistance has been maintained during the mid-1980s, but private investment virtually collapsed in 1985.*

|  | 1974–1976[b] | 1982 | 1983 | 1984 | 1985 |
|---|---|---|---|---|---|
|  |  |  | *($ millions)* |  |  |
| **OFFICIAL FLOWS** | **16,817** | **35,191** | **32,471** | **34,934** | **32,783** |
| Official Development Assistance (ODA) | 13,145 | 27,777 | 27,590 | 28,738 | 29,428 |
| Bilateral | 9,186 | 18,445 | 18,627 | 19,690 | 21,916 |
| Grants[c] | 6,062 | 13,423 | 14,224 | 15,498 | 17,840 |
| Loans[d] | 3,125 | 5,022 | 4,403 | 4,192 | 4,076 |
| Contributions to multilateral institutions | 3,959 | 9,332 | 8,963 | 9,049 | 7,512 |
| Grants | 1,809 | 4,137 | 4,001 | 4,176 | 4,184 |
| Capital subscription payments | 2,106 | 5,192 | 4,961 | 4,889 | 3,345 |
| Concessional loans | 43 | 4 | 4 | −17 | −17 |
| Other Official Flows[e] | 3,672 | 7,414 | 4,881 | 6,196 | 3,355 |
| **PRIVATE FLOWS** | **19,646** | **46,557** | **35,411** | **47,322** | **10,677** |
| Direct and Portfolio Investment[f] | 15,956 | 39,228 | 30,162 | 43,083 | 9,171 |
| Private Export Credits | 3,690 | 7,328 | 5,249 | 4,239 | 1,506 |
| **GRANTS BY PRIVATE VOLUNTARY AGENCIES** | **1,320** | **2,317** | **2,318** | **2,587** | **2,865** |
| **Total** | **37,783** | **84,065** | **70,200** | **84,844** | **46,325** |
| Total (as percentage of GNP) | 0.97 | 1.15 | 0.92 | 1.07 | 0.55 |
| ODA (as percentage of GNP) | 0.34 | 0.38 | 0.36 | 0.36 | 0.35 |

Note: Figures include capital subscriptions to multilateral organizations made in the form of notes payable on demand. After 1975, such subscriptions are reported in the year in which they are issued rather than the year in which they are cashed.
[a]Members of the Development Assistance Committee (DAC).
[b]Annual average.
[c]Technical assistance, food aid, and other grants.
[d]New development lending, food-aid loans, rescheduled debt, equities, and other bilateral assets.
[e]Official export credits (including official funds in support of private export credits), debt relief, equities and other bilateral assets, and contributions to multilateral institutions on terms not concessional enough to qualify as ODA.
[f]Includes bilateral and multilateral portfolio investment.
Source: OECD (DAC), *Development Co-operation, 1986 Report* (Paris: 1987), Table 36.

## C-4. Net Flow of U.S. Resources to Developing Countries and Multilateral Institutions: Official Flows Negated by Private Flow Reversal ($ millions)

*The severe reversal of flows of U.S. private investment resources in 1985 resulted in a near-complete negation of U.S. Official Development Assistance. Consequently, total net flows dropped from $28.6 billion in 1984 to $1.8 billion in 1985.*

|  | 1974–1976[a] | 1982 | 1983 ($ millions) | 1984 | 1985 |
|---|---|---|---|---|---|
| **OFFICIAL FLOWS** | **4,923** | **9,780** | **8,137** | **9,734** | **9,581** |
| Official Development Assistance (ODA) | 4,065 | 8,202 | 8,081 | 8,711 | 9,403 |
| Bilateral | 2,778 | 4,861 | 5,563 | 6,457 | 8,182 |
| Grants[b] | 1,710 | 3,791 | 4,540 | 5,644 | 7,310 |
| Loans[c] | 1,068 | 1,070 | 1,023 | 813 | 872 |
| Contributions to multilateral institutions | 1,287 | 3,341 | 2,518 | 2,254 | 1,221 |
| Grants | 383 | 854 | 852 | 953 | 973 |
| Capital subscription payments | 904 | 2,473 | 1,650 | 1,304 | 252 |
| Concessional loans | 0 | 14 | 16 | −3 | −4 |
| Other Official Flows[d] | 858 | 1,578 | 56 | 1,023 | 178 |
| **PRIVATE FLOWS** | **5,835** | **19,099** | **13,580** | **17,387** | **−9,278** |
| Direct and Portfolio Investment[e] | 5,449 | 18,794 | 11,939 | 16,404 | −9,396 |
| Private Export Credits | 386 | 305 | 1,641 | 983 | 118 |
| **GRANTS BY PRIVATE VOLUNTARY AGENCIES** | **776** | **1,280** | **1,320** | **1,464** | **1,513** |
| **Total** | **11,534** | **30,159** | **23,037** | **28,585** | **1,816** |
| Total (as percentage of GNP) | 0.73 | 0.98 | 0.69 | 0.78 | 0.05 |
| ODA (as percentage of GNP) | 0.26 | 0.27 | 0.24 | 0.24 | 0.24 |

Note: Figures include capital subscriptions to multilateral organizations made in the form of notes payable on demand. After 1975, such subscriptions are reported in the year in which they are issued rather than the year in which they are cashed.
[a] Annual average.
[b] Technical assistance, food aid, and other grants.
[c] New development lending, food-aid loans, rescheduled debt, equities, and other bilateral assets.
[d] Official export credits (including official funds in support of private export credits), debt relief, equities and other bilateral assets, and contributions to multilateral institutions on terms not concessional enough to qualify as ODA.
[e] Includes bilateral and multilateral portfolio investment.
Source: OECD (DAC), *Development Co-operation, 1986 Report* (Paris: 1987), Table 35.

# C-5. Official and Private Aid: Private American Generosity Above Average, U.S. Government Aid Last Among 18 Nations ($ millions, constant 1985, $ per capita, and percentages)

*The United States government's development aid (as a percentage of GNP) for the Third World ranks last among 18 industrial-country donor nations and is still far short of the United Nations target of 0.7 per cent of GNP for net ODA. However, aid given directly by individual Americans ranks above average.*

| | Private Voluntary Assistance | | | | Official Development Assistance | | | |
| --- | --- | --- | --- | --- | --- | --- | --- | --- |
| | Total Contribution ($ millions) | | Average Contribution Per Capita ($) | | Total Contribution ($ millions) | | Contribution as Share of GNP (percentages) | |
| | 1975 | 1985 | 1975 | 1985 | 1975 | 1985 | 1975 | 1985 |
| Norway | 16 | 52 | 3.90 | 12.54 | 271 | 575 | 0.66 | 1.03 |
| Netherlands | 35 | 98 | 2.54 | 6.77 | 891 | 1,135 | 0.75 | 0.91 |
| Sweden | 57 | 78 | 6.98 | 9.34 | 835 | 840 | 0.82 | 0.86 |
| Denmark | 9 | 16 | 1.81 | 3.13 | 303 | 440 | 0.58 | 0.80 |
| France | 22 | 65 | 0.43 | 1.18 | 3,085 | 3,995 | 0.62 | 0.78 |
| Belgium | −30 | 4 | −3.01 | 0.41 | 557 | 438 | 0.59 | 0.54 |
| Australia | 50 | 52 | 3.62 | 3.30 | 748 | 749 | 0.60 | 0.49 |
| Canada | 98 | 171 | 4.30 | 6.74 | 1,298 | 1,631 | 0.55 | 0.49 |
| Germany | 303 | 424 | 4.89 | 6.95 | 2,491 | 2,942 | 0.40 | 0.47 |
| Finland | 3 | 13 | 0.69 | 2.65 | 71 | 211 | 0.18 | 0.40 |
| Austria | 16 | 18 | 2.17 | 2.38 | 95 | 248 | 0.17 | 0.38 |
| United Kingdom | 79 | 169 | 1.40 | 2.98 | 1,273 | 1,531 | 0.37 | 0.34 |
| Italy | 4 | 8 | 0.08 | 0.14 | 269 | 1,098 | 0.11 | 0.31 |
| Switzerland | 47 | 54 | 7.39 | 8.27 | 153 | 303 | 0.19 | 0.31 |
| Japan | 15 | 101 | 0.13 | 0.84 | 1,693 | 3,797 | 0.23 | 0.29 |
| New Zealand | 9 | 8 | 3.06 | 2.46 | 97 | 54 | 0.52 | 0.25 |
| Ireland | n.a. | 22 | n.a. | 6.18 | n.a. | 39 | n.a. | 0.24 |
| United States | 1,186 | 1,513 | 5.55 | 6.32 | 5,911 | 9,403 | 0.26 | 0.24 |
| DAC Total | 1,921 | 2,866 | 2.95 | 4.13 | 20,042 | 29,429 | 0.33 | 0.35 |

Note: Countries are ranked according to 1985 ODA as a percentage of GNP.
Sources: OECD (DAC), *Development Co-operation, 1986 Report* (Paris: 1987), Tables 29, 38 and 40, and *1977 Review*, Tables A.9, and H.1.

# C-6. Official Development Assistance: Not Always Given to the Neediest
## ($ millions, $ per capita, and percentages)

*Less than half of bilateral development aid goes to the 46 countries with the lowest incomes. A substantial portion of aid grants go to relatively well-off countries on the basis of political and military considerations.*

| | United States | | | DAC Countries[a] | |
|---|---|---|---|---|---|
| | Total ODA ($ millions) | ODA Per Capita[b] ($) | U.S. as a percentage of DAC | Total ODA ($ millions) | ODA Per Capita[b] ($) |
| **Low-Income Countries** | 1,640.0 | 0.65 | 22.1 | 7,436.8 | 2.93 |
| Africa | 1,131.0 | 3.82 | 25.8 | 4,390.0 | 14.83 |
| Asia | 453.0 | 0.20 | 15.5 | 2,930.3 | 1.32 |
| Latin America | 56.0 | 9.03 | 54.7 | 102.4 | 16.52 |
| Oceania | 0.0 | 0.00 | 0.0 | 14.1 | 141.00 |
| **Lower Middle-Income Countries** | 2,767.0 | 4.02 | 44.9 | 6,166.3 | 8.90 |
| Africa | 1,628.0 | 6.99 | 57.5 | 2,833.4 | 12.17 |
| Asia | 183.0 | 0.56 | 12.7 | 1,436.5 | 4.41 |
| Latin America | 916.0 | 12.15 | 62.6 | 1,462.9 | 19.40 |
| Oceania | 2.0 | 0.45 | 0.7 | 296.8 | 67.45 |
| Europe | 38.0 | 0.70 | 27.8 | 136.7 | 2.51 |
| **Upper Middle-Income Countries** | 423.0 | 0.69 | 22.5 | 1,878.4 | 3.14 |
| Africa | 13.0 | 0.19 | 1.9 | 682.3 | 9.95 |
| Asia | 36.0 | 0.22 | 10.5 | 342.3 | 2.09 |
| Latin America | 286.0 | 0.86 | 41.1 | 695.4 | 2.09 |
| Oceania | 1.0 | 1.43 | 3.8 | 26.3 | 37.57 |
| Europe | 87.0 | 2.50 | 65.9 | 132.1 | 3.80 |
| **High-Income Countries** | 1,948.0 | 1.83 | 66.3 | 2,937.8 | 2.76 |
| Africa | 0.0 | 0.00 | 0.0 | 3.2 | 0.84 |
| Asia | 1,948.0 | 12.51 | 94.7 | 2,056.5 | 13.21 |
| excluding Israel | 0.0 | 0.00 | 0.0 | 78.1 | 0.52 |
| Latin America | 0.0 | 0.00 | 0.0 | 484.3 | 134.53 |
| Oceania | 0.0 | 0.00 | 0.0 | 315.7 | 15.86 |
| **Total** | 6,778.0 | 1.39 | 36.8 | 18,419.3 | 3.76 |

Note: Figures are for net disbursements of ODA in 1985 and only include bilateral ODA given to specific countries. Annex D-1 lists the countries in each category. Population data from Annex D-1.
[a]Including the United States.
[b]Calculated using the total number of countries in the category, regardless of whether or not each received ODA.
Source: OECD, *Geographical Distribution of Financial Flows to Developing Countries, 1982/1985*, (Paris: 1987).

# C-7. U.S. Foreign Aid Compared to Personal Consumption Expenditures, 1986 ($ billions)

*U.S. foreign aid, particularly the part aimed at furthering development in low-income countries, is relatively small in comparison to a variety of U.S. personal consumption expenditures.*

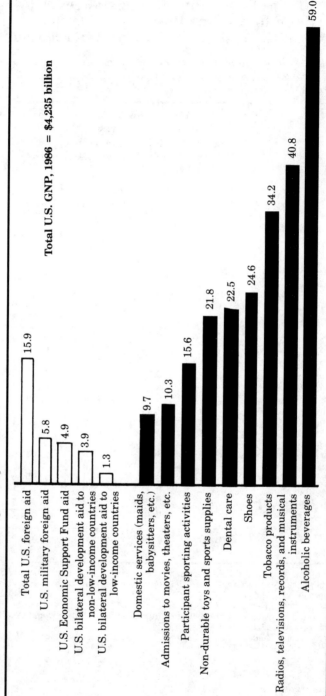

Total U.S. GNP, 1986 = $4,235 billion

- Total U.S. foreign aid — 15.9
- U.S. military foreign aid — 5.8
- U.S. Economic Support Fund aid — 4.9
- U.S. bilateral development aid to non-low-income countries — 3.9
- U.S. bilateral development aid to low-income countries — 1.3
- Domestic services (maids, babysitters, etc.) — 9.7
- Admissions to movies, theaters, etc. — 10.3
- Participant sporting activities — 15.6
- Non-durable toys and sports supplies — 21.8
- Dental care — 22.5
- Shoes — 24.6
- Tobacco products — 34.2
- Radios, televisions, records, and musical instruments — 40.8
- Alcoholic beverages — 59.0

Sources: U.S. Department of Commerce, *Survey of Current Business* (July 1987), p. 32, and U.S. Agency for International Development, *U.S. Overseas Loans and Grants, 1945-1986.*

# C-8. U.S. Bilateral Aid: Changes in Regional Focus ($ millions)

*U.S. aid is heavily skewed to security assistance. U.S. aid to the Middle East and Central America has risen in conjunction with increased attention to security issues in those regions.*

| | Development Assistance | | | | | | Security Assistance[a] | | | | | |
| | Nixon 1969–72 | Nixon 1973–74 | (administration) Ford 1975–76 | Carter 1977–80 | Reagan 1981–84 | Reagan 1985–86 | Nixon 1969–72 | Nixon 1973–74 | (administration) Ford 1975–76 | Carter 1977–80 | Reagan 1981–84 | Reagan 1985–86 |
| | ($ millions) | | | | | | ($ millions) | | | | | |
|---|---|---|---|---|---|---|---|---|---|---|---|---|
| Near East and South Asia[b] | 764 | 507 | 795 | 590 | 629 | 658 | 394 | 395 | 431 | 726 | 1,466 | 2,090 |
| Egypt and Israel | 47 | 38 | 186 | 244 | 275 | 226 | 253 | 1,449 | 1,665 | 3,685 | 4,204 | 5,764 |
| East Asia | 710 | 748 | 350 | 363 | 249 | 272 | 3,537 | 3,491 | 983 | 364 | 425 | 648 |
| Central America | 73 | 82 | 123 | 96 | 199 | 364 | 7 | 8 | 14 | 13 | 383 | 766 |
| Other Latin America | 421 | 309 | 300 | 316 | 399 | 513 | 58 | 106 | 135 | 41 | 159 | 302 |
| Africa | 288 | 279 | 311 | 517 | 730 | 1,035 | 54 | 33 | 89 | 202 | 555 | 611 |
| Europe | 16 | 4 | 10 | 57 | 49 | 9 | 43 | 63 | 39 | 288 | 393 | 626 |
| Oceania | 52 | 68 | 70 | 33 | 7 | 13 | 1 | 0 | 0 | 0 | 0 | 2 |

Note: Years are fiscal years. The transition quarter between FY76 and FY77 is not included.
[a]Security assistance includes all military assistance programs and Economic Support Funds.
[b]Excludes Israel and Egypt.
Source: U.S. Agency for International Development, *U.S. Overseas Loans and Grants*, various issues.

# C-9. Twenty Major Recipients of U.S. Military Aid, Fiscal Year 1986: Israel and Egypt Receive the Majority of the Aid ($ millions and percentages)

*Most U.S. military aid goes to a few countries in the Middle East. For many of these aid recipients, U.S. development assistance is very small in comparison to military aid and Economic Support Funds (formerly called security support assistance).*

| | Total | Development Assistance | Economic Support Funds | Military Assistance | Development Aid as a Percentage of Total Aid |
|---|---|---|---|---|---|
| | | ($ millions) | ($ millions) | | (percentage) |
| Israel | 3,621.0 | 0.0 | 1,898.4 | 1,722.6 | 0.0 |
| Egypt | 2,539.1 | 224.1 | 1,069.2 | 1,245.8 | 8.8 |
| Turkey | 738.1 | 0.0 | 119.6 | 618.5 | 0.0 |
| Greece | 431.9 | 0.0 | — | 431.9 | 0.0 |
| Spain | 385.2 | 0.0 | — | 385.2 | 0.0 |
| Pakistan | 668.2 | 117.0 | 239.3 | 311.9 | 17.5 |
| South Korea | 164.5 | 0.0 | — | 164.5 | 0.0 |
| El Salvador | 444.4 | 140.7 | 181.9 | 121.8 | 31.7 |
| Portugal | 189.0 | 0.0 | 76.6 | 112.4 | 0.0 |
| Philippines | 504.2 | 98.8 | 300.3 | 105.1 | 19.6 |
| Thailand | 125.3 | 32.8 | 5.0 | 87.5 | 26.2 |
| Jordan | 178.4 | 0.0 | 95.3 | 83.1 | 0.0 |
| Tunisia | 104.8 | 16.5 | 22.8 | 65.5 | 15.7 |
| Honduras | 197.7 | 70.1 | 66.5 | 61.1 | 35.5 |
| Morocco | 120.6 | 68.2 | 16.5 | 35.9 | 56.6 |
| Indonesia | 123.5 | 102.5 | — | 21.0 | 83.0 |
| Kenya | 79.3 | 44.3 | 14.4 | 20.6 | 55.9 |
| Somalia | 89.1 | 46.9 | 22.0 | 20.2 | 52.6 |
| Sudan | 138.2 | 111.2 | 10.0 | 17.0 | 80.5 |
| Oman | 28.7 | 0.0 | 19.6 | 9.1 | 0.0 |
| **Total (20 countries)** | **10,871.2** | **1,073.1** | **4,157.4** | **5,640.7** | **9.9** |
| | | | | | |
| **Total (all countries)** | **15,945.0** | **5,206.0** | **4,900.0** | **5,839.0** | **32.6** |
| Near East and South Asia | 8,758.3 | 859.3 | 3,471.6 | 4,427.4 | 9.8 |
| Europe | 630.7 | 2.3 | 130.6 | 497.8 | 0.4 |
| East Asia | 998.7 | 266.4 | 351.4 | 380.9 | 26.7 |
| Latin America | 1,728.6 | 832.1 | 658.1 | 238.4 | 48.1 |
| Africa | 1,421.0 | 931.9 | 284.5 | 204.6 | 65.6 |
| Oceania and other | 15.2 | 12.8 | 1.9 | 0.5 | 84.2 |

Source: A.I.D., *U.S. Overseas Loans and Grants*, July 1, 1945–September 30, 1986.

# People, Development, and Environment

*The disparity between living conditions in the wealthier countries and those in the poorer nations remains enormous. Infant mortality is roughly 5 times higher in developing countries than in industrial countries; life expectancy is 13 years shorter in developing countries; 39 per cent of the people in developing countries are illiterate; and income per capita is but 7 per cent of industrial-country income. Although great strides have been taken to improve life in developing countries, population growth still results in a continuing increase in the number of "absolute poor" people. In Africa, food consumption declined during 1980-84, falling still further below the standard requirement for an active working life. There are, moreover, strong links between development and environmental. Different types of development and poverty alleviation efforts differ in their effects on the environment—on deforestation, on soil erosion and water pollution, and on air pollution.*

# D-1. Economic and Social Indicators of Development

| | Popu-lation mid-1987 (*mil.*) | Annual Growth Rate of Popu-lation (%) | Physical Quality of Life Index (PQLI)[a] 1985 | Per Capita GNP 1985 ($) | Ave.Ann. Growth Rate of Real GNP Per Capita 1965–85 (%) |
|---|---|---|---|---|---|
| WORLD (176) | 5,021 | 1.7 | 73 | 2,899 | 2.5 |
| DEVELOPED COUNTRIES (32) | 1,158 | 0.6 | 96 | 10,169 | 1.7 |
| DEVELOPING COUNTRIES (144) | 3,863 | 2.1 | 66 | 720 | 2.7 |
| AFRICA (53) | 601 | 2.8 | 49 | 683 | 1.1 |
| ASIA (40) | 2,877 | 1.9 | 69 | 1,023 | 3.5 |
| LATIN AMERICA (36) | 417 | 2.2 | 80 | 1,663 | 2.5 |
| OCEANIA (13) | 25 | 1.2 | 91 | 8,195 | 1.7 |
| EUROPE (32) | 831 | 0.6 | 93 | 7,073 | 2.7 |
| NORTH AMERICA (2) | 270 | 0.7 | 98 | 16,401 | 1.8 |
| Low-Income (46) | 2,534 | 1.9 | 64 | 279 | 2.7 |
| Lower Middle-Income (43) | 693 | 2.5 | 65 | 724 | 2.9 |
| Upper Middle-Income (37) | 611 | 2.2 | 78 | 2,133 | 2.8 |
| High-Income (50) | 1,183 | 0.6 | 95 | 10,180 | 1.8 |
| **AFRICA (53)** | | | | | |
| Low-Income (31) | 296.0 | 2.9 | 43 | 231 | −0.3 |
| * Benin | 4.3 | 3.0 | 40 | 260 | 0.2 |
| * Burkina Faso | 7.3 | 2.8 | 29 | 150 | 1.3 |
| * Burundi | 5.0 | 2.9 | 41 | 230 | 1.9 |
| * Cape Verde | 0.3 | 2.6 | 65 | 430 | 5.0 |
| * Central African Republic | 2.7 | 2.5 | 43 | 260 | −0.2 |
| * Chad | 4.6 | 2.0 | 34 | 100c | −2.3 |
| * Comoros | 0.4 | 3.3 | 57 | 240 | −0.3 |
| * Equitorial Guinea | 0.3 | 1.8 | 38 | 340c | n.a. |
| * Ethiopia | 46.0 | 2.3 | 25 | 110 | 0.2 |
| * Gambia | 0.8 | 2.1 | 28 | 230 | 1.1 |
| Ghana | 13.9 | 2.8 | 55 | 380 | −2.2 |
| * Guinea | 6.4 | 2.4 | 28 | 320 | 0.8 |
| * Guinea-Bissau | 0.9 | 2.0 | 29 | 180 | −1.5 |
| Kenya | 22.4 | 3.9 | 58 | 290 | 1.9 |
| Madagascar | 10.6 | 2.8 | 57 | 240 | −1.9 |
| * Malawi | 7.4 | 3.2 | 37 | 170 | 1.5 |
| * Mali | 8.4 | 2.9 | 28 | 150 | 1.4 |
| * Mauritania | 2.0 | 3.0 | 33 | 420 | 0.1 |
| Mozambique | 14.7 | 2.6 | 41 | 160 | n.a. |
| * Niger | 7.0 | 2.9 | 28 | 250 | −2.1 |
| * Rwanda | 6.8 | 3.7 | 45 | 280 | 1.8 |
| * Sao Tome & Principe | 0.1 | 2.7 | 69 | 320 | 0.8 |
| Senegal | 7.1 | 2.8 | 36 | 370 | −0.6 |
| * Sierra Leone | 3.9 | 1.8 | 26 | 350 | 1.1 |
| * Somalia | 7.7 | 2.5 | 29 | 280 | −0.7 |
| * Sudan | 23.5 | 2.8 | 41 | 300 | 0.0 |
| * Tanzania | 23.5 | 3.5 | 63 | 290 | 0.0 |

| Life Expectancy at Birth (years) | Infant Mortality per 1,000 Live Births | Literacy (%) | Per Capita Military Spending 1983 ($) | Per Capita Public Education Spending 1983 ($) | Exports f.o.b. 1986 ($ mil.) | Imports c.i.f. 1986 ($ mil.) | U.S. Bilateral Economic Aid[b] FY 1986 ($ mil.) |
|---|---|---|---|---|---|---|---|
| 64 | 59 | 69 | 154 | 134 | 2,138,350 | 2,222,739 | 7,469.0 |
| 74 | 15 | 99 | 524 | 487 | 1,654,327 | 1,722,553 | 1,954.7 |
| 61 | 72 | 61 | 43 | 28 | 484,023 | 500,186 | 5,514.3 |
| | | | | | | | |
| 52 | 111 | 45 | 31 | 29 | 72,704 | 77,344 | 2,412.6 |
| 62 | 63 | 62 | 53 | 46 | 509,308 | 436,816 | 3,458.7 |
| 66 | 57 | 84 | 28 | 68 | 92,071 | 85,705 | 1,329.9 |
| 73 | 20 | 87 | 236 | 552 | 30,162 | 34,752 | 0.9 |
| 73 | 23 | 96 | 429 | 343 | 1,127,108 | 1,115,361 | 266.9 |
| 76 | 11 | 99 | 862 | 747 | 306,997 | 472,761 | 0.0 |
| | | | | | | | |
| 60 | 73 | 55 | 14 | 8 | 59,501 | 91,258 | 1,739.6 |
| 58 | 84 | 67 | 33 | 28 | 80,949 | 92,492 | 3,129.0 |
| 66 | 55 | 79 | 96 | 85 | 227,210 | 212,077 | 626.1 |
| 74 | 16 | 97 | 554 | 491 | 1,770,690 | 1,826,912 | 1,974.3 |
| | | | | | | | |
| 48 | 126 | 41 | 10 | 11 | 10,282 | 15,816 | 808.9 |
| | | | | | | | |
| 49 | 115 | 26 | 6 | 15 | 129 | 541 | 2.8 |
| 45 | 144 | 13 | 5 | 6 | 88 | 397 | 23.7 |
| 48 | 118 | 34 | 11 | 8 | 155 | 201 | 5.2 |
| 63 | 69 | 50 | n.a. | n.a. | 4 | 110 | 7.2 |
| 49 | 137 | 41 | 6 | 10 | 117 | 127 | 4.6 |
| 45 | 138 | 26 | 10 | 3 | 120 | 203 | 19.2 |
| 55 | 84 | 51 | n.a. | n.a. | 16 | 60 | 1.2 |
| 45 | 132 | 37 | n.a. | n.a. | 37 | 28 | 1.6 |
| 45 | 168 | 8 | 12 | 5 | 496 | 1,257 | 78.3 |
| 43 | 169 | 25 | n.a. | 14 | 69 | 168 | 8.5 |
| 53 | 94 | 53 | 2 | 5 | 876 | 875 | 24.2 |
| 40 | 153 | 28 | 12 | 11 | 448 | 352 | 19.6 |
| 39 | 138 | 31 | n.a. | n.a. | 6 | 63 | 2.8 |
| 54 | 91 | 59 | 14 | 17 | 1,339 | 1,831 | 58.7 |
| 52 | 109 | 68 | 7 | 10 | 351 | 442 | 4.7 |
| 45 | 156 | 41 | 4 | 5 | 282 | 287 | 36.4 |
| 46 | 174 | 17 | 8 | 7 | 94 | 426 | 21.6 |
| 47 | 132 | 17 | 31 | 21 | 326 | 385 | 7.9 |
| 47 | 123 | 38 | 13 | n.a. | 166 | 485 | 31.5 |
| 44 | 140 | 14 | 2 | 9 | 261 | 316 | 31.7 |
| 48 | 127 | 47 | 5 | 8 | 163 | 274 | 10.9 |
| 65 | 74 | 57 | n.a. | n.a. | 6 | 15 | 1.3 |
| 47 | 137 | 28 | 11 | 20 | 589 | 1,087 | 66.3 |
| 40 | 175 | 29 | 3 | 10 | 176 | 180 | 12.5 |
| 46 | 152 | 12 | 19 | 4 | 101 | 423 | 68.9 |
| 48 | 112 | 31 | 13 | 18 | 563 | 1,278 | 121.2 |
| 52 | 110 | 85 | 15 | 14 | 379 | 1,003 | 3.2 |

| | Popu-lation mid-1987 (*mil.*) | Annual Growth Rate of Popu-lation (%) | Physical Quality of Life Index (PQLI)[a] 1985 | Per Capita GNP 1985 ($) | Ave.Ann. Growth Rate of Real GNP Per Capita 1965–85 (%) |
|---|---|---|---|---|---|
| * Togo | 3.2 | 3.1 | 48 | 230 | 0.3 |
| * Uganda | 15.9 | 3.4 | 51 | 220c | −2.6 |
| Zaire | 31.8 | 3.1 | 55 | 170 | −2.1 |
| Zambia | 7.1 | 3.5 | 62 | 390 | −1.6 |
| **Lower Middle-Income (14)** | **232.8** | **2.8** | **52** | **722** | **2.4** |
| Angola | 8.0 | 2.5 | 37 | 840c | n.a. |
| * Botswana | 1.2 | 3.4 | 66 | 840 | 8.3 |
| Cameroon | 10.3 | 2.7 | 58 | 810 | 3.6 |
| Congo | 2.1 | 3.4 | 64 | 1,110 | 3.8 |
| * Djibouti | 0.3 | 2.5 | 31 | 1,180c | n.a. |
| Egypt | 51.9 | 2.6 | 60 | 610 | 3.1 |
| Ivory Coast | 10.8 | 3.0 | 49 | 660 | 0.9 |
| * Lesotho | 1.6 | 2.6 | 61 | 470 | 6.5 |
| Liberia | 2.4 | 3.2 | 43 | 470 | −1.4 |
| Mauritius | 1.1 | 1.2 | 83 | 1,090 | 2.7 |
| Morocco | 24.4 | 2.5 | 54 | 560 | 2.2 |
| † Nigeria | 108.6 | 2.8 | 47 | 800 | 2.2 |
| Swaziland | 0.7 | 3.1 | 58 | 670 | 2.7 |
| Zimbabwe | 9.4 | 3.5 | 67 | 680 | 1.6 |
| **Upper Middle-Income (7)** | **68.6** | **2.6** | **64** | **2,138** | **2.3** |
| † Algeria | 23.5 | 3.2 | 62 | 2,550 | 3.6 |
| † Gabon | 1.2 | 1.6 | 54 | 3,670 | 1.5 |
| Namibia | 1.3 | 3.3 | 47 | 1,520e | n.a. |
| Reunion | 0.6 | 1.9 | 85 | 3,580e | n.a. |
| Seychelles | 0.1 | 1.9 | 88 | 2,770c | n.a. |
| South Africa | 34.3 | 2.3 | 66 | 2,010 | 1.1 |
| Tunisia | 7.6 | 2.5 | 66 | 1,190 | 4.0 |
| **High-Income (1)** | **3.8** | **3.0** | **66** | **7,170** | **−1.3** |
| † Libya | 3.8 | 3.0 | 66 | 7,170 | −1.3 |
| **ASIA (40)** | | | | | |
| **Low-Income (12)** | **2,231.5** | **1.8** | **66** | **285** | **3.2** |
| * Afghanistan | 14.2 | 2.6 | 21 | 280c | n.a. |
| * Bangladesh | 107.1 | 2.7 | 43 | 150 | 0.4 |
| * Bhutan | 1.5 | 2.0 | 26 | 160 | n.a. |
| Burma | 38.8 | 2.1 | 71 | 190 | 2.4 |
| China, Peoples Republic | 1,062.0 | 1.3 | 80 | 310 | 4.8 |
| India | 800.3 | 2.1 | 55 | 270 | 1.7 |
| Kampuchea | 6.5 | 2.1 | 50 | 160c | n.a. |
| * Maldives | 0.2 | 3.8 | 67 | 290 | 1.9 |
| * Nepal | 17.8 | 2.5 | 36 | 160 | 0.1 |

| Life Expectancy at Birth (years) | Infant Mortality per 1,000 Live Births | Literacy (%) | Per Capita Military Spending 1983 ($) | Per Capita Public Education Spending 1983 ($) | Exports f.o.b. 1986 ($ mil.) | Imports c.i.f. 1986 ($ mil.) | U.S. Bilateral Economic Aid[b] FY 1986 ($ mil.) |
|---|---|---|---|---|---|---|---|
| 51 | 97 | 41 | 6 | 16 | 252 | 531 | 15.9 |
| 49 | 108 | 57 | 4 | 4 | 453 | 332 | 15.3 |
| 51 | 102 | 61 | 3 | 10 | 1,532 | 1,548 | 72.4 |
| 52 | 84 | 76 | 21 | 32 | 688 | 591 | 29.6 |
| **54** | **102** | **45** | **32** | **28** | **25,223** | **31,132** | **1,545.7** |
| 44 | 143 | 41 | 131 | 45 | 1,787 | 1,080 | 3.4 |
| 57 | 71 | 71 | 29 | 80 | —d | —d | 22.4 |
| 55 | 89 | 56 | 18 | 30 | 1,790 | 1,809 | 28.8 |
| 58 | 77 | 63 | 45 | 77 | 795 | 527 | 0.8 |
| 48 | 152 | 12 | n.a. | n.a. | 45 | 281 | 3.4 |
| 61 | 93 | 45 | 50 | 28 | 3,761 | 12,132 | 1,293.3 |
| 52 | 105 | 43 | 9 | 37 | 3,348 | 1,917 | 1.8 |
| 54 | 106 | 74 | 17 | 18 | —d | —d | 19.3 |
| 50 | 127 | 35 | 12 | 26 | 899 | 1,938 | 58.8 |
| 66 | 25 | 83 | 3 | 49 | 662 | 676 | 2.2 |
| 59 | 90 | 33 | 35 | 53 | 2,312 | 3,962 | 84.7 |
| 50 | 109 | 43 | 18 | 16 | 8,823 | 5,650 | 2.0 |
| 54 | 124 | 68 | 17 | 57 | —d | — | 12.0 |
| 57 | 77 | 74 | 52 | 64 | 1,001 | 1,160 | 12.8 |
| **58** | **80** | **64** | **71** | **96** | **30,787** | **25,843** | **58.0** |
| 61 | 81 | 50 | 47 | 106 | 7,953 | 8,251 | 0.0 |
| 51 | 108 | 62 | 88 | 170 | 1,211 | 878 | 1.9 |
| 48 | 116 | 50 | n.a. | 33 | —d | —d | 0.0 |
| 69 | 18 | 79 | n.a. | n.a. | 126 | 988 | 0.0 |
| 69 | 14 | 88 | n.a. | n.a. | 54 | 92 | 2.5 |
| 55 | 78 | 76 | 92 | 97 | 19,713d | 12,781d | 14.3 |
| 63 | 78 | 54 | 51 | 57 | 1,730 | 2,853 | 39.3 |
| **60** | **90** | **66** | **892** | **310** | **6,412** | **4,553** | **0.0** |
| 60 | 90 | 66 | 892 | 310 | 6,412 | 4,553 | 0.0 |
| **62** | **65** | **57** | **15** | **8** | **48,757** | **74,766** | **853.0** |
| 38 | 187 | 24 | 21 | 4 | 636 | 1,026 | 8.9 |
| 51 | 123 | 33 | 2 | 2 | 889 | 2,502 | 185.3 |
| 44 | 133 | 5 | n.a. | n.a. | n.a. | n.a. | 0.5 |
| 59 | 66 | 78 | 7 | 4 | 506 | 668 | 16.2 |
| 69 | 35 | 69 | 22 | 8 | 31,366 | 43,503 | 0.0 |
| 56 | 89 | 44 | 8 | 8 | 10,317 | 18,830 | 196.7 |
| 46 | 145 | 75 | n.a. | n.a. | 3 | 17 | 1.6 |
| 53 | 68 | 82 | n.a. | n.a. | 30 | 79 | 0.7 |
| 47 | 133 | 26 | 2 | 4 | 144 | 316 | 21.2 |

| | Population mid-1987 (*mil.*) | Annual Growth Rate of Population (%) | Physical Quality of Life Index (PQLI)[a] 1985 | Per Capita GNP 1985 ($) | Ave.Ann. Growth Rate of Real GNP Per Capita 1965–85 (%) |
|---|---|---|---|---|---|
| Pakistan | 104.6 | 2.9 | 43 | 380 | 2.6 |
| Sri Lanka | 16.3 | 1.8 | 87 | 380 | 2.9 |
| Vietnam | 62.2 | 2.6 | 80 | 220[c] | n.a. |
| **Lower Middle-Income (8)** | **326.1** | **2.3** | **70** | **628** | **4.1** |
| † Indonesia | 174.9 | 2.1 | 63 | 530 | 4.8 |
| Korea, Dem. People's Rep. | 21.4 | 2.5 | 85 | 1,170[f] | n.a. |
| * Laos | 3.8 | 2.5 | 52 | 500[c] | n.a. |
| Mongolia | 2.0 | 2.6 | 80 | 880[g] | n.a. |
| Philippines | 61.5 | 2.8 | 79 | 580 | 2.3 |
| Thailand | 53.6 | 2.1 | 82 | 800 | 4.0 |
| * Yemen, Arab Republic | 6.5 | 3.4 | 28 | 550 | 5.3 |
| * Yemen, People's Dem. Rep. | 2.4 | 3.0 | 39 | 530 | n.a. |
| **Upper Middle-Income (9)** | **163.9** | **2.5** | **75** | **2,673** | **5.7** |
| † Iran | 50.4 | 3.2 | 59 | 3,690[c] | n.a. |
| † Iraq | 17.0 | 3.3 | 62 | 1,970[c] | n.a. |
| Jordan | 3.7 | 3.7 | 77 | 1,560 | 5.8 |
| Korea, Rep | 42.1 | 1.4 | 88 | 2,150 | 6.6 |
| Lebanon | 3.3 | 2.2 | 79 | 2,220[c] | n.a. |
| Macao | 0.4 | 1.7 | 84 | 3,450[c] | n.a. |
| Malaysia | 16.1 | 2.4 | 81 | 2,000 | 4.4 |
| Syria | 11.3 | 3.8 | 71 | 1,570 | 4.0 |
| Taiwan | 19.6 | 1.2 | 94 | 3,250[c] | n.a. |
| **High-Income (11)** | **155.1** | **1.0** | **94** | **10,725** | **4.7** |
| Bahrain | 0.4 | 2.8 | 81 | 9,420 | n.a. |
| Brunei[i] | 0.2 | 2.6 | 90 | 17,570 | − 1.2 |
| Hong Kong[i] | 5.6 | 0.9 | 95 | 6,230 | 6.1 |
| • Israel | 4.4 | 1.7 | 96 | 4,990 | 2.5 |
| • Japan | 122.2 | 0.6 | 99 | 11,300 | 4.7 |
| † Kuwait | 1.9 | 3.2 | 84 | 14,480 | − 0.3 |
| Oman | 1.3 | 3.3 | 46 | 6,730 | 5.7 |
| † Qatar | 0.3 | 3.0 | 73 | 16,270 | − 7.0 |
| † Saudi Arabia | 14.8 | 3.1 | 56 | 8,850 | 5.3 |
| Singapore[i] | 2.6 | 1.1 | 91 | 7,420 | 7.6 |
| † United Arab Emirates | 1.4 | 2.6 | 74 | 19,270 | n.a. |
| U.S.S.R. (see Europe) | | | | | |
| **LATIN AMERICA (36)** | | | | | |
| **Low-Income (1)** | **6.2** | **2.3** | **48** | **310** | **0.7** |
| * Haiti | 6.2 | 2.3 | 48 | 310 | 0.7 |
| **Lower Middle-Income (14)** | **75.4** | **2.5** | **77** | **899** | **1.0** |

| Life Expectancy at Birth (years) | Infant Mortality per 1,000 Live Births | Literacy (%) | Per Capita Military Spending 1983 ($) | Per Capita Public Education Spending 1983 ($) | Exports f.o.b. 1986 ($ mil.) | Imports c.i.f. 1986 ($ mil.) | U.S. Bilateral Economic Aid[b] FY 1986 ($ mil.) |
|---|---|---|---|---|---|---|---|
| 51 | 115 | 30 | 23 | 8 | 3,383 | 5,367 | 356.3 |
| 70 | 36 | 87 | 5 | 10 | 1,163 | 1,829 | 65.6 |
| 65 | 49 | 84 | n.a. | n.a. | 320 | 629 | 0.0 |
| **59** | **76** | **79** | **26** | **22** | **31,026** | **29,046** | **575.3** |
| 55 | 96 | 74 | 15 | 18 | 14,824 | 10,724 | 102.5 |
| 68 | 27 | 85 | 94 | 39 | 1,380[g] | 1,720[g] | 0.0 |
| 45 | 151 | 84 | n.a. | n.a. | 14 | 70 | 0.0 |
| 63 | 49 | 90 | 119 | n.a. | 53 | 47 | 0.0 |
| 63 | 48 | 86 | 12 | 14 | 4,787 | 5,213 | 399.1 |
| 64 | 43 | 91 | 32 | 32 | 9,776 | 9,303 | 37.8 |
| 45 | 154 | 14 | 108 | 53 | 50 | 1,412 | 35.9 |
| 46 | 145 | 42 | 82 | 36 | 142 | 557 | 0.0 |
| **65** | **58** | **70** | **248** | **113** | **100,351** | **92,149** | **112.4** |
| 60 | 111 | 51 | 261 | 136 | 9,005 | 9,775 | 0.0 |
| 61 | 73 | 47 | 717 | 61 | 7,634 | 8,847 | 0.0 |
| 65 | 49 | 75 | 193 | 102 | 804 | 3,694 | 95.3 |
| 69 | 27 | 92 | 115 | 100 | 35,624 | 33,335 | 0.0 |
| 66 | 44 | 77 | 126 | 102 | 582 | 2,089 | 17.1 |
| 67 | 12 | 79 | n.a. | n.a. | 1,034 | 874 | 0.0 |
| 68 | 28 | 73 | 160 | 141 | 13,832 | 10,819 | 0.0 |
| 64 | 54 | 60 | 249 | 102 | 1,136 | 2,616 | 0.0 |
| 73 | 7 | 92 | 197 | n.a. | 30,700[h] | 20,100[h] | 0.0 |
| **75** | **13** | **90** | **441** | **580** | **329,174** | **240,855** | **1,918.0** |
| 69 | 30 | 72 | 444 | 322 | 2,501 | 2,390 | 0.0 |
| 74 | 12 | 79 | 1,318 | 360 | 2,156 | 1,114 | 0.0 |
| 76 | 9 | 88 | n.a. | n.a. | 35,420 | 35,360 | 0.0 |
| 75 | 14 | 95 | 1,323 | 455 | 7,130 | 10,491 | 1,898.4 |
| 77 | 6 | 99 | 102 | 558 | 210,804 | 127,660 | 0.0 |
| 72 | 22 | 70 | 962 | 724 | 7,707 | 5,634 | 0.0 |
| 54 | 109 | 30 | 1,737 | 250 | 2,687 | 2,741 | 19.6 |
| 72 | 35 | 40 | 614 | 1105 | 2,106 | 1,095 | 0.0 |
| 62 | 61 | 24 | 2,686 | 869 | 24,776 | 22,114 | 0.0 |
| 73 | 9 | 86 | 291 | 339 | 22,490 | 25,506 | 0.0 |
| 70 | 35 | 48 | 1,694 | 433 | 11,397 | 6,750 | 0.0 |
| **54** | **123** | **38** | **5** | **3** | **461** | **654** | **77.7** |
| 54 | 123 | 38 | 5 | 3 | 461 | 654 | 77.7 |
| **64** | **69** | **83** | **50** | **48** | **16,007** | **18,843** | **887.5** |

| | Population mid-1987 (mil.) | Annual Growth Rate of Population (%) | Physical Quality of Life Index (PQLI)[a] 1985 | Per Capita GNP 1985 ($) | Ave.Ann. Growth Rate of Real GNP Per Capita 1965–85 (%) |
|---|---|---|---|---|---|
| Bolivia | 6.5 | 2.6 | 59 | 470 | − 0.2 |
| Cuba | 10.3 | 1.2 | 98 | 960[c] | n.a. |
| Dominica | 0.1 | 1.9 | 88 | 1,150 | 0.4 |
| Dominican Republic | 6.5 | 2.5 | 75 | 790 | 2.9 |
| † Ecuador | 10.0 | 2.8 | 79 | 1,160 | 3.5 |
| El Salvador | 5.3 | 2.6 | 74 | 820 | − 0.2 |
| Grenada | 0.1 | 1.9 | 86 | 970 | − 0.1 |
| Guyana | 0.8 | 2.0 | 86 | 500 | − 0.2 |
| Honduras | 4.7 | 3.1 | 67 | 720 | 0.4 |
| Jamaica | 2.5 | 2.0 | 92 | 940 | − 0.7 |
| Nicaragua | 3.5 | 3.4 | 74 | 770 | − 2.1 |
| Paraguay | 4.3 | 2.9 | 83 | 860 | 3.9 |
| Peru | 20.7 | 2.5 | 71 | 1,010 | 0.2 |
| St. Vincent & the Grenadines | 0.1 | 2.0 | 84 | 850 | 1.2 |
| **Upper Middle-Income (15)** | **332.9** | **2.2** | **81** | **1,829** | **2.9** |
| Antigua & Barbuda | 0.1 | 1.0 | 88 | 2,020 | 0.2 |
| Argentina | 31.5 | 1.6 | 90 | 2,130 | 0.2 |
| Belize | 0.2 | 2.7 | 86 | 1,190 | 2.7 |
| Brazil | 141.5 | 2.1 | 77 | 1,640 | 4.3 |
| Chile | 12.4 | 1.6 | 91 | 1,430 | − 0.2 |
| Colombia | 29.9 | 2.1 | 82 | 1,320 | 2.9 |
| Costa Rica | 2.8 | 2.7 | 94 | 1,300 | 1.4 |
| Guatemala | 8.4 | 3.2 | 64 | 1,250 | 1.7 |
| Mexico | 81.9 | 2.5 | 84 | 2,080 | 2.7 |
| Panama | 2.3 | 2.2 | 90 | 2,100 | 2.5 |
| St. Kitts-Nevis | 0.0 | 1.6 | 85 | 1,550 | 2.4 |
| St. Lucia | 0.1 | 2.5 | 85 | 1,240 | 2.8 |
| Suriname | 0.4 | 2.1 | 84 | 2,580 | 3.4 |
| Uruguay | 3.1 | 0.8 | 91 | 1,650 | 1.4 |
| † Venezuela | 18.3 | 2.7 | 87 | 3,080 | 0.5 |
| **High-Income (6)** | **2.6** | **1.6** | **90** | **5,846** | **2.0** |
| Bahamas | 0.2 | 1.8 | 89 | 7,070 | − 0.5 |
| Barbados[i] | 0.3 | 0.9 | 95 | 4,630 | 2.3 |
| Guadeloupe | 0.3 | 1.3 | 87 | 6,340[j] | n.a. |
| Martinique | 0.3 | 1.1 | 89 | 4,820[c] | n.a. |
| Netherlands Antilles[i] | 0.2 | 1.4 | 91 | 6,110[d] | n.a. |
| Trinidad & Tobago[i] | 1.3 | 2.0 | 90 | 6,020 | 2.3 |
| **OCEANIA (13)** | | | | | |
| **Low-Income (2)** | **0.1** | **1.3** | **n.a.** | **450** | **n.a.** |
| * Kiribati, Rep. of | 0.1[k] | 1.2[k] | n.a. | 450[e] | n.a. |
| * Tuvalu | 0.0[k] | 1.8[k] | n.a. | 450[f] | n.a. |

| Life Expectancy at Birth (years) | Infant Mortality per 1,000 Live Births | Literacy (%) | Per Capita Military Spending 1983 ($) | Per Capita Public Education Spending 1983 ($) | Exports f.o.b. 1986 ($ mil.) | Imports c.i.f. 1986 ($ mil.) | U.S. Bilateral Economic Aid[b] FY 1986 ($ mil.) |
|---|---|---|---|---|---|---|---|
| 53 | 117 | 74 | 7 | 18 | 657 | 685 | 74.6 |
| 77 | 16 | 96 | 130 | 117 | 6,500[h] | 8,600[h] | 0.0 |
| 75 | 40 | 80 | n.a. | n.a. | 50 | 54 | n.a. |
| 64 | 70 | 77 | 15 | 25 | 212 | 861 | 101.8 |
| 66 | 67 | 82 | 20 | 48 | 2,940 | 2,074 | 60.4 |
| 64 | 65 | 72 | 31 | 28 | 789 | 1,186 | 322.6 |
| 68 | 14 | 85 | n.a. | n.a. | 21 | 49 | n.a. |
| 65 | 33 | 96 | 28 | 52 | 242 | 231 | 3.2 |
| 62 | 76 | 59 | 16 | 28 | 925 | 890 | 136.6 |
| 73 | 20 | 92 | 15 | 102 | 583 | 969 | 126.6 |
| 59 | 69 | 88 | 90 | 40 | 315 | 544 | 0.0 |
| 66 | 43 | 88 | 23 | 20 | 234 | 579 | 3.3 |
| 59 | 94 | 85 | 64 | 42 | 2,505 | 2,089 | 58.4 |
| 69 | 33 | 82 | n.a. | n.a. | 34 | 32 | n.a. |
| **66** | **53** | **85** | **23** | **72** | **71,540** | **58,672** | **364.7** |
| 70 | 32 | 90 | n.a. | n.a. | 6 | 80 | n.a. |
| 70 | 34 | 96 | 39 | 52 | 7,477 | 5,067 | 0.0 |
| 66 | 23 | 91 | n.a. | n.a. | 84 | 135 | 12.1 |
| 65 | 67 | 78 | 16 | 59 | 24,551 | 16,390 | 0.7 |
| 70 | 22 | 97 | 82 | 96 | 4,226 | 3,132 | 1.1 |
| 65 | 48 | 88 | 17 | 41 | 5,174 | 4,077 | 11.5 |
| 74 | 19 | 94 | 0 | 58 | 1,213 | 1,137 | 162.8 |
| 60 | 65 | 55 | 21 | 20 | 1,471 | 1,106 | 116.7 |
| 67 | 50 | 90 | 12 | 60 | 16,579 | 12,899 | 11.9 |
| 72 | 25 | 88 | 34 | 105 | 576 | 4,685 | 33.4 |
| 64 | 41 | 98 | n.a. | n.a. | 6 | 27 | n.a. |
| 70 | 18 | 78 | n.a. | n.a. | 104 | 107 | n.a. |
| 66 | 33 | 90 | n.a. | n.a. | 306 | 289 | 0.0 |
| 72 | 29 | 94 | 83 | 54 | 1,355 | 1,066 | 14.4 |
| 70 | 37 | 87 | 58 | 325 | 8,412 | 8,475 | 0.1 |
| **69** | **20** | **95** | **61** | **341** | **4,063** | **7,536** | **0.0** |
| 70 | 23 | 89 | n.a. | n.a. | 649 | 2,222 | 0.0 |
| 73 | 13 | 98 | 36 | 228 | 280 | 572 | n.a. |
| 67 | 19 | 90 | n.a. | n.a. | 112 | 847 | 0.0 |
| 68 | 13 | 93 | n.a. | n.a. | 216 | 831 | 0.0 |
| 71 | 25 | 95 | n.a. | n.a. | 1,434 | 1,732 | 0.0 |
| 69 | 22 | 96 | 67 | 367 | 1,372 | 1,332 | 0.0 |
| **n.a.** | **n.a.** | **n.a.** | **n.a.** | **n.a.** | **1** | **22** | **n.a.** |
| n.a. | n.a. | n.a. | n.a. | n.a. | 1 | 19 | n.a. |
| n.a. | n.a. | n.a. | n.a. | n.a. | 0 | 3 | n.a. |

| | Popu-lation mid-1987 (*mil.*) | Annual Growth Rate of Popu-lation (%) | Physical Quality of Life Index (PQLI)[a] 1985 | Per Capita GNP 1985 ($) | Ave.Ann. Growth Rate of Real GNP Per Capita 1965–85 (%) |
|---|---|---|---|---|---|
| **Lower Middle-Income (5)** | **4.4** | **2.5** | **55** | **678** | **0.6** |
| Papua New Guinea | 3.6 | 2.4 | 54 | 680 | 0.4 |
| Solomon Islands | 0.3 | 3.6 | 51 | 510 | 3.5 |
| Tonga | 0.1[k] | 1.3[k] | 80 | 730 | n.a. |
| * Vanuatu | 0.2 | 3.3 | 42 | 880 | n.a. |
| * Western Samoa | 0.2 | 2.4 | 86 | 660 | n.a. |
| **Upper Middle-Income (1)** | **0.7** | **2.3** | **83** | **1,710** | **2.9** |
| Fiji | 0.7 | 2.3 | 83 | 1,710 | 2.9 |
| **High-Income (5)** | **19.9** | **0.8** | **99** | **10,115** | **1.9** |
| • Australia | 16.2 | 0.8 | 100 | 10,830 | 2.0 |
| French Polynesia | 0.2 | 2.4 | n.a. | 7,840[i] | n.a. |
| Nauru | 0.0[k] | 1.3[k] | n.a. | 9,000[c] | n.a. |
| New Caledonia | 0.2 | 1.8 | n.a. | 5,760[i] | n.a. |
| • New Zealand | 3.3 | 0.8 | 96 | 7,010 | 1.4 |
| **EUROPE (32)** | | | | | |
| **Lower Middle-Income (2)** | **54.5** | **2.1** | **73** | **1,070** | **2.6** |
| Albania | 3.1 | 2.0 | 82 | 900[i] | n.a. |
| Turkey | 51.4 | 2.1 | 73 | 1,080 | 2.6 |
| **Upper Middle-Income (5)** | **44.8** | **0.5** | **92** | **2,415** | **3.8** |
| Cyprus | 0.7 | 1.1 | 93 | 3,790 | n.a. |
| • Greece[i] | 10.0 | 0.2 | 97 | 3,550 | 3.6 |
| Malta | 0.4 | 0.8 | 94 | 3,310 | 8.1 |
| Portugal | 10.3 | 0.3 | 91 | 1,970 | 3.3 |
| Yugoslavia | 23.4 | 0.7 | 91 | 2,070 | 4.1 |
| **High-Income (25)** | **731.9** | **0.5** | **95** | **7,805** | **2.5** |
| • Austria | 7.6 | 0.0 | 96 | 9,120 | 3.5 |
| • Belgium | 9.9 | 0.0 | 97 | 8,280 | 2.8 |
| • Bulgaria | 9.0 | 0.1 | 92 | 6,300[f] | n.a. |
| • Czechoslovakia | 15.6 | 0.3 | 93 | 8,280[f] | n.a. |
| • Denmark | 5.1 | −0.1 | 98 | 11,200 | 1.8 |
| • Finland | 4.9 | 0.3 | 99 | 10,890 | 3.3 |
| • France | 55.6 | 0.4 | 100 | 9,540 | 2.8 |
| • Germany, Democratic Republic | 16.7 | 0.0 | 94 | 9,800[f] | n.a. |
| • Germany, Federal Republic | 61.0 | −0.2 | 97 | 10,940 | 2.7 |
| • Hungary | 10.6 | −0.2 | 93 | 7,200[f] | 5.8 |
| • Iceland | 0.2 | 0.9 | 100 | 10,710 | 2.4 |
| • Ireland | 3.5 | 0.8 | 96 | 4,850 | 2.2 |

| Life Expectancy at Birth (years) | Infant Mortality per 1,000 Live Births | Literacy (%) | Per Capita Military Spending 1983 ($) | Per Capita Public Education Spending 1983 ($) | Exports f.o.b. 1986 ($ mil.) | Imports c.i.f. 1986 ($ mil.) | U.S. Bilateral Economic Aid[b] FY 1986 ($ mil.) |
|---|---|---|---|---|---|---|---|
| 53 | 65 | 45 | 12 | 58 | 1,143 | 1,219 | 0.9 |
| 52 | 68 | 45 | 12 | 58 | 1,029 | 986 | 0.9 |
| 58 | 44 | 15 | n.a. | n.a. | 65 | 73 | n.a. |
| 64 | 20 | 78 | n.a. | n.a. | 5 | 40 | n.a. |
| 56 | 101 | 10 | n.a. | n.a. | 30 | 70 | n.a. |
| 65 | 33 | 98 | n.a. | n.a. | 14 | 50 | n.a. |
| 65 | 29 | 86 | 22 | 115 | 247 | 379 | n.a. |
| 65 | 29 | 86 | 22 | 115 | 247 | 379 | n.a. |
| 77 | 9 | 99 | 285 | 659 | 28,771 | 33,132 | 0.0 |
| 78 | 9 | 99 | 310 | 714 | 22,541 | 26,211 | 0.0 |
| n.a. | n.a. | n.a. | n.a. | n.a. | 34 | 494 | 0.0 |
| n.a. | n.a. | n.a. | n.a. | n.a. | 78 | 29 | n.a. |
| n.a. | n.a. | n.a. | n.a. | n.a. | 188 | 401 | n.a. |
| 74 | 11 | 99 | 161 | 391 | 5,930 | 5,997 | 0.0 |
| 64 | 82 | 74 | 58 | 38 | 7,550 | 12,252 | 119.6 |
| 70 | 43 | 75 | 46 | n.a. | 345[g] | 335[g] | 0.0 |
| 64 | 84 | 74 | 59 | 40 | 7,205 | 11,917 | 119.6 |
| 73 | 22 | 92 | 123 | 112 | 24,285 | 35,034 | 91.0 |
| 74 | 16 | 89 | 94 | 137 | 492 | 1,269 | 14.4 |
| 75 | 14 | 98 | 246 | 146 | 5,652 | 11,358 | 0.0 |
| 73 | 12 | 95 | 39 | 120 | 498 | 885 | 0.0 |
| 74 | 19 | 85 | 80 | 109 | 7,345 | 9,766 | 76.6 |
| 72 | 27 | 92 | 92 | 98 | 10,298 | 11,756 | 0.0 |
| 73 | 18 | 98 | 475 | 380 | 1,095,273 | 1,068,075 | 56.3 |
| 74 | 11 | 98 | 119 | 550 | 22,473 | 26,823 | 0.0 |
| 75 | 11 | 99 | 308 | 575 | 68,819[m] | 68,624[m] | 0.0 |
| 71 | 16 | 95 | 188 | 293 | 13,350[h] | 13,550[h] | 0.0 |
| 70 | 15 | 99 | 238 | 263 | 17,400[h] | 17,450[h] | 0.0 |
| 75 | 7 | 99 | 292 | 804 | 21,158 | 22,844 | 0.0 |
| 76 | 6 | 99 | 187 | 612 | 16,356 | 15,335 | 0.0 |
| 78 | 8 | 99 | 438 | 468 | 124,946 | 129,399 | 0.0 |
| 72 | 10 | 99 | 361 | 336 | 24,700[h] | 23,250[h] | 0.0 |
| 75 | 10 | 99 | 385 | 582 | 243,315 | 191,068 | 0.0 |
| 71 | 20 | 98 | 132 | 309 | 13,000[h] | 12,500[h] | 0.0 |
| 77 | 6 | 100 | 0 | 452 | 1,098 | 1,119 | 0.0 |
| 74 | 10 | 99 | 93 | 348 | 12,571 | 11,612 | 50.0 |

| | Population mid-1987 (*mil.*) | Annual Growth Rate of Population (%) | Physical Quality of Life Index (PQLI)[a] 1985 | Per Capita GNP 1985 ($) | Ave.Ann. Growth Rate of Real GNP Per Capita 1965–85 (%) |
|---|---|---|---|---|---|
| • Italy | 57.4 | 0.1 | 98 | 6,520 | 2.6 |
| • Luxembourg | 0.4 | 0.0 | 97 | 14,260 | 4.0 |
| • Liechtenstein | 0.0[k] | 1.7[k] | 94 | 15,000[l] | n.a. |
| • Netherlands | 14.6 | 0.4 | 99 | 9,290 | 2.0 |
| • Norway | 4.2 | 0.2 | 99 | 14,370 | 3.3 |
| • Poland | 37.8 | 0.8 | 94 | 6,190[f] | n.a. |
| • Romania | 22.9 | 0.5 | 91 | 5,200[f] | n.a. |
| • San Marino | 0.0[k] | 0.9[k] | n.a. | 7,300[o] | n.a. |
| • Spain | 39.0 | 0.5 | 98 | 4,290 | 2.6 |
| • Sweden | 8.4 | 0.1 | 99 | 11,890 | 1.8 |
| • Switzerland | 6.6 | 0.2 | 99 | 16,370 | 1.4 |
| • U.S.S.R. | 284.0 | 0.9 | 91 | 7,120[f] | n.a. |
| • United Kingdom | 56.8 | 0.2 | 97 | 8,460 | 1.6 |
| **NORTH AMERICA (2)** | | | | | |
| **High-Income (2)** | **269.7** | **0.7** | **98** | **16,401** | **1.8** |
| • Canada | 25.9 | 0.8 | 98 | 13,680 | 2.4 |
| • United States | 243.8 | 0.7 | 98 | 16,690 | 1.7 |

Note: All regional and income group averages are weighted by population; a country is excluded if data are not available for the particular indicator in question. Low-income countries have per capita GNPs under $470. Lower middle-income countries have per capita GNPs in the range of $470–1,189. Upper middle-income countries have per capita GNPs in the range of $1,190–4,129. High-income countries have per capita GNPs of $4,130 or above.

* = Least Developed Countries, according to DAC Review 1986.

† = OPEC members.

• = Considered by ODC to be a developed country because of its per capita GNP of $4,130 or more and PQLI of 90 or above.

[a]The Physical Quality of Life Index (PQLI) is a composite index based on life expectancy at age one, infant mortality, and literacy (see Statistical Note at the beginning of these Annexes for information on the method of computation). In general, the PQLI numbers presented here measure the physical quality of life as of 1985. The PQLI numbers were prepared for ODC by Professor M.D. Morris, Director of the Center for Comparative Study of Development at Brown University, Providence, Rhode Island 02912, with the assistance of Dr. Chen-kuo Pang.

[b]U.S. bilateral economic aid includes development assistance, Economic Support Funds, and PL480 food aid. Aid not specifically going to an individual country (e.g. regional and inter-regional activities) is not included in regional subtotals or world total.

[c]1984 figure. DAC, *Development Co-operation*, 1986 Report.

[d]All external trade for South African Common Customs Area is listed under South Africa.

[e]1984 figure. World Bank, *World Bank Atlas*, 1987.

[f]1984 figure. U.S. Central Intelligence Agency, *World Factbook*, 1986.

[g]1985 figure. *CIA World Factbook*.

[h]1985 figure. *GATT International Trade 1985–86.*

| Life Expectancy at Birth (years) | Infant Mortality per 1,000 Live Births | Literacy (%) | Per Capita Military Spending 1983 ($) | Per Capita Public Education Spending 1983 ($) | Exports f.o.b. 1986 ($ mil.) | Imports c.i.f. 1986 ($ mil.) | U.S. Bilateral Economic Aid[b] FY 1986 ($ mil.) |
|---|---|---|---|---|---|---|---|
| 77 | 12 | 97 | 168 | 393 | 97,827 | 99,925 | 0.0 |
| 74 | 9 | 100 | 126 | 779 | —[n] | —[n] | 0.0 |
| 70 | 6 | 100 | n.a. | n.a. | 476[n] | n.a.[n] | 0.0 |
| 77 | 8 | 99 | 319 | 751 | 80,550 | 75,738 | 0.0 |
| 77 | 8 | 99 | 446 | 977 | 18,261 | 20,289 | 0.0 |
| 72 | 19 | 98 | 125 | 155 | 11,100[h] | 10,400[h] | 6.3 |
| 72 | 24 | 93 | 48 | 73 | 12,400[h] | 11,000[h] | 0.0 |
| n.a. | 10 | 97 | n.a. | n.a. | 8[o] | 40[o] | 0.0 |
| 77 | 10 | 95 | 103 | 120 | 27,206 | 35,056 | 0.0 |
| 77 | 6 | 99 | 398 | 1043 | 37,315 | 32,228 | 0.0 |
| 77 | 8 | 99 | 364 | 821 | 37,456 | 41,049 | 0.0 |
| 70 | 29 | 99 | 778 | 319 | 86,400[h] | 82,450[h] | 0.0 |
| 75 | 9 | 99 | 486 | 482 | 107,088 | 126,326 | 0.0 |
| **76** | **11** | **99** | **862** | **747** | **306,997** | **472,761** | **0.0** |
| 76 | 8 | 99 | 257 | 951 | 89,706 | 85,686 | 0.0 |
| 76 | 11 | 99 | 926 | 725 | 217,291 | 387,075 | — |

[i]Despite attaining GNP per capita of $4,130 or above and a PQLI of 90 or above, Barbados, Brunei, Hong Kong, Singapore, and Trinidad and Tobago are considered to be developing countries by the ODC. Greece's income fell below the threshold level only recently and therefore is still considered to be a developed country.

[j]1985 figure. *World Bank Atlas,* 1987.

[k]U.S. Department of Commerce, Bureau of the Census, "World Population Profile, 1985." Growth rate is average annual rate for 1987.

[l]1984 estimate. *CIA World Factbook, 1986.*

[m]All external trade for the Belgium-Luxembourg Customs Union is listed together under Belgium.

[n]Department of State, Background Notes, Liechtenstein, 1985.

[o]1983 estimate. Worldmark Encyclopedia on the Nations, 1984.

Sources: Per capita public education and military spending data are from Ruth Leger Sivard, *World Military and Social Expenditures* (1986). Export and import data are from IMF, *Direction of Trade Statistics Yearbook 1986.* Population and population growth data are from the Population Reference Bureau, "1987 Population Data Sheet." Population growth rates apply to the early 1980s. Per capita GNP and growth rates are from the World Bank, *World Development Report, 1986.* U.S. aid data are from U.S. A.I.D. *U.S. Overseas Loans and Grants* (September 1986). Literacy data are primarily from UNICEF, *The State of the World's Children 1987.* Infant mortality and life expectancy data are from the World Bank, *World Development Report 1986.*

# D-2. PQLI Map of the World

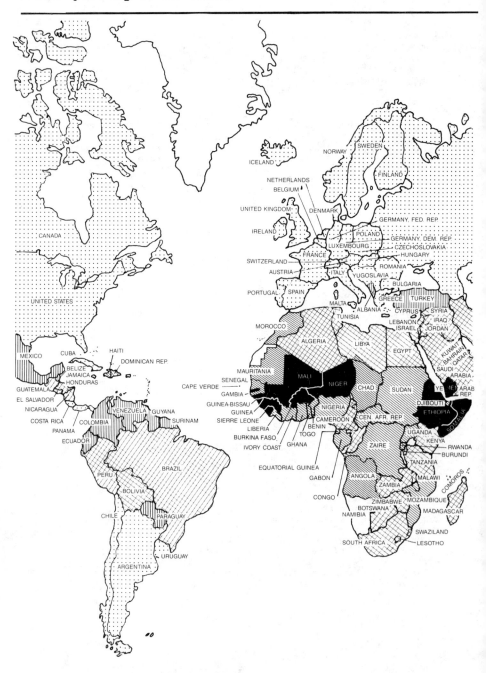

Notes: Each country's PQLI (Physical Quality of Life Index) is based on an average of life expectancy at age one, infant mortality, and literacy.

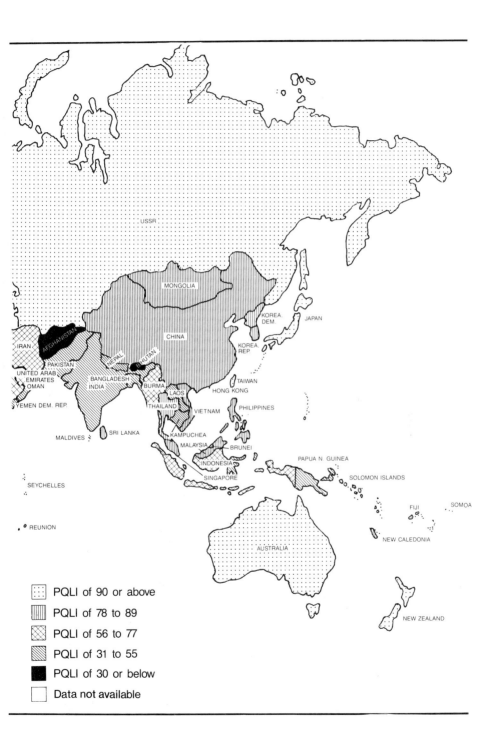

PQLI of 90 or above

PQLI of 78 to 89

PQLI of 56 to 77

PQLI of 31 to 55

PQLI of 30 or below

Data not available

## D-3. Developed- and Developing-Country Shares of World Expenditures and Human Resources (percentages)

*Disparities between the rich and the poor nations of the world remain very high. Despite having more than three-quarters of the world's population, the developing countries account for less than one-quarter of world production, exports, and various public expenditures.*

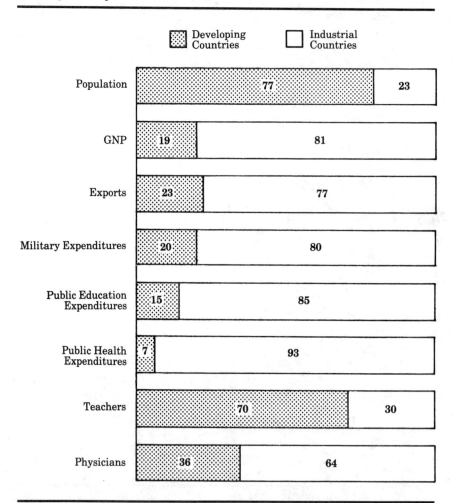

Notes: World population, 5.0 billion in mid-1987; world GNP, $14.6 trillion in 1985; world exports, $2.1 trillion in 1986; world military expenditures, $728 billion in 1983; world public education expenditures, $644 billion in 1983; world public health expenditures, $545 billion in 1983; teachers worldwide, 33.5 million in 1983; physicians worldwide, 4.6 million in 1983.

Sources: Population, GNP, exports, military expenditures, and public education expenditures are based on Table D-1. Public health expenditures, teachers, and physicians figures are based on Ruth Leger Sivard, *World Military and Social Expenditures*, 1986.

## D-4. Global Production: Third World Share is Rising ($ trillions, constant 1982)

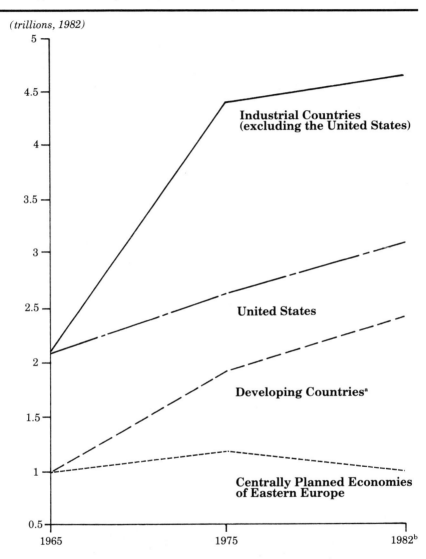

(trillions, 1982)

Industrial Countries
(excluding the United States)

United States

Developing Countries[a]

Centrally Planned Economies
of Eastern Europe

[a]Includes Asian socialist countries.
[b]Preliminary.

Source: UNCTAD, *Handbook of International Trade and Development Statistics, 1985*, Table 6.3

# D-5. Rates of Income Growth: Debtor Nation Growth Slows (percentages)

*Falling from 5–6 per cent growth per year in the 1970s, debtor-country income growth was sharply negative in 1982–83 and has been anemic since then—roughly half of the 1970s rate.*

| | 1969–78[a] | 1979 | 1980 | 1981 | 1982 | 1983 | 1984 | 1985 | 1986 |
|---|---|---|---|---|---|---|---|---|---|
| | | | | | *(percentages)* | | | | |
| **Developing Countries** | **6.1** | **4.2** | **3.5** | **2.1** | **1.6** | **1.4** | **4.1** | **3.2** | **3.5** |
| By region | | | | | | | | | |
| Africa | 5.1 | 3.2 | 3.7 | 1.8 | 0.8 | -1.9 | 1.7 | 2.0 | 1.6 |
| Asia | 5.8 | 4.4 | 5.4 | 5.5 | 5.0 | 7.6 | 7.9 | 5.9 | 5.7 |
| Europe | 6.0 | 3.8 | 1.5 | 2.3 | 2.4 | 1.1 | 3.6 | 2.1 | 3.2 |
| Middle East | 8.2 | 1.8 | -2.5 | -2.0 | -0.2 | 0.2 | 0.9 | -1.0 | 0.0 |
| Western Hemisphere | 5.8 | 6.1 | 5.4 | 0.7 | -1.0 | -3.0 | 3.2 | 3.5 | 4.0 |
| By financial criteria | | | | | | | | | |
| Countries with recent debt-servicing problems | 5.5 | 5.2 | 4.5 | 1.1 | -0.1 | -2.5 | 2.6 | 2.7 | 3.2 |
| Countries without debt-servicing problems | 5.9 | 4.1 | 4.8 | 4.9 | 4.2 | 6.2 | 6.9 | 5.3 | 5.1 |
| **Industrial Countries** | **3.4** | **3.4** | **1.3** | **1.4** | **-0.4** | **2.7** | **4.7** | **3.0** | **2.4** |
| United States | 2.8 | 2.5 | -0.2 | 1.9 | -2.5 | 3.6 | 6.4 | 2.7 | 2.5 |
| Other industrial countries | 3.6 | 3.1 | 2.3 | 0.5 | 0.4 | 1.7 | 3.3 | 2.9 | 2.0 |

Note: Based on GDP for developing countries and GNP for industrial countries.
[a] Annual average.
Source: IMF, *World Economic Outlook*, April 1987, Tables A2 and A5.

# D-6. Absolute Poverty in the Third World: Still Rising (millions of people and percentages)

*While estimates of poverty are quite speculative, the number of people living in "absolute" poverty is growing, albeit at a rate slower than population growth. In the case of Sub-Saharan Africa, however, a larger percentage of the people are poor than in 1970.*

|  | 1970 | | 1985[a] | |
|---|---|---|---|---|
|  | Number of "Absolute" Poor (*millions*) | Share of Region's Population (*percentage*) | Number of "Absolute" Poor (*millions*) | Share of Region's Population (*percentage*) |
| Developing Countries[b] | 300 | 18 | 350–400 | 13–14 |
| South Asia | 136 | 19 | 200 | 18 |
| Sub-Saharan Africa | 60 | 21 | 100–150 | 21–32 |
| East Asia[b] | 47 | 21 | 20 | 9 |
| Latin America | 25 | 10 | 20 | 5 |
| Middle East and North Africa | 31 | 18 | 10 | 4 |

Note: The absolute poor are defined as those who ordinarily do not have enough income to obtain calories to prevent stunted growth and serious health risks (i.e. they consume less than 80 per cent of the calories required to live a normally active life according to FAO/WHO standards).
[a] Data for 1985 is speculative.
[b] Does not include the People's Republic of China.
Source: Adapted from Shahid Javed Burki, "The African Food Crisis: Looking Beyond the Emergency" (Paper presented at the Conference on South–South Cooperation: Experience and Prospects, at Harare, Zimbabwe, November 11–14, 1985).

## D-7. Average Daily Caloric Intake: The African Diet Worsens (percentage of daily caloric requirement)

*The mid-1980s have witnessed deep declines in food consumption by Africans. In 1984, average caloric intake per person was well below the standard requirement for an active working life and less than two–thirds of the caloric intake in industrial countries.*

| | 1970 | 1975 | 1980 | 1982 | 1984 | Annual Rates of Change | |
| --- | --- | --- | --- | --- | --- | --- | --- |
| | | | | | | 1970–80 | 1980–84 |
| | | | *(percentages)* | | | *(percentages)* | |
| Developing Countries | 92.7 | 94.6 | 101.8 | 103.9 | 104.9 | 0.9 | 0.8 |
| Africa | 93.1 | 92.9 | 95.6 | 94.5 | 87.3 | 0.4 | − 2.4 |
| Far East | 91.5 | 90.7 | 97.7 | 99.1 | n.a. | 0.7 | n.a. |
| Latin America | 105.3 | 106.8 | 110.8 | 110.2 | 114.5 | 0.5 | 0.9 |
| Near East | 98.4 | 107.8 | 116.3 | 118.9 | 122.3 | 1.7 | 1.3 |
| Developed Countries | 128.1 | 130.0 | 132.1 | 132.4 | n.a. | 0.3 | n.a. |

Note: Annual index numbers are based on three-year averages centering on the year indicated. Figures refer to the calories required for an active working life in the regions concerned.

Source: Adapted from U.N. World Food Council, "Current World Food Situation," March 1982 and April 1986 issues; and Food and Agriculture Organization, "Current World Food Situation" (May 1987).

# D-8. Soil Erosion: Damages Drinking Water and Agricultural Output

*The large river basins of Asia, home to the largest concentrations of the world's poor, are rapidly eroding—creating hazardous drinking water conditions. Soil erosion also washes away valuable topsoil and thereby reduces agricultural production. By the turn of the century, agricultural production is expected to be reduced by 25 per cent in Africa, 21 per cent in Latin America, and 18 per cent for all developing countries due to soil erosion.*

| River | Outflow | Area of Drainage Basin (thousand square km) | Water Pollution[a] (million metric tons) | Soil Erosion[b] (metric tons per hectare) |
|---|---|---|---|---|
| **Asia:** | | | | |
| Huang (Yellow) | Yellow Sea | 668 | 1,600 | 479 |
| Ganges | Bay of Bengal | 1,076 | 1,455 | 270 |
| Irrawady | Bay of Bengal | 430 | 299 | 139 |
| Mekong | South China Sea | 795 | 170 | 43 |
| **Latin America:** | | | | |
| Amazon | Atlantic Ocean | 5,776 | 363 | 13 |
| **Africa:** | | | | |
| Nile | Mediterranean Sea | 2,978 | 111 | 8 |
| Congo | Atlantic Ocean | 4,014 | 65 | 3 |
| Niger | Gulf of Guinea | 1,114 | 5 | 0 |

[a]Average annual suspended load.
[b]Estimated annual soil erosion from field.
Sources: World Resources Institute, *World Resources 1986*, (New York, 1986), p. 53; U.N. Food and Agriculture Organization, *Protect and Produce* (1984).

# D-9. Deforestation in Tropical Countries (thousands of hectares and percentages)

*Deforestation in a number of countries is proceeding at a rate that greatly undermines living conditions for humans as well as other species.*

| Region/Country | Closed Forest Area, 1980 (thousand hectares) | Area Deforested Annually (thousand hectares) | Annual Rate of Deforestation 1981–85 (percent) |
|---|---|---|---|
| **Latin America** | | | |
| Paraguay | 4,070 | 190 | 4.7 |
| Costa Rica | 1,638 | 65 | 4.0 |
| Ecuador | 14,250 | 340 | 2.4 |
| Nicaragua | 4,496 | 105 | 2.3 |
| Colombia | 46,400 | 820 | 1.8 |
| Guatemala | 4,442 | 72 | 1.6 |
| Honduras | 3,797 | 48 | 1.3 |
| Mexico | 46,250 | 470 | 1.0 |
| Panama | 4,165 | 36 | 0.9 |
| Brazil | 357,480 | 1,360 | 0.4 |
| Peru | 69,680 | 260 | 0.4 |
| Venezuela | 31,870 | 125 | 0.4 |
| Bolivia | 44,010 | 87 | 0.2 |
| **Asia** | | | |
| Nepal | 1,941 | 80 | 4.1 |
| Sri Lanka | 1,659 | 58 | 3.5 |
| Thailand | 9,235 | 244 | 2.6 |
| Malaysia | 20,996 | 255 | 1.2 |
| Laos | 8,410 | 100 | 1.2 |
| Philippines | 9,510 | 91 | 1.0 |
| Vietnam | 8,770 | 60 | 0.7 |
| Indonesia | 113,895 | 600 | 0.5 |
| Kampuchea, Dem. | 7,548 | 25 | 0.3 |
| Burma | 31,941 | 102 | 0.3 |
| India | 51,841 | 132 | 0.3 |
| Papua New Guinea | 34,230 | 22 | 0.1 |
| **Africa** | | | |
| Ivory Coast | 4,458 | 290 | 6.5 |
| Nigeria | 5,950 | 300 | 5.0 |
| Liberia | 2,000 | 42 | 2.1 |
| Guinea | 2,050 | 36 | 1.8 |
| Ghana | 1,718 | 22 | 1.3 |
| Madagascar | 10,300 | 128 | 1.2 |
| Angola | 2,900 | 34 | 1.2 |
| Zambia | 3,010 | 30 | 1.0 |
| Cameroon | 17,920 | 80 | 0.4 |
| Zaire | 105,750 | 160 | 0.2 |
| Congo | 21,340 | 22 | 0.1 |
| Gabon | 20,500 | 15 | 0.1 |

Source: International Institute for Environment and Development and the World Resources Institute, *World Resources 1987* (Basic Books, New York, 1987), pp. 284–285.

# D-10. Populations Experiencing Fuelwood Deficits[a] (millions)

*Deforestation, energy shortages, and poverty are interconnected. The pressures of population growth and lack of income to pay for fuels have combined to push the world's poor into consuming vital fuelwoods at a rate faster than they can be grown. Consequently, nearly 1.3 billion people (mostly in rural areas) experienced fuelwood shortages in 1980. This number is expected to rise to nearly 3 billion by the year 2000.*

| | 1980 | | | | 2000[b] | |
| | Acute Scarcity | | Deficit | | Acute Scarcity or Deficit | |
| | Total Population | Rural Population | Total Population | Rural Population | Total Population | Rural Population |
| | *(millions)* | | | | *(millions)* | |
|---|---|---|---|---|---|---|
| Africa | 55 | 49 | 146 | 131 | 535 | 464 |
| Near East and North Africa | 0 | 0 | 104 | 69 | 268 | 158 |
| Asia and Pacific | 31 | 29 | 832 | 710 | 1,671 | 1,434 |
| Latin America | 26 | 18 | 201 | 143 | 512 | 342 |
| Total | 112 | 96 | 1,283 | 1,052 | 2,986 | 2,398 |

[a]Total population and rural population (total population less that of towns with more than 100,000 inhabitants) in zones whose fuelwood situation has been classified.
[b]Estimate.
Source: U.N. Food and Agriculture Organization, *Fuelwood Supplies in Developing Countries* (Rome, 1983), pp. 16–17.

# D-11. Air Pollutants: Developing-Country Emissions Rise Rapidly (millions of metric tons of carbon dioxide percentages)

*Between 1950 and 1983 the level of carbon dioxide emissions tripled. A large portion is due to industrial countries, but the fastest growth of emissions has been in developing countries and the biggest polluters relative to economic activity are the centrally planned economies of Eastern Europe.*

| | 1950 | | 1965 | | 1983 | | 1950–83 Annual Rate of Growth |
| --- | --- | --- | --- | --- | --- | --- | --- |
| | *(millions of metric tons)* | *(percentage of world)* | *(millions of metric tons)* | *(percentage of world)* | *(millions of metric tons)* | *(percentage of world)* | *(percentage)* |
| **Developing Regions** | 117 | 7.5 | 397 | 13.6 | 1,220 | 25.5 | 10.7 |
| Latin America | 36 | 2.3 | 87 | 3.0 | 224 | 4.7 | 8.3 |
| Africa | 26 | 1.7 | 55 | 1.9 | 143 | 3.0 | 7.7 |
| Middle East | 4 | 0.3 | 29 | 1.0 | 116 | 2.4 | 15.8 |
| South and Southeast Asia | 27 | 1.7 | 79 | 2.7 | 254 | 5.3 | 10.2 |
| Centrally Planned Asia | 22 | 1.4 | 146 | 5.0 | 482 | 10.1 | 14.4 |
| **Developed Countries** | 1,436 | 92.5 | 2,532 | 86.4 | 3,563 | 74.5 | 4.0 |
| United States | 679 | 43.7 | 935 | 31.9 | 1,138 | 23.8 | 2.3 |
| Western Europe | 377 | 24.3 | 643 | 22.0 | 753 | 15.7 | 3.1 |
| Japan | 27 | 1.7 | 101 | 3.4 | 224 | 4.7 | 9.6 |
| Other | 353 | 22.7 | 853 | 29.1 | 1,448 | 30.3 | 6.3 |
| Eastern Europe | 291 | 18.7 | 748 | 25.5 | 1,279 | 26.7 | 6.6 |
| **World** | 1,553 | 100.0 | 2,929 | 100.0 | 4,783 | 100.0 | 5.0 |

[a]Emissions from fossil fuel consumption.
Source: World Resources Institute, *World Resources 1986*, (New York, 1986), p. 318.

**About the Overseas Development Council**

The Overseas Development Council is a private, non-profit organization established in 1969 for the purpose of increasing American understanding of the economic and social problems confronting the developing countries and of how their development progress is related to U.S. interests. Toward this end, the Council functions as a center for policy research and analysis, a forum for the exchange of ideas, and a resource for public education. The Council's current program of work encompasses four major issue areas: trade and industrial policy, international finance and investment, development strategies and development cooperation, and U.S. foreign policy and the developing countries. ODC's work is used by policy makers in the Executive Branch and the Congress, journalists, and those concerned about U.S.-Third World relations in corporate and bank management, international and non-governmental organizations, universities, and educational and action groups focusing on specific development issues. ODC's program is funded by foundations, corporations, and private individuals; its policies are determined by a governing Board and Council. In selecting issues and shaping its work program, ODC is also assisted by a standing Program Advisory Committee.

Victor H. Palmieri is chairman of the ODC, and J. Wayne Fredericks is vice chairman. The Council's president is John W. Sewell.


Overseas Development Council
1717 Massachusetts Ave., N.W.
Washington, D.C. 20036
Tel. (202) 234-8701

# The Project Directors and Editors

*Growth, Exports, and Jobs in a Changing World Economy: Agenda 1988* is the ninth volume in the Overseas Development Council's series of policy books, U.S.-Third World Policy Perspectives. The co-editors of this series—often collaborating with guest editors contributing to the series—are Richard E. Feinberg and Valeriana Kallab.

**John Sewell** has been president of the Overseas Development Council since January 1980. From 1977 to 1979, he was the Council's executive vice president, directing ODC's programs of research and public education. Prior to joining the Council in 1971, he directed the communications program of The Brookings Institution. He also served in the Foreign Service of the United States and the Research Bureau of the Department of State. Mr. Sewell is a frequent lecturer, commentator, and author on U.S. relations with the developing countries. He is the author (with Christine E. Contee) of "Foreign Aid and Gramm-Rudman," an assessment of the U.S. foreign aid program, published in *Foreign Affairs* (Summer 1987). A contributor to several of ODC's past *Agenda* assessments of U.S. policies and performance in U.S.-Third World relations, he is also co-author of *Rich Country Interests and Third World Development,* and of *The Ties That Bind: U.S. Interests in Third World Development.*

**Stuart K. Tucker** is a fellow at the Overseas Development Council. Prior to joining ODC in 1984, he was a research consultant for the Inter-American Development Bank, the Urban Institute, and the Roosevelt Center for American Policy Studies. He has written on U.S. international trade policy, including the linkage between the debt crisis and U.S. exports and jobs, the impact of the U.S. Caribbean Basin Initiative, and U.S. agricultural trade policy. He also prepared the Statistical Annexes in ODC's *Agenda 1985-86* and in *Hard Bargaining Ahead: U.S. Trade Policy and Developing Countries,* edited by Ernest H. Preeg and issued in ODC's U.S.-Third World Policy Perspectives series in 1985.

**Valeriana Kallab** is vice president and director of publications of the Overseas Development Council and series co-editor of the ODC's U.S.-Third World Policy Perspectives series. She has been responsible for ODC's published output since 1972. Before joining ODC, she was a research editor and writer on international economic issues at the Carnegie Endowment for International Peace in New York.

**Richard E. Feinberg** is vice president of the Overseas Development Council and co-editor of the Policy Perspectives series. Before joining ODC in 1981, he served as the Latin American specialist on the Policy Planning Staff of the U.S. Department of State, and as an international economist in the Treasury Department and with the House Banking Committee. He is the author of numerous books as well as journal and newspaper articles on U.S. foreign policy, Latin American politics, and international economic and financial issues.

# Contributing Authors

**Manuel Castells** is professor of planning at the University of California at Berkeley and senior research fellow at the Berkeley Roundtable on the International Economy (BRIE). Before his appointment to Berkeley in 1979, he taught for ten years at the École des Hautes Études en Sciences Sociales (Paris). He has also held visiting appointments at the Universities of Montreal, Chile, Mexico, Wisconsin-Madison, Boston, Southern California, Copenhagen, Geneva, Madrid, Hong Kong, and Singapore. He has published twelve books in different languages, including *The Economic Crisis and American Society* (1980) and *Information Technology, Economic Restructuring, and Urban Development* (1988). His current work focuses on the impact of high technology on the international division of labor.

**Laura D'Andrea Tyson** is a principal faculty member of the Berkeley Roundtable on the International Economy (BRIE) and an associate professor of economics at the University of California at Berkeley. She has served as a consultant to the World Bank, the Office of Technology Assessment, the Rand Corporation, the President's Commission on Industrial Competitiveness, and the Council on Competitiveness. Her major publications include: *American Industry in International Competition* (with John Zysman); "Creating Advantage in High Technology Industries" (with Michael Borrus and John Zysman) in Paul Krugman, ed., *Strategic Trade Policy and the New International Economics;* and "The U.S. Trade Deficit: A Black Hole in the World Economy" (with Lester Thurow) in *Foreign Policy,* June 1987. She is currently working on a book on trade and employment patterns in the U.S. economy (forthcoming, Ballinger Publications). In addition to her work on U.S. competitiveness, she has published a number of books and articles on the Eastern European economies.

**Jonathan D. Aronson** is a professor in the School of International Relations and the Annenberg School of Communications at the University of Southern California. His work focuses on the politics of international trade and monetary relations, with particular emphasis on trade in services, international telecommunications, and international banking. In 1982-83, he was a Council on Foreign Relations International Affairs Fellow in the Office of the U.S. Trade Representative. His most recent books are *When Countries Talk: International Trade in Telecommunications Services* (with Peter Cowhey) and *Trade Talks: America Better Listen!* (with Michael Aho). He is currently preparing a new book on international corporate alliances for the Council on Foreign Relations.

**Robert L. Paarlberg** is associate professor of political science at Wellesley College, and associate at the Harvard University Center for International Affairs. He is the author of three books on international agricultural policy, including, most recently, *Food Trade and Foreign Policy* (Cornell, 1985) and *Fixing Farm Trade: Policy Options for the United States* (Ballinger, for the New York Council on Foreign Relations, 1987). His current research on international agricultural policy reform is being supported by the National Center for Food and Agricultural Policy at Resources for the Future.

**Raymond F. Mikesell** has been professor of economics at the University of Oregon since 1957 and previously taught at the University of Virginia and the University of Washington. He has published widely in the fields of international finance, economic development, and resource economics. His latest book, *Nonfuel Minerals: Foreign Policy Dependence and National Security,* was published by the University of Michigan Press for the Twentieth Century Fund in 1987. He has served as a consultant to the U.S. Department of State, the U.S. Agency for International Development (AID), the Executive Office of the President, the World Bank, and the United Nations, and was a member of the National Materials Advisory Board, 1981-84.

**Ray Marshall** is professor of economics and public affairs at the University of Texas at Austin, where he has taught since 1962. From 1977 to 1981, he served as U.S. Secretary of Labor. He is the author of numerous books and articles on employment issues, including *Unheard Voices: Labor and Economic Policy in a Competitive World* and *The Jobs Challenge: Pressures and Possibilities* (co-edited). His current research interests include labor and economic policy; the competitiveness of American industry; technology, the economy, and education; and the employment problems of women.

# Overseas Development Council
# Board of Directors*

# ODC Program Advisory Committee

Chairman: John P. Lewis
*Woodrow Wilson School of Public
and International Affairs
Princeton University*

Nancy Birdsall
*The World Bank*

Colin Bradford, Jr.
*International Relations Program
Yale University*

Lawrence J. Brainard
*Bankers Trust Company*

Mayra Buvinic
*International Center for
Research on Women*

Shahid Javed Burki
*The World Bank*

Albert Fishlow
*University of California*

James Galbraith
*Lyndon B. Johnson School
of Public Affairs
University of Texas at Austin*

Denis Goulet
*University of Notre Dame*

Davidson R. Gwatkin
*The World Bank*

Catherine Gwin
*New York, New York*

Edward K. Hamilton
*Hamilton, Rabinovitz,
& Alschuler, Inc.*

Chandra Hardy
*The World Bank*

G.K. Helleiner
*University of Toronto*

Albert O. Hirschman
*Institute for Advanced Study
Princeton, New Jersey*

Michael M. Horowitz
*Institute for Development
Anthropology, Inc. and
State University of New York*

Gary Horlick
*O'Melveny and Myers*

Gary Hufbauer
*School of Foreign Service
Georgetown University*

Peter B. Kenen
*Princeton University*

Tony Killick
*Overseas Development Institute*

Paul R. Krugman
*Sloan School of Management
Cambridge, Massachusetts*

John Mellor
*International Food Policy
Research Institute*

Theodore H. Moran
*Landegger Program,
School of Foreign Service
Georgetown University*

Henry R. Nau
*George Washington University*

Kenneth A. Oye
*Princeton University*

Dwight H. Perkins
*Institute for International Development
Harvard University*

Gustav Ranis
*Economic Growth Center
Yale University*

John Schnittker
*Schnittker Associates*

Ronald K. Shelp
*New York City Partnership, Inc.
and New York Chamber of
Commerce and Industry*

Robert Solomon
*The Brookings Institution*

Lance Taylor
*Massachusetts Institute of Technology*

Norman Uphoff
*Cornell University*

Bernard Wood
*North-South Institute*

Overseas Development Council
1717 Massachusetts Ave., N.W.
Washington, D.C. 20036
Tel. (202) 234-8701

# U.S.-THIRD WORLD POLICY PERSPECTIVES

Other titles in this series: